Understanding
Early Years Policy

Education at SAGE

SAGE is a leading international publisher of journals, books, and electronic media for academic, educational, and professional markets.

Our education publishing includes:

- accessible and comprehensive texts for aspiring education professionals and practitioners looking to further their careers through continuing professional development

- inspirational advice and guidance for the classroom

- authoritative state of the art reference from the leading authors in the field

Find out more at: **www.sagepub.co.uk/education**

Peter Baldock, Damien Fitzgerald & Janet Kay

Understanding Early Years Policy

3rd Edition

Los Angeles | London | New Delhi
Singapore | Washington DC

SAGE Publications Ltd
1 Oliver's Yard
55 City Road
London EC1Y 1SP

SAGE Publications Inc.
2455 Teller Road
Thousand Oaks, California 91320

SAGE Publications India Pvt Ltd
B 1/I 1 Mohan Cooperative Industrial Area
Mathura RoadA
New Delhi 110 044

SAGE Publications Asia-Pacific Pte Ltd
3 Church Street
#10–04 Samsung Hub
Singapore 049483

Commissioning Editor: Jude Bowen
Assistant Editor: Miriam Davey
Production Editor: Jeanette Graham
Assistant Production Editor: Nicola Marshall
Copyeditor: Sharon Cawood
Proofreader: Beth Crockett
Indexer: Anne Solomito
Marketing Manager: Lorna Patkai
Cover design: Wendy Scott
Typeset by: Dorwyn, Wells, Somerset, UK
Printed by: MPG Books Group, Bodmin, Cornwall

First edition published 2005
Reprinted 2006 three times
Second edition published 2009
Reprinted 2009, 2010 twice, 2011
This third edition first published 2013

Library of Congress Control Number: 2012940990

British Library Cataloguing in Publication data

A catalogue record for this book is available from the British Library

ISBN 978-1-4462-0705-5
ISBN 978-1-4462-0706-2 (pbk)

We are dedicating this third edition to Pete Baldock, our co-author, colleague and friend for many years, who sadly died in 2011. Pete's contributions to planning and writing the book were inspirational from the start, and he continued to write new material even during his final illness. We have gained an enormous amount from knowing Pete and from working with him. He is greatly missed.

Contents

Acknowledgements

We are grateful to Michelle Smith and Mark O'Hara for their valuable comments on an earlier draft of the first edition of the book. We are also grateful to colleagues working in Wales, Scotland and Northern Ireland for their comments on an earlier draft of Chapter 5.

Peter Baldock also wanted to thank Varonika Najvarona, Vivian Chan, Trevor Higginbottom, Michael Collins, Kathy Bartlett and Rimas Tankile Morris for their help with Chapter 6 in this new third edition of the book.

Key for Icons

Chapter objectives

Activity

Points for reflection

Case study

Summary

Further reading

About the Authors

Peter Baldock was a teacher and a member of staff at an international organization before spending more than 20 years in community development, always with a particular interest in early years. He also worked in regulation and inspection, and was an Associate Tutor for the Open University. He sadly passed away in 2011, and he completed his work on this new edition whilst fighting serious illness. He is much missed.

Damien Fitzgerald has worked as a Registered Nurse, teacher and special needs coordinator in early years and primary education and as an LEA support teacher. He is currently a Principal Lecturer at Sheffield Hallam University in Childhood Studies and is engaged in varied research.

Janet Kay worked as a qualified social worker with children and families for some years before moving into teaching in further and then higher education. She currently works as a Principal Lecturer in Children and Childhood at Sheffield Hallam University.

Preface

Policy has an important impact on the daily life of early years practitioners. Every setting has its own policies. The policies of central and local government establish expectations of those settings and do much to determine their level of resources. All practitioners, but especially those in managerial positions, have to be conscious of these issues. Questions of policy figure significantly on vocational courses, including programmes leading to Early Years Professional Status (EYPS), and others such as those leading to degrees or Foundation Degrees in Early Childhood Studies.

At the same time, there are few books available at the moment designed primarily to help students or practitioners negotiate their way around this area. Authors dealing with social policy in general have yet to catch up with the importance now attached to early years services by politicians and the public. There are books and articles that argue for changes in policy, but their objective is at least as much to persuade readers to support those changes as it is to help them understand the process of policy-making. Four years ago, we saw the need for a book that would help students and practitioners learn how to understand that process, identify the context in which new policies arise and work out how to influence policy themselves. The first edition of this book was written as a result.

It was not a detailed account of the policies of the government in power at the time we wrote it. Such a reference book would have duplicated information available on the Internet and elsewhere and it would have needed updating on a regular, at least annual, basis to remain accurate. What we tried to do was to explain what policy is and how it comes about in a way that would be relevant for some time to come through any likely changes in detailed policy. We seem to have been successful in this, but changes since we wrote the second edition have suggested the need for this new, updated, third edition. We have used the opportunity of this third edition to make some further changes and to bring the story up to date. There is, however, one new topic that has been introduced.

In the preface to the first edition, we acknowledged the fact that, as people who worked in early years in England, we were considering the subject from an

English perspective and warned that the reader should assume that it was the situation in England that was being discussed unless we said otherwise quite specifically. Reviewers who were generally kind about the book pointed out that this limited its usefulness. In addition, the process of devolution has not stood still but has developed in many ways that underline the importance of paying specific attention to the rest of the United Kingdom (hereafter UK) outside England. The countries that make up the UK have a great deal in common and, therefore, differences between them on early years policy can provide interesting comparisons that can be used to debate the best way forward in this area. Devolution has also had an impact on policy-making itself – not just adding another tier of decision-making, but also creating a new driving force as each of the three devolved nations attempts to prove itself. As a result of considerations such as these, we added another chapter to the second edition that spoke about policy in Wales, Scotland and Northern Ireland. In this new, third edition, we have added a new chapter on the international dimension of early years policy.

The book now has nine chapters. Chapter 1 explains what policy is and why it is important. Chapter 2 outlines the development of policy in this field. Chapter 3 describes the factors that influence the development of the aspirations and objectives that constitute basic policy. Chapter 4 describes the process by which aspirations and objectives are translated into specific legislative and administrative measures. Chapter 5 deals with the impact of devolution on policy-making. Chapter 6 looks at the international dimension of early years policy. Chapter 7 looks at the impact of policy on practitioners, children and parents. Chapter 8 deals with the analysis of policy and considers the relevance of different perspectives (of politicians, professionals, parents and children) and the extent to which a coherent early years policy is in the making. Finally, there is a concluding summary. Chapters 1–8 include activities, discussion points or suggestions for reflection designed to help you think further about the issues raised. Chapter 2 also includes a timeline as a summary of developments in the period from 1945 to 2012. The book closes with a list of useful websites and a glossary of terms used as further aids.

The authors owe a debt of gratitude to the students and colleagues with whom we have worked over the last few years and whose questions, observations and comments during discussion have done much to inform what we have said. We remain responsible for the final outcome.

What is Policy and Why is it Important?

Chapter 1

This chapter explores:

▶ the role practitioners can play in influencing policy development and implementation

▶ the significance of policy

▶ three levels of policy-making: the basic assumptions about values and facts that usually underpin policy decisions; the broad objectives; and the detailed arrangements required to meet those objectives

▶ the characteristics of policies

▶ written statements of policy

▶ controversy in the debate on policy.

Working with young children every day is fascinating and demanding. It is easy to see why so many early years practitioners remain entirely focused on the task in hand and do not spend time discussing policy, which is typically seen as something produced by people in suits somewhere else that just has to be implemented. A common joke has the person in charge explaining 'There is no reason for it – it's just our policy'. Those who are actually working with children and their families may feel they can do little but put up with the consequences of changes in policy. Thinking about them and their implications is for someone else to do.

This book takes a different approach. We believe that the policies adopted by those in power make an enormous difference to the way practitioners are able to work. We also argue that policies are not just conjured up out of the air. People who make policies have reasons for what they do. We may not agree with them, but they are reasons, not mere whims. We need to understand those reasons in order to implement more effectively those policies that appear to be useful and to challenge more effectively those that do not. We want to argue against the sense of helplessness. Practitioners can do more than just cope.

Among the sources of policy are what practitioners themselves have to say and they can have a considerable impact on the way that policies are implemented. A good practitioner will give time to think how he/she can help policy develop in useful directions.

What is policy?

Levin (1997) points out that the word 'policy' is used in several different ways and identifies four of these. (The examples given are not from Levin himself, but have been chosen because of their relevance to our overall subject.)

▶ A stated intention (for example, in 1999 the government announced its intention to transfer responsibility for the regulation of childminding and day care in England from local authorities to Ofsted – the Office for Standards in Education).

▶ Action taken on an issue by those with responsibility (for example, the issuing of new guidance and regulations on the early years curriculum or young children's day care. Sometimes the word 'policy' is used to cover all the actions the government or some other body has undertaken in a particular field. Thus we speak of 'the government's childcare policy' meaning everything it has done in relation to childcare).

▶ An organizational or administrative practice (for example, if the government sets up a funding regime for early years settings, there will be policies governing the type of setting that is eligible to receive the money).

▶ An indication of the formal status of a course of action (policies on, for example, childcare are to be found in documents that have some status, such as a government Green Paper or a manifesto published for a general election by a political party).

Although the word does carry different meanings and it is important to be aware of these, there are common elements. Levin says that any policy will entail:

▶ belongingness: a policy will belong to some body or another – a political party, a government department, an individual setting, and so on

▶ commitment: a policy entails a commitment to a particular approach or course of action on the part of that body

▶ status: the fact that a proposal or set of ideas is described as a policy suggests that it has been formally adopted in some way by the body that owns it

▶ specificity: a policy will entail specific ways of dealing with specific issues, although the extent to which it is specific on the detail will vary.

These four attributes of policy reflect the fact that policies are considered. People do not usually do things in a completely random way in their everyday lives. The same is also true of policy-makers. We define 'policy' as: an attempt by those working inside an organization to think in a coherent way about what it is trying to achieve (either in general or in relation to a specific issue) and what it needs to do to achieve it.

Such thinking is conducted at three levels (although any policy statement may focus on one or two of these):

▸ basic assumptions about the relevant facts and the values that should inform the approach to them

▸ broad objectives

▸ detailed arrangements required to meet those objectives.

In many statements of policy, the underlying values and statements about what are described as the facts of the situation are presented quite baldly, as though there can be no argument about them. This is because such statements usually come from people in charge and, however much they may have consulted people before issuing the document, they now want to get on with things. It should become clear, in the chapters that follow, that the facts of the situation and the values people bring to bear on them are constantly changing and are often matters of controversy. It is also the case that the distinction between values and facts is far from clear much of the time and people may state as matters of fact things that merely reflect their personal beliefs. In short, we should not take for granted the basic assumptions about values and facts that usually underpin policy decisions even when there is wide consensus on these, perhaps especially when there is consensus.

In the same way, we need to look critically at the second level of policy-making – the broad objectives. Objectives have to be defined clearly, otherwise the policy-makers do not know whether they have been successful and cannot think clearly about further measures their objectives might imply. However, clarity is not always in evidence.

Policy-makers will often argue in favour of a policy on one set of grounds while also having other considerations in mind. For example, both the Labour and Conservative governments have often adopted policies that have restricted the powers and autonomy of local councils. There is an inevitable tension between central government, which wishes to set policies for the nation, and local authorities that have to implement policies (especially as the political party controlling a local council may be the one in opposition in Parliament). Yet it is difficult to identify a situation where a government has stated explicitly that restricting the autonomy of local government is one of its major aims. Instead, they are more likely to talk about policies that have

3

that effect as being designed to secure greater fairness or effectiveness in the delivery of services.

Clarity can also be undermined by ambivalence on the part of policy-makers. For example, a policy designed to give more families access to affordable child-care may be designed to give parents greater freedom of choice or to reduce dependence on benefits (so that it is expected most parents will take up those opportunities). Yet it may be the case that the policy is not described consistently in terms of either of those alternative objectives in spite of the fact that they can be in conflict with each other.

In a large organization, such as the national government, there can also be inconsistency between policies arising in different contexts. For example, at the time of the 2005 general election the Labour Party had policies intended to promote:

▶ the recruitment of more older people into the childcare workforce

▶ the continuing contribution of private providers of day care operating on a small scale (with one or two settings) and of the voluntary and community sector

▶ the development of a better qualified childcare workforce.

At the same time, it intended to fund the growing demand for post-16 education among young people, partly by depending more on employers for the training of older employees.

A case could be made for each of these policies, but there was a clear tension between them, as discussed further in Chapter 7. Smaller-scale providers (as opposed to local authorities or large commercial organizations) could not afford to fund the training of their older staff or to recruit older staff for whose training they would have to pay. This meant that the developing policy on the funding of post-16 education was restricting the scope for recruiting older people into the childcare workforce and training them. The government of Tony Blair spoke, when it came to power, of wanting to create 'joined-up government', but found this was more difficult in practice than it had anticipated.

The third level of policy-making is that of the detailed arrangements that need to be made if the broad objectives are to be achieved. The law may have to be changed. Organizational structures may have to be put in place. New funding may have to be found. Particular efforts may have to be made to secure support for the broad objectives. Chapter 4 gives many examples of these and other aspects of implementation of policy.

There are always choices to be made in determining what kinds of arrangements will best meet the stated objectives. For example, if it is decided to make it easier for parents to afford childcare, this can be done by:

▸ measures (such as tax credits) to make it easier for parents to find the money for childcare

▸ subsidies paid directly to independent childcare providers or subsidised provision by local authorities or other parts of the public sector.

Whichever of these is chosen (and governments often adopt measures that have elements of both approaches), the arrangements are likely to be connected with the way in which broad objectives are conceived and with objectives in other fields (such as general economic policy).

Policy-makers might also want to offset possible disadvantages in one set of arrangements by creating others without changing the first. For example, the recent Labour Government sought to prevent the expansion in childcare in England from leading to a decline in the quality of what is on offer by:

▸ giving financial support to training and providing other quality-enhancing measures in the early years field

▸ issuing curriculum guidance

▸ issuing national standards on care

▸ enforcing care and education standards in England by giving Ofsted regulatory powers in these fields.

So far we have been talking about government policy, but, if policy is the attempt to think coherently about objectives and the means to achieve them, then policy-making is something that will occur at every organizational level.

Politicians in government will have their own policies, but the UK is not a tightly controlled hierarchical organization where the prime minister decides what he wants to happen and everyone does as he wishes. As described in Chapter 3, the policies of government are heavily influenced by the views of a wide range of organizations as well as the media and the general public. Once policies have been determined, the government is dependent on many different agencies, and, again, the general public, for their successful implementation, as discussed further in Chapter 4. It is also important to bear in mind that in the field of early education and childcare, the national government and Parliament have direct responsibility mainly for England and that the devolved regimes in other parts of the UK now take the lead on this issue in their own countries (as described in Chapter 5).

Different departments of the Civil Service and government agencies such as Ofsted (or Ofsted's equivalents in Wales, Scotland and Northern Ireland) will need their own policies to work up the general directions from the politicians into detailed organizational and financial arrangements.

Local authorities and the National Health Service (NHS) will have their own policies for young children. The Labour governments of 1997–2010 took various steps to secure cooperation between them, but the Coalition Government that came to power in 2010 has strong reservations about some of the mechanisms it employed.

Early years settings will have their own policies and procedures on a whole range of practice issues. In some cases, the individual setting will be part of a wider organization, such as the education department or one of the national nursery chains, and will have policies common throughout the wider body.

Activity

Take one of the early years policies of the government or of your local authority as an example.

Describe the effects of that policy on any setting with which you are familiar.

The policy could be relevant to the general situation of the setting. It could have helped to make the setting more or less financially viable than it would otherwise have been or it could have affected the type of service offered (for example, the age range or the number of children with special needs received). The policy could also have affected daily practice in a variety of ways.

How has the policy come to have those effects? Have they always been what the policy-makers intended?

What are the characteristics of policies?

If a policy is the outcome of an attempt to think clearly and coherently about a particular issue, then it should have certain characteristics:

▶ The underlying assumptions about values and facts will be apparent.

▶ The broad objectives will be clear. It will be obvious who is intended to benefit from the policy and in what way, and objectives will be compatible with each other.

▶ The costs will be known and accepted by those responsible for implementation.

▶ Structural, financial and other arrangements will be made that are best designed to meet those objectives. Resources of all kinds will match the objectives adopted.

▶ The implications for day-to-day practice will be clear or, at least, the basis will be laid for those implications to be determined.

▶ Plans will be in place for communicating the policy and its implications to all those who need to know about it.

▶ The body making the policy will ensure that this particular policy is compatible with other policies on related topics that it has in place.

▶ The implementation of policy will be reviewed periodically in an effective way, so that policy can be modified if necessary.

Of course, many policies fail to meet all of these requirements all of the time. No one is perfect.

To take one example, those outlining a policy may be clear as to the identity of those it is hoped will benefit, but less clear on the identity of those who may be put at a disadvantage (a key part of the costs). Thus it may be understood but not clearly stated that:

▶ tax advantages are being given to families with young children, *but* these will not be shared by other taxpayers

▶ financial assistance with childcare costs must be as simple as possible for parents, *but* this may mean additional paperwork or delays in payment for providers

▶ minimum standards will be required of early years services, *therefore* those unable to reach those standards will be forced to cease operation

▶ services may be required to cooperate more closely to the benefit of users *and* this may mean a loss or renegotiation of professional identity and status for some particular groups of staff.

Of course, the claim will often be made that *in the longer run* the whole of society will benefit from the improvements the policy will bring, so that the short-term disadvantages to some people are acceptable.

Written statements of policy

Policies are normally given a written form. This is not, however, always the case. Custom and practice can govern what is done in the absence of any written policy. Sometimes custom and practice can be more powerful than written policy and take things in a different direction. This is true of central and local government, but is often more obvious in the case of an individual setting. A nursery may have a written policy that there should be close cooperation with parents but undermine that policy by administrative or security practices or the use of professional jargon that have the effect of 'freezing out' parents.

Sometimes practice is not so much about what people do as what they do not do. A kind of negative policy creation can take place. The absence of measures designed to make a setting inclusive and welcoming to children with special needs or from minority cultures can become, in effect, a policy to be exclusive and discriminatory, even though no one would state that that was intended (or, probably, even think it).

Policies should be clear about all the aspects defined in the previous section. Written statements of policy help to achieve this in two ways:

▶ The process of composing a written statement can itself help to clarify ideas that may be shared but not sufficiently articulated, or uncover disagreements that had not previously surfaced so that these can be resolved.

▶ A written statement is an essential step in communicating the policy to others (even though it is not usually adequate in itself). The others include, of course, those joining at a later date the body for which the policy was created.

Written policy statements can take three basic forms:

▶ general statements that focus on the underlying assumptions and broad objectives

▶ policy statements that spell out those assumptions and objectives in more detailed terms. This might include the identification of issues and possible ways forward on which the policy-makers' views are still tentative and on which they wish to consult

▶ detailed statements about the manner in which policy will be implemented.

Written policies are only useful to the extent that reference is made to them on a regular basis and their effectiveness is monitored and reviewed. Again, it may be easier to consider this at the level of the individual setting. Childcare inspectors have sometimes found that settings have excellent sets of written policies and procedures of which the staff seem completely unaware. This is pointless. The important thing is the quality of the experience of the children, not the quality of the document in the manager's office. The procedures are only important to the extent that they are helpful to staff and both govern and reflect their responses to the situations they encounter.

This is why it is dangerous to leave the composition of policy documents to a few experts. If a group of parents new to this kind of thing are trying to set up a pre-school in the local church hall and struggling to raise funds and do the other things they need to do, it may seem helpful if someone from outside offers to produce all their policy documentation for them. In the longer, run it can be a recipe for disaster.

Activity

Select a policy statement from a setting in which you are working or have worked (including work as a volunteer or student on placement) and consider the following questions:

▶ Have you read the policy statement?

▶ Have you received any kind of briefing or training in its implementation?

▶ Were you involved in any way in the drafting of the document?

▶ Do you understand the reasoning behind the requirements it makes of staff?

▶ Are there any changes you would like to see made to the statement? If so, which changes and why?

▶ Do you understand what the policy statement requires you to do as a member of staff?

▶ Does your ability to understand the policy statement depend on your involvement in developing it?

Controversy in the debate on policy

The next chapter gives an account of the development of government policy up to 2011. Chapter 3 deals with the influences that lead to broad changes in policy, while Chapter 4 explores the ways in which policies are put into practice through changes in the law or administrative arrangements. Our main focus is on what are conventionally called early childhood services (day care for young children, pre-school education, playwork and some support services for parents). We also say a little about services that cater for all children, but do not usually have special agencies for younger children, such as child protection services. We say very little about some areas of general policy that also have an important impact on the lives of young children – economic policy, the welfare benefits system or the management of the built environment, for example. All three chapters underline some of the problematic aspects of policy. It can be easy to present the development of early years services as something inevitably moving in a single direction, with the main question being how quickly we will get to what is seen as the desired state of affairs. It is a key message of this book that change is a more complex process than that.

In the year or so before the general election of 2010, clearer differences began to emerge between the two major parties, with, for example, Labour showing itself willing to make Sure Start Children's Centres an increasingly universal service, while the Conservatives wanted them to focus on those families most in need.

There are also controversies among the general public and practitioners around issues such as the possible disadvantages of day care, the role of different professions in early years services, the best ways of working with young children to help them benefit from later schooling and whether the state should or should not interfere more in family life.

All of these disputes are important and, at the time of writing, it is still unclear whether the Coalition Government will take us in a significantly new direction in relation to any of these.

Summary

- ▶ There is nothing simple about the subject with which this book deals. However, that is not a reason to run away from policy issues and attempt to concentrate exclusively on the day-to-day job with all its problems and rewards.

- ▶ Policy is important because we have to think about what we are trying to do and why and how we are doing it.

- ▶ There are opportunities for influencing policy.

- ▶ If we ignore policy issues, they will not go away. With or without our participation, people will make decisions on the organizational context in which early years practitioners operate, the qualifications they need, their pay and other conditions, the resources that will be made available and, above all, what they should be doing with the children day by day.

- ▶ Children need more than our enthusiasm. They need us to think about what we are doing. In the end, that is what 'policy' means.

Further reading

The chapters that follow will offer suggestions on further reading on some of the particular topics with which they deal. The field is changing rapidly, but earlier publications are still useful in spelling out some of the general issues and showing how far things have (and have not) moved in the recent past. Among books that can be recommended are:

Penn, H. (ed.) (2000) *Early Childhood Services: Theory, Policy and Practice*, Oxford: Oxford University Press.

Pugh, G. and Duffy, B. (eds) (2010) *Contemporary Issues in the Early Years: Working Collaboratively for Children* (5th edn), London: Paul Chapman Publishing.

It is also worth looking at early years policy in the context of wider social policy. Levin, P. (1997) *Making Social Policy* (Buckingham: Open University Press) was quoted earlier in this chapter. It will help you to understand the complexity of policy-making as a human endeavour, although it was written too early to reflect the changes in early childhood policy since Labour first returned to power in 1997.

For those who want to keep up to date on developments in early years policy, there are two important sources:

The weekly publication *Nursery World* has useful news items and a lively letters page, and often covers significant policy issues in its longer articles.

Government websites are an important source of official information, as are the websites of such bodies as your local authority early years team and national voluntary organizations, such as the Day Care Trust. (See Useful Websites after References at the end of this book.)

Chapter 2

The Development of Early Years Policy So Far

This chapter outlines:

▶ the relevance of the historical background to a fuller understanding of current policy on early childhood services

▶ some key features of the development of those services up until the election of the Labour Party to power in 1997

▶ the ways in which policy on those services developed from 1997 to 2010

▶ the changing situation under the Coalition government and the prospects for the future direction of policy on early childhood services.

The importance that the recent Labour government attached to early childhood services was relatively new. There were few such services at all until the early years of the 19th century and those that were established in that period (or beforehand) relied mainly on philanthropists and voluntary organizations rather than on central or local government. Things began to change in the 19th century, but never at the pace that was achieved in France, for example, and it was only towards the end of the 20th century that the idea that early childhood services could be an important aspect of government policy began to take hold.

This historical background is significant because it underlines the fact that there is nothing guaranteed or permanent about current policy on early childhood services. It seemed in the period that Tony Blair was prime minister that a new consensus was developing on the place of such services in the welfare state. The even greater commitment to them shown by the government of Gordon Brown and the evident wish of leaders of the Conservative Party to distance themselves from that approach opened up a fault line in the consensus that was aggravated by the recession and the subsequent restrictions on all public spending. Early childhood services are still not as well established as other aspects of the welfare state.

In spite of this, the historical background is rarely taken into account when such services are discussed. There are books that acknowledge its significance in relation to specific issues (Bilton, 1998) or services in general (Penn, 2005). There are also studies of specific aspects of our history, such as the valuable work by Brehony on the influence of Froebel and his followers in this country (in, for example, an article published in 2000). Such publications tend to be exceptions. It is only very recently that a comprehensive survey of the history of early childhood services in England has been published and that book reflects, as much as it corrects, the relatively low coverage of the topic else-where (Baldock, 2011).

Developments from the 16th century to the mid-20th century

The development of early childhood services followed on from changes in attitudes to childhood itself. There were many reasons for change, but the most fundamental explanation lies in the way the economic organization of our society was transformed from the time of the Tudors and with increasing rapidity from the end of the 18th century. The escalating pace of agricultural modernization, industrialization and urbanization gradually broke up the family as a unit of production and turned it into a unit of consumption. The worlds of work and home became increasingly separated. The roles of men and women within the family became differentiated in new ways. A world of childhood more strongly separated from adult society began to emerge (at least in the homes of families in more comfortable circumstances).

While the main driving force was economic change, other factors also came into play. Religion was one. The Reformation and the Civil War of the 17th century undermined the already limited role the church had formerly played in providing care and education for children whose parents were unable to do so. Debate on the responsibilities of parents followed. One particularly influential figure across Europe was the Czech Protestant theologian Comenius who, in a book first published in 1633, argued that children under 7 should be educated in the 'school of the mother', i.e. kept at home with mothers who would devote much of their time to the upbringing of those children (Comenius, 1956). Catholic thinkers were more prepared to see a role for the institutional church in work with young children. Long after most people had forgotten the theological origins of the differences, it remained the case that countries that had been largely Protestant (such as Britain) were more reluctant to see very young children cared for or educated outside the family home than countries, such as France and Spain, that had remained largely Catholic.

As religious belief began to fade from the picture, science became more significant in shaping attitudes to early childhood. From the 1890s, people began to study the cognitive development as well as the physical growth of small children, and in the early 20th century the picture was further modified with new perspectives on emotional development, especially those put forward by Freudians, such as Melanie Klein.

In the 18th century, England failed to follow Scotland in the development of a system of basic education. In fact, fewer English children were in school in 1800 than there had been when Elizabeth I came to the throne in 1558. As the pace of industrialization and urbanization grew, many people saw the need for schools for children under 7. Infant schools were established by philanthropists on a voluntary basis, first in London then across much of the UK. The ideas of Froebel on education were spread by the many German immigrants in London, Manchester and other major cities from the middle of the century onwards. Central Government became tentatively involved. A key date was 1839 when the Privy Council established its own Education Committee. However, the state's involvement was opposed by many (because it would limit the influence of the churches) and progress was slow. A universal system of elementary schooling was established by an Act of Parliament in 1870 and measures to strengthen that reform followed later. There was still reluctance to accept fully that government now had the leading responsibility in this field. The age at which schooling should start was set at 5 years. This was lower than in much of Europe because English policy-makers believed that the schooling of the majority of children by the state was something of an unfortunate necessity and should be got out of the way as soon as possible.

If there was reluctance to see the state take on responsibility for schooling, there was even more reluctance to see it provide day care for working mothers. A few employers recognized the potential benefits to themselves of providing their female employees with childcare where it was needed. There were also a large number of women called 'baby-farmers' who were paid by working-class parents to provide childminding and fostering services and even acted as unofficial adoption agents. However, many opposed paid employment by the mothers of young children. A day nursery system for lower-paid families had barely begun to emerge by the 20th century and the number of day nurseries in the UK actually dropped quite drastically between the two world wars. There was some pressure on the school system from parents to take very young children and this was seen as a source of difficulty in itself, since schools lacked the skills, equipment or space to cope with toddlers. It is also worth noting that while lower-income mothers were blamed for seeking the paid help of others to care for their children, mothers in more affluent families found themselves increasingly unable to cope without the help of nannies and in 1892 Emily Ward opened the first training college for them – the Norland Institute.

The First World War reinforced a lesson that had been learned from the Boer War a few years previously – that many working-class men were in too poor a state of health to be adequate soldiers. There was a new emphasis during that war on the need for advice and other forms of support for young mothers and on the provision of play opportunities for older children in order to secure the health of future generations of soldiers. The impact was so significant that it led Dwork to give her book about maternal and child welfare services in this period the deliberately disconcerting title *War is Good for Babies* (1987). The period after the war might have seen further improvements. However, concerns about the health of pre-school children meant that the medical profession often had a dominant say in education and day care for children under 5. This was resented by leaders of the teaching profession (who opposed, for example, the development of separate nursery schools). More significantly, the economic problems of the inter-war years discouraged any real investment in early childhood services, which – as in later recessions – were seen as being among the most obvious forms of expenditure to cut.

There were, nevertheless, many arguing for better services. This is an aspect of the history of the period that is frequently forgotten. When the Women's Liberation Movement was formed in the 1970s, its adherents often described it as the 'second wave of feminism', as though nothing had happened between the victory of the Suffragettes in securing votes for women in 1918 and their own movement. But then the members of the Women's Liberation Movement were for the most part young and it is one of the characteristics of the young to feel more uncomplicated affection for their grandparents than for their parents. In fact, feminist struggles continued throughout the inter-war period. When Bradford City Council closed down many of its nursery schools and play centres in the early 1930s, the politicians making the decisions were mainly men and those opposing them mainly women. More significantly, the gender dimension of the dispute was highlighted in the arguments in the local press and elsewhere.

The pressure for better childcare that was there already played an important part in securing such services during the Second World War. It is sometimes said that the government opened up day nurseries soon after the start of the war because it needed women for war-time production and took the cynical decision to close them down afterwards when it was no longer dependent on their contribution. There is some truth in this, but it is an over-simplification. Other aspects of what happened should be taken into account:

▸ Initially, the pressure for wartime day nurseries came from women's organizations. Many in government and among their professional advisers were reluctant to agree. They believed that, as children's day care is very labour intensive, the provision of nurseries would make no substantial difference to the war effort. There were also fears that children in nurseries would be especially vulnerable to both infectious diseases and enemy bombing.

▶ In so far as the government did want to see mothers freed up for wartime production, they would have preferred to see this being made possible by some kind of childminding. However, the two officially sponsored forms of childminding – the Volunteer Housewives Scheme and the Guardians Scheme – were both flops.

▶ A good deal of the day care that was provided during the war came, not just from day nurseries, but from play centres and extended hours nursery classes – services whose importance has often been ignored.

▶ The pace of closure of wartime nurseries after the war varied from place to place. In Sheffield, for example, it was not until 1953 that large-scale closures took place.

Before the war, many women had looked forward to improved early childhood services as the economic difficulties eased. After the war, the same women assumed that such services would form part of the new welfare state. It did not happen. The UK was in serious financial difficulties after the war and early childhood services were again among the first casualties of restrictions on public expenditure.

Developments from 1951 to 1997

In 1951 a long period of Conservative rule began (interrupted by periods of Labour Party rule in the 1960s and 1970s). This did not mean an immediate retreat from the newly established 'welfare state'. There was a considerable consensus on matters of policy, with the Conservatives accepting the welfare state and the Labour Party supporting many of the policies of the Conservatives on foreign affairs and defence. However, consolidation of the welfare state meant working within the framework already established (building more council houses, for example) rather than developing new institutions. The trauma of the war led many to seek a return to what was seen as normality, only with more financial security and better health services. There was little challenge to the established model of family life – many people wanted to get back to it again. The age at which couples married and had their first children dropped to a lower level in the 1950s and 1960s than at any other point in the 20th century.

However, as material comfort became better established, other problems began to emerge. The separation of work and home was being reinforced by the development of new residential areas – council estates, new towns and owner-occupied suburbs. Life in these areas was more comfortable, but in many ways more lonely than in older working-class neighbourhoods. Doctors began to talk about the spread of 'sub-clinical neurosis', the press of 'new town blues'. The reduction in the amount of hard physical work involved in running a home (because of the then greater availability of domestic equipment, such as vacuum cleaners and washing machines) left women with time on their hands. The cost of those new homes also made the idea of paid employment more attractive. More and more women looked to go out to work even when their children were young.

The government was unhappy about this. One of the major policy changes introduced towards the end of the 1940s was an Act of Parliament regulating childminders and private nurseries, which were seen as a potential problem rather than as a resource for families. Local authority day nurseries were intended for families that were failing in some way. There were moves to improve the training of nursery nurses, but the qualifications offered by the National Nursery Examination Board were at a low level and many of those that secured them became nannies rather than working in day care. Innovation came from community organizations – not the government or the professions. The best-known example was the pre-school playgroup movement launched by a group of London housewives in 1960, which soon became a national organization (now called the Pre-school Learning Alliance). There were also moves to establish holiday playcare schemes that were similarly based on very local initiatives. Both playgroups and playschemes were designed primarily for the benefit of children rather than to make it easier for mothers to seek paid employment. However, they did undermine the idea that care in organized settings was only needed for families that were in some sense failing. They provided positive lessons of what could be achieved with young children and facilitated greater cooperation between providers and parents in planning for them than many of the services provided by the state.

The Labour Party, which was in power for much of the period from the middle of the 1960s to the end of the 1970s, made only tentative efforts to improve early childhood services. In 1968 the law on regulation was revised to bring more childminding arrangements within its scope and to encourage attention to avoiding accidental harm as well as infectious diseases. The Family Advice Centres launched in a few places towards the end of the 1960s anticipated in some ways the later Sure Start Children's Centres, but had too little support and died out. The Plowden Committee set up to consider nursery classes and schools in England and the similar body under Professor Gittins in Wales had a significant impact on approaches to teaching, but favoured only modest increases in the scale of nursery education and even the degree of expansion they supported was lost in the economic problems of the 1970s.

The pressure from parents for more early childhood services grew only gradually. Little was done by the state. There were ventures from the voluntary and commercial sectors, but the major expansion in childcare was in the number of registered childminders and research conducted in the 1970s highlighted the poor quality of many registered childminders, who lacked any consistent form of training or support, not to mention the many unregistered ones.

In 1979, Margaret Thatcher became the UK's first woman prime minister. It might have been expected that this would bring about a new and improved situation for other career women. However, the Conservative Party was anxious to bring back adherence to older 'family values' and also wanted to restrict rather than enhance the role of the state in social life. The one really important contribution to early childhood services they made was to set up a much more effective regulatory regime for children's day care and childminding as part of their 1989 Children Act. Even that was something they took on reluctantly under pressure from voluntary-sector organizations and, once the Act was implemented, they expressed unhappiness about the way local authorities were implementing it. When Thatcher's successor John Major was prime minister, there were new moves on pre-school education. A serious start was made on devising a curriculum for children aged 3–5 and a system of vouchers was devised for nursery education. Even the latter was a half-hearted measure since it appears that the primary motivation was to try out the idea of vouchers before applying the scheme to the main school system.

Initiatives to develop early childhood services in the 1980s took place largely outside government. The number of private and voluntary day nurseries increased. Several voluntary bodies that had been set up some time earlier to provide health services for families with young children lost much of that role with a major reform of the National Health Service in 1974 and began to focus on day nursery provision and parent support. Teams set up in the social services departments to regulate childminding and nurseries began to offer advice and support as well as to regulate. Leaders of the teaching profession began to argue that there was a lack of direction in early childhood services and that giving a clear lead role to education was the best way to tackle this.

Pressure from outside government and the established professions grew significantly. A critical aspect of this was the establishment of a number of new third-sector organizations:

▶ The National Childminding Association (NCMA), which had been established in 1977, continued to develop its role in the improvement of childminding as a profession.

▶ In 1980 a National Child Care Campaign was launched in London.

▶ In 1982 the National Out of School Alliance (now 4Children) was set up as an independent body to press for better out of school care.

▶ In 1986 the Daycare Trust was launched with plans to strengthen the case for better day care by publishing research.

▶ In 1987 an independent Children's Information Service was opened in Sheffield, specifically as a pilot for a possible nationwide network of such agencies.

▶ 1989 the National Children's Bureau set up the Early Childhood Forum, an important medium of exchange between people pressing for change.

▶ In 1990 the Childcare Association, representing private nurseries, was established, although this body did not survive for long and was effectively replaced in 2000 by the National Day Nurseries Association (NDNA).

Activity

Study a book or official document dealing with an aspect of early years services that was published before 1970.

▶ To what extent are the values and assumptions that underpin the document ones that would be widely accepted today?

▶ Are there any references or assertions in the text that you find puzzling? (If so, can further reading help you understand what was meant?)

▶ To what extent does the text demonstrate an appreciation of the whole early years scene (whether or not it deals with a particular topic)?

What have you learned from this exercise about the ways in which attitudes to young children and early childhood services have changed in the period since the text was published?

The Labour governments of 1997–2010 and the new emphasis on early childhood services

In 1985, while in opposition, the Labour Party produced a booklet explaining how they would – if they secured power – initiate a new deal for early childhood services. Twelve years passed before they were able to win a general election and put their ideas into practice. They were, however, able to initiate changes in many of the large cities where they controlled the local authorities. In particular, several of them set up 'integrated' services for young children and encouraged employers to consider workplace nurseries or other ways of subsidizing their employees' childcare costs. It was widely expected that they would do a great deal when they came to power nationally in 1997.

However, there were important differences of perspective within the Labour Party's leadership. Tony Blair, who became leader of the party in 1994 and was prime minister from 1997 to 2007, supported moves to facilitate both day care and pre-school education, but his own interest in and knowledge of the subject appear to have been slight. This is clear from the fact that early childhood services go unmentioned in the many books that describe his time in power, whether from vantage points on the inside or from a more distant perspective. It is also clear from the scant mention Blair gave the topic in a book outlining his political creed. He speaks in one brief passage of childcare being important so that single mothers can get off welfare and back to work, but has nothing else to say on the subject (Blair, 1996: 68). His own direct interventions in the field as prime minister were ill-judged and poorly informed. One occurred quite early in his premiership when he contemplated taking responsibility for early childhood services from his Education Minister and handing it back to Health. This seems to have resulted from his impatience with the slow pace of progress in establishing enough services to make a significant dent in welfare dependency, rather than from any principled position as to where such services should fit within the welfare state (Blunkett, 2006: 156–7). Another occurred just before he resigned as prime minister when he said that Sure Start was one of the public services that he believed was doing badly, but failed to identify what he thought the problems – or the solutions – were (Wintour, 2006). Some of his ministers agreed with him. Estelle Morris, the Minister for Education, said in 2002 that she considered that everything that needed to be done to improve early childhood services was now accomplished and it was time the government turned to other issues. The reaction was so hostile that she back-tracked a little, but her statement was one indication of the low importance some senior members of Blair's government ascribed to the issue (Tweed, 2002).

Blair may not have seen early childhood services as a priority, but statements from the Labour Party had stimulated activity amongst those in the field and pressure began to build for more to be done. Moreover, Blair's Chancellor Gordon Brown seems to have seen the issue as more crucial than Blair himself did (Blunkett, 2006: 28). Thus, during Blair's second period of office, partly as a result of the scandal caused by the death of Victoria Climbié and the report of events compiled by Lord Laming in 2003, there was a renewed emphasis on the reform of early childhood services. Once Brown was prime minister himself and his close ally Ed Balls was put in charge of the new Department for Children, Schools and Families, the issue climbed even higher up the political agenda.

There were three main strands to the policy on early childhood services during Blair's first period in office:

▶ A National Childcare Strategy was published in a Green Paper (DfEE, 1998). The objective of the strategy was to encourage the development of new services and at the same time maximize the choice to parents. Because of the centrality given to the principle of parental choice, provision was not to be secured by any central plan that might have entailed establishing an early years centre in every neighbourhood, but by helping parents to pay for both childcare and pre-school education through tax credits and in other ways. In other words, the emphasis was entirely on assisting those with demands to secure the services they wanted rather than on the state supplying services either directly or by sub-contracting providers from the voluntary or commercial spheres. The option of setting up a national system of local services was just not considered. It was too 'old Labour' and too expensive.

▶ To offset some of the potential defects of a market-led policy, effort was put into securing greater coherence. In part, this was one aspect of the wider system of regular spending reviews instituted by Labour, although it was significant that work with children required a special set of arrangements within that system because so many departmental boundaries were crossed. Local authorities were required to establish Early Years Development and Childcare Partnerships (EYDCPs) to pull together the work of different local authority departments, the NHS at local level and various agencies outside the state. These were later judged not to have worked well (with most going out of existence by the end of 2004). However, the principle of partnership, which lay behind them, also underpinned later legislation to establish Local Area Agreements within local authority areas and Children's Trusts.

▶ A new system of regulation of childminding and day care was established in England under Ofsted, with a similar system in Wales under the new Welsh Assembly (later developments were to follow in Scotland and Northern Ireland). The Care Standards Act 2000 was not implemented until after the general election of 2001, but it entailed a number of significant changes. It highlighted the fact that the argument over which profession was to take the lead in early childhood services had been won by Education. It made it possible to combine the inspection processes for day care and nursery education. It paved the way for a system of regulation based on actual outcomes (i.e. what the experience of being cared for was like for the children involved) rather than inputs (i.e. detailed regulations on how providers were expected to operate). This required a new professionalism of both providers and childcare inspectors. The new system also laid the basis for consistency across England in the judgements that were made on services that were inspected and arranged for their publication on the Internet. It separated quite radically the arrangements for regulation from those for support to services (which stayed with local authorities) with the intention at least of ensuring proper attention to both tasks. These were all important changes. They also marked a shift from preventing the bad to supporting improvements in quality. They must be seen alongside a number of initiatives that were taken to encourage the development of innovative services at local level. There are likely to be changes in the system of regulation in the future, but 2001 was probably the last time that a change in the law on regulation was a major part of any government's policy on early childhood services.

Blair's second period of office saw the consolidation of much of this. As well as the implementation of changes in the law, it also saw:

▶ the publication of *Birth to Three Matters*, an important official document on the quality of work with children under 3 that complemented the *Curriculum Guidance for the Foundation Stage* (Abbott, 2002)

▶ the Green Paper *Every Child Matters* (which laid down principles for work with all children and young people, including changes in the system to safeguard them from neglect or abuse) (DfES, 2003)

▶ the development of a network of Children's Centres, starting in the poorest parts of the country, the purpose of which was to secure cooperation between agencies and innovative work at local level.

What undermined much of this was that the National Childcare Strategy was failing in its primary objective. It was not making it sufficiently easy for parents to access good quality and affordable childcare and, therefore, was doing too little to reduce child poverty and welfare dependency. There were detailed arguments between academics and others as to the scale on which these failures were happening and there was no doubt that many local Sure Start projects were making a positive difference to the families that used their services. The fact remained that (as has happened in other countries) the impact of tax credits, nursery grants or other systems to help parents secure access to pre-school education and to childcare (including out-of-school-hours care for younger school-age children) did not lead to improvements in availability on the scale that had been anticipated.

When Brown became prime minister in 2007, Ed Balls attempted to deal with these difficulties largely by the expenditure of enormous energy.

▶ Great effort was put into promoting the idea of Sure Start Children's Centres.

▶ Children's Trusts were given a new legislative basis as part of an Act of Parliament passed in 2009.

▶ A Children's Workforce Development Council was established to promote new ideas on ways in which professions concerned with children could be helped to work together more effectively, including a significant expansion in the amount of shared elements in professional training.

▶ Local authorities and NHS Primary Care Trusts in particular were leaned on to work more closely together on the elaboration and implementation of joint plans for children and young people.

▶ The Foundation Stage curriculum guidance introduced in 2000 was heavily revised and the 'stage' itself extended from covering children aged 3–5 years to covering children from birth until close on their sixth birthday.

Much of this was to the good, although there were complaints that too many resources were going into high-level discussions on joint planning and too few into implementation, that serious problems were still arising in child protection (with some of the measures taken since Laming appearing to have aggravated rather than eased them) and that the new Foundation Stage curriculum was too detailed and lent itself to burdensome paperwork.

The main problem remained that of the *supply* of early childhood services. The Daycare Trust warned in 2009 that childcare costs were continuing to rise in a way that caused parents enormous problems without any obvious gains being made by providers or their staff. The number of providers was falling. Some of this may have been due to inadequate providers leaving the business and some providers offering a wider range of services, but it was clear that major difficulties lay ahead.

Activity

Talk to someone who was working in an early years setting in 1997, preferably someone still working in the field today.

▶ Ask her/him about the ways in which things have changed since that period. What are the most important of the changes that have taken place in that person's opinion?

▶ What is her/his understanding of the thinking behind the changes of which s/he is most aware?

▶ How have the changes s/he has seen impacted on daily practice and the expectations of parents?

▶ Does s/he see the changes as making things better, on the whole, or worse for practitioners, children and parents?

▶ What do you make of her/his experience?

The Coalition government of 2010

In the spring of 2010, the general election resulted in defeat for Labour, but no overall majority for the Conservatives who went into coalition with the Liberal Democrats to form a government. Although Sarah Teather, the first Minister for

Children in the new government, was a Liberal Democrat, it was evident that the Conservatives had a stronger and more detailed approach to the issue and that early childhood services was one of the areas where their views were likely to prevail. In the period from the electoral defeat of the Conservatives in 1997 to the rise of David Cameron to the leadership of the party at the end of 2005, Conservative leaders had made little reference to the Labour government's new emphasis on young children. It seemed safe to assume that, while considerably less enthusiastic than some in the Labour Party, they had no intention of reversing what had happened. It gradually became clear that, with Cameron as Conservative leader, this was no longer a safe assumption.

Before the election of 2010, David Willetts, a leading Conservative, had twice made public statements about the need to slow down the development of Sure Start (Morton, 2009; Faux, 2010). Balls in response highlighted the progress of Sure Start as one of the successes of the Labour government. Once the Coalition government was established, work began on chipping away at the changes the Labour Party had introduced. Some of these moves were symbolic. The crucial government department was once more called simply the Department of Education, although the functions relating to children that the previous government had transferred to that sphere were retained. Another gesture was the discouragement everyone was given from making use of the phrase 'Every Child Matters' or referring to the five outcomes for children that policy should be serving. Since no one is ever likely to object to children being healthy, safe, materially secure or able to enjoy life and make a positive contribution to society, this step can only have been a re-branding exercise, underlining the split from the past. Other measures included a reduction in the funding and role, and eventual closure in 2011, of the Children's Workforce Development Council, the establishment of a review under Dame Clare Tickell of the new Foundation Stage which simplified the guidance (something that the Liberal Democrats had also actively sought) and a commitment to recruit 4,200 more health visitors in order to achieve a greater focus on support to families in their own homes rather than in group settings.

The key change – one signalled by the Conservatives long before the election – was to abandon the idea of Sure Start being a universal service and concentrate effort on those families in the greatest difficulties. Teather, in an article published in 2010, spoke of Sure Start as a 'universal service' whilst saying she wanted to 'better target those most in need'. If this was not confused thinking, the statement was certainly confusing. The new prime minister was rather clearer on the principle. In a speech given in August 2010, Cameron said that the 'sharp-elbowed middle classes' should keep out of Sure Start, which was 'for those who are suffering the greatest disadvantage' (Hope, 2010). This was in sharp contrast to the stated aim of the Labour government to develop Sure Start as a universal service. Many were worried that it threatened a return to the situation that had prevailed for much of the period from the 1950s to the 1990s where local authority day nursery provision was seen as a service for failing families and consequently stigmatized. The collapse of a large number of community-based early childhood services, as their funding was withdrawn or drastically reduced, added to the potential for this to happen, since the manner in which those services were established and operated had produced some reduction of distance between providers and clientele.

At the time of writing, it is clear that the Labour Party's attempted revolution in early years services is faltering. Some providers and other agencies might well continue to make progress. Some might even find the new policy context one that suited them, especially private providers operating in more affluent areas. It was also true that government ministers continued to protest that they were committed to securing the best possible services for young children. However, it was far from clear that the new crucial role for such services that some had sought in the period of Labour rule now had the established status of other aspects of the welfare state.

Summary ☐

This chapter has described:

- ▶ some of the factors that have influenced the opinions of the public, professionals and politicians about the place of early childhood services in the general scheme of things

- ▶ the slow progress made before the end of the 20th century in establishing services for young children

- ▶ the continuing difficulty that such services are not seen as being as integral to the welfare state as certain other services are and that, as a consequence, they are especially vulnerable in times of economic recession

- ▶ the attempt by some in the Labour Party to give early childhood services a more central position and the extent to which they have failed.

Early childhood services are not making incremental progress as awareness of needs and the forms of provision that are best take hold. Things are more complex and controversy-ridden than that. The next chapter deals in more detail with some of the social and political forces that lie behind changes in policy.

Further reading

Baldock, P. (2011) *Developing Early Childhood Services: Past, Present and Future,* Maidenhead: Open University Press. Offers the only history of the full range of services available for young children.

Cunningham, H. (2006) *The Invention of Childhood*, London: BBC Books. Offers a good introduction to the historical study of childhood in this country.

Key Dates in the Development of Early Years Policy, 1962–2012

This timeline sets out some of the principal dates in the development of early years in the UK over the last half-century (starting in 1962) in order to give you an overview and help you put particular events in their historical context.

NB: Only those general elections that led to a change of government are included.

1962 • The Nursery Schools Campaign becomes the National Association of Pre-School Playgroups (now the Pre-Schools Learning Alliance)

1963 • The Children and Young Persons Act provides the legislative base for Family Advice Centres

1964 • The Labour Party wins the general election

1965 • The Ministry of Health conducts an inquiry on childminding

1966 • The Handicapped Adventure Playground Association is launched – a significant event in the development of inclusion in play settings

1967 • The Plowden Report is published

1968 • The Health Services and Public Health Act tightens up the regulation of day care and childminding

1969 • The Children and Young Persons Act (among other things) increases the powers of local authorities to intervene in families

1970 • The Conservatives win the general election

1971 • Social Services Departments begin operating

1972 • The White Paper *Education: A Framework for Expansion* urges education departments to cooperate more closely with the voluntary and community sector in early childhood provision

1973 • A Major research project on childminding by Brian and Sonia Jackson begins

1974 • The Labour Party wins the general election

1975 • The Children Act is passed in response to child abuse scandals

1976 • The DES/DHSS report *Low Cost Day Care for the Under-Fives* is produced
• The National Conference at Sunningdale speaks of the dangers of

emotional deprivation for children in day care – this is highly influential for many years to come

1977 • The National Childminding Association (NCMA) is launched

1978 • A government circular on the coordination of early childhood services is released

1979 • The Conservative Party wins the general election

1980 • The National Child Care Campaign is launched

1981 • The Brierley Report leads to reforms at the National Nursery Examination Board

1982 • The National Out of School Alliance (Later 4Children) is launched

1983 • Changes in tax law create difficulties for assistance with childcare which employers offer their staff

1984 • The Workplace Nurseries Campaign is launched

1985 • The Labour Party presents its 'Charter' for under-5s

1986 • The Daycare Trust is launched
     • An 'integrated' service for early childhood is formed in Strathclyde (this is copied over the next decade in several local authorities run by the Labour Party)

1987 • The Clark Report speaks of the need for greater coordination of early childhood services

1988 • The National Curriculum is introduced in schools

1989 • The Children Act (among other things) extends the system of regulation of early years day care and childminding
     • The UN Convention on the Rights of the Child is published

1990 • The Rumbold Report on the education of 3–5-year-olds is published
     • The Scottish Childminding Association is launched

1991 • Guidance on the regulation of early childhood services is published by the government
     • The number of playgroups and childminders reaches an all-time high
     • The UK formally adopts the UN Convention on the Rights of the Child

1992 • The Schools Act establishes Ofsted

- Part X of the 1989 Children Act (on regulation of early childhood services) is implemented

1993
- A government circular accuses local authorities of being too rigid in the regulation of early childhood services
- The *First Class* report by Ofsted on reception classes is produced

1994
- The Council for Awards in Children's Care and Education (CACHE) is formed

1995
- A hearing in the High Court confirms that official Guidance and Regulations on the registration and inspection of early childhood services does not have the force of law

1996
- *Desirable Outcomes for Children's Learning on Entering Compulsory Education* is published by the Schools Curriculum and Assessment Authority – the start of what later became the Early Years Foundation Stage (EYFS)
- The Nursery Education and Grant-Maintained Schools Act sets out the voucher system for nursery education

1997
- The Labour Party wins the general election

1998
- The National Childcare Strategy is launched

1999
- Working Families Tax Credit is introduced
- The National Early Years Training Organisation is launched
- The Protection of Children Act comes into force

2000
- The National Day Nurseries Association is launched
- *Curriculum Guidance for the Foundation Stage* is published
- The Care Standards Act (among other things) lays down the legislative basis for the transfer of early childhood services regulation from local authorities to Ofsted in England and the Assembly in Wales

2001
- Local authorities are obliged for the first time to provide information, advice and training services in the early years field
- New regulatory regimes take over in England and Wales
- The First Children's Commissioner is appointed in Wales
- *For Scotland's Children* is published by the Scottish Executive

2002
- The Criminal Records Bureau begins work
- *Birth to Three Matters* is published
- The *Inter-departmental Review of Childcare* is published
- A single Sure Start unit is established in the DfES

2003
- The Laming Report on the Victoria Climbié case is produced

- *Every Child Matters* is published
- A 'children's centres' programme is announced
- The Children's Commissioner for Northern Ireland takes up their position

2004
- The *Common Core Prospectus* for early years is drafted
- A system of 'light touch' regulation of nannies is announced
- The EPPE (*Effective Provision of Pre-School Education*) report is published
- The ten-year strategy for childcare in England is published
- The Children Act comes into force
- The Children's Commissioner for Scotland is appointed
- The Childcare Working group is set up by the Welsh Assembly Government

2005
- The Children's Commissioner for England is appointed
- The Children's Workforce Development Council for England is launched
- The evaluation of Sure Start is published

2006
- The Childcare Act comes into force
- The first set of candidates secure the new EYPS
- The Welsh Assembly publishes its strategic plan for education for 2006–2010

2007
- A critical report on children's centres is published by the National Audit Office
- Ofsted's range of responsibilities is significantly extended
- The new SNP government in Scotland appoints the country's first Minister for Children and the Early Years
- A new Department for Children, Schools and Families is established
- The final version of the Welsh Foundation Stage guidance is published
- The new qualifications framework for Scotland is published
- The Department for Education in Northern Ireland assumes responsibility for Sure Start in the province
- Critical reports on the ways in which government policy on funding early childhood services is working are issued by the Child Care Trust and HEDRA Consulting

2008
- The new EYFS in England is implemented

2009
- The Apprentices, Skills, Children and Learning Act (among other things) alters the law in relation to children's centres, Safeguarding Boards and Children's Trusts

2010
- The general election leads to a coalition government being formed by

the Conservative Party and the Liberal Democrats
- A review of the Early Years Foundation Stage is set up
- Cuts in public spending begin
- Ofsted figures show an 'alarming' drop in the number of childcare places in England
- Private providers threaten to pull out of the nursery education grant system
- Dunford reviews the role of the Children's Commissioner for England
- The Frank Field report *The Foundation Years: preventing poor children becoming poor adults: the report of the Independent Review on Poverty and Life Chances* is published

2011
- There is a continued decline in the number of childcare places
- A survey by 4Children and the Daycare Trust suggests that some 250 children's centres in England could close
- 4Children is asked to set up a group to lead work with the government on early childhood services, as part of the Department for Education's grant programme for the voluntary sector
- An advisory group on early years policy is set up by the government
- Funding is announced for childcare strategy in Northern Ireland
- The government Green Paper *Support and Aspiration: A New Approach to SEN and Disability* sets out a new approach to supporting children and families with special educational needs and disabilities
- The Tickell report on EYFS is published
- The Munro review of child protection (final report) is produced
- The Graham Allen report: *Early Intervention: The Next Steps* is published

2012
- Nutbrown reviews education and childcare qualifications (interim report March 2012, final report June 2012)
- A Revised Statutory Framework for the Early Years Foundation Stage is produced

Figure 2.1 *Key dates in the development of early years policy*

Chapter 3

Influences on Early Years Policy Development

This chapter explores:

▸ the range of influences on the formation and development of early years policy

▸ the ways in which policy is developed

▸ the first two levels of policy-making as described in Chapter 1 (underlying factors and broad objectives). The third level (detailed arrangements required to meet those objectives) is discussed in Chapter 4.

In this chapter, we explore case studies of policy development to demonstrate who is involved in policy-making and how particular policies come into being. The social and cultural contexts of early years policy development are discussed along with the influence of social change and public opinion on the policy process. The roles of central and local government and key government agencies are also discussed with reference to the influence of early years agencies, organizations, practitioners and academics on how policy is developed.

The development of early years policy is often part of much wider policy agendas, and the goals of early years policy may be broader than simply developing and structuring services for young children and their families. For example, within the New Labour political agenda (1997–2010), much of the development of early years services was part of a much bigger strategy to tackle poverty and raise standards of educational outcomes for children. The aims of early years policy were multi-layered and complex, interweaving early years developments with other linked social goals.

During this period, the development of early years services was part of the Every Child Matters policy agenda and other policy related to reducing social exclusion and poverty, the aims of which included:

▸ improving educational standards, particularly basic skills, especially among socially disadvantaged children

▸ increasing employability among school-leavers and reducing the number of NEETS (not in employment, education or training) aged 16–24

▶ providing childcare so parents (particularly mothers) can go into work, education or training

▶ reducing the number of people dependent on the state in both the short and the long term

▶ ensuring better standards of health and welfare for all children

▶ reducing anti-social behaviour and crime rates.

The Coalition government formed in May 2010 has made some significant changes both to the underpinning principles of early years policy and to actual policies. The emphasis on social exclusion and poverty reduction has been downplayed, while the role of early intervention has become very central, influenced by Graham Allen's report *Early Intervention: The Next Steps* (Allen, 2011), which outline the rationale for early intervention, both in terms of child development and the economic use of resources. This is reflected in the planned introduction (at the time of writing) of checks on 2-year-olds to assess any learning or developmental problems to facilitate early intervention. This check will be part of the *Healthy Child* programme and be done alongside health visitor checks in the same time period. However, the focus on family responsibility is also noticeable as parents will receive a report on their child's progress. Although current early years policies, embodied in *Families in the Foundation Stage* (2012), also still focus on the attainment gap and improving progress for all children, as did *Every Child Matters*, the significance of the social and economic dimensions of inequalities in achievement and life chances has given way to increased emphasis on parental engagement, choice and control. Similarly, the roles of professionals are discussed in the context of increased parental responsibility for children's learning and welfare. The focus on family responsibility is placed in the context of parents getting more choice and more flexibility to manage family life and work, such as being able to use the 15 hours of free nursery education and care for longer days and over a minimum of two rather than three days to fit with work hours. It is clear that the universal principles behind Every Child Matters are being replaced with increased expectations on families and more targeted professional interventions.

As with all changes of government, there have been areas of continuity as well as change. The planned extension from 12.5 to 15 hours of free education and care for 3- and 4-year-olds was taken forward within a few months of the Coalition government coming to power, and free early education and care for disadvantaged 2-year-olds was extended to 20 per cent of these, with a further extension to 40 per cent planned. However, changes to the EYFS have been more radical, clearly reflecting current political agendas. Based on the Tickell review (2011), the EYFS, to be re-introduced in September 2012, has been simplified, and focuses much more directly on preparing children for school. The six areas of learning have been changed to seven, but with a clear remit to focus mainly on three of these. They are:

▶ personal, social and emotional development

▶ physical development

▶ communication and language.

Tickell (2011) argues that these three areas are essential for preparation for school as they provide the child with the skills and confidence to access the curriculum, especially literacy. Tickell found the original EYFS to be over-bureaucratic with much repetition and not at all user-friendly for parents because of its complexities. One of the goals of simplification is to try and engage parents more fully with their children's development and learning in line with wider government policy to promote the Big Society, and to place responsibility and power in the hands of individuals and communities. The school-readiness theme is also evident in the closer alignment of the EYFS early learning goals with the KS1 curriculum. And changes to Sure Start Children's Centres are once again a move away from universal services to targeted services. (These are discussed later in this chapter.)

The discussion above illustrates how developments in early years policies cannot be viewed in isolation from the wider political agendas which shape them. A change in government not only produces new policies but also new policy goals and underpinning principles, depending on those agendas. But, why is it important to have an understanding of where early years policy comes from, and what determines the content of such policy? Practitioners need to understand the varied and interrelated factors influencing policy development in the early years, in order to be able to understand their own and others' roles in this process. It is also important to recognize that policy is neither exempt from trends nor made in isolation, but that it is a product of the prevailing social context within which it develops. Practitioners need to understand that policy will change and develop; that it can be questioned; can be considered wrong; and can be influenced by their own views and actions.

Early years policy as a social construct

Social policies, including early years policies, are not created in a vacuum but develop within a historical, cultural and ideological framework. Policy is subject to trends and the influence of dominant viewpoints. It is based on previous policy, which may continue to shape it. It may be influenced by single events or long-term trends. It can be influenced by feedback from those who implement it or research by academics or practitioners. Policy is not developed outside 'real life' but is dependent on what happens in practice whilst at the same time influencing this.

Early years policy can be described as a social construct because its nature and content are dependent at any point in time on the social and cultural context within which it is made and implemented. As such, early years policy will change over time and develop within the society in which it is made. Early years policy is subject not only to wider social and cultural trends and developments, but also specific events within the field of early years. Often, policy developments are the result of the interactions between a complex range of factors.

Historical perspectives on early years policy, like any other policy, are dependent on viewing past events from the ideology and value-systems of the present, resulting in changed perceptions of the relevance of those policies. For example, Moss (2003) discusses how childcare policy has changed over time and how 'best practice' in the past seems 'grotesquely inappropriate' today. Moss concludes:

> care – policy and practice is situated within particular temporal, spatial and cultural contexts. What we see as best practice today may not seem so in another generation, nor will it necessarily be viewed as such from the perspectives of those countries and groups who prefer different approaches or who have different traditions. An historical perspective is a reminder of the provisional and contingent status of all policies, and the practices and provisions to which they give rise. (2003: 16)

For example, one of the authors remembers visiting a residential nursery in the 1970s where children under 2 were cared for either because they were waiting to be placed for adoption or because they were in the short- or long-term care of the local authority. At the time, this type of care was diminishing rapidly as changing views of the needs of infants, particularly around attachment needs, led to the development of policies which determined that all young children should be placed in family care. Within current thinking, this type of group care of young infants goes against everything we know about the needs of children of this age, exemplified by the human rights outcry against such nurseries in countries like Romania and China. However, in the past, young children were routinely raised in orphanages and children's homes, sometimes from birth, and this was considered a positive aspect of child welfare.

In the next section, the various influences on early years policy development are illustrated in an extended case study of how the original Sure Start Local Programmes were developed. This case study is intended to demonstrate the ways in which a range of influences shape policy development at a particular time and how these influences interact with each other.

Case study of early years policy development: Sure Start Local Programmes

One early years policy development that clearly exemplifies the varied range of interrelated factors which come together to influence policy at a particular point in time and place is that of Sure Start Local Programmes (SSLPs). This highly significant development in early years policy evolved in the way it did because of the conjunction of a range of events at a time when the political agenda created an opportunity for this type of project. In 1997, the New Labour government came to power with a remit to tackle poverty and social exclusion. A comprehensive spending review was undertaken to look at how public money was being spent and to make reforms to take into account the spending priorities of the new government. Although most of this review was done on a department-by-department basis, some areas of policy, such as early years, were not the responsibility of one department and so were subject to 'cross-cutting' reviews across a number of departments. The early years 'cross-cutting' review was also influenced by the perception that early years services were failing the most needy children and families. The departments involved were many.

> As well as the obvious departments like health (including personal social services), education and employment (including childcare), there were also social security (benefits for children and families), environment, transport and the regions (urban regeneration and housing), home office (policy on the family), the Lord Chancellor's Department (family law), culture, media and sport (children's play) and the Treasury (the money) – not forgetting the Scots, Welsh and Northern Irish, each with their own subtly different mix of policies (Glass, 1999: 2).

The sheer number of departments involved led to the appointment of Tessa Jowell, the Minister for Public Health, as the chair of the group, not as departmental representative, but in her own right. This was significant in that she strongly influenced changes in the remit to look at under 7s and refocused the review on birth to 3s and pre-conception as the period most likely to influence long-term changes in outcomes for children. Although usually this type of review would mainly have been done through relevant departments as outlined above, early in the review many other agencies became involved either through being contacted by government officials or through their own interventions.

This meant that the development of SSLPs was influenced right from the start by organizations such as the Pre-school Learning Alliance (PLA), National Children's Bureau (NCB), various early years services and academics involved in the field. This involvement by those in practice led to a series of seminars where government officials and ministers met with those directly involved in early years services from 'a wide range of disciplines including child development, social work, health and demography as well as practitioners and local politicians' (Glass, 1999: 3). It also led to the commissioning of a review of research into 'what worked' to support children and families by Marjorie Smith of the Thomas Coram Research Unit (Smith et al., 1998).

The result of all this range of activity was the conclusion, in the review, that services needed to be developed to support children and families in their earliest years of life to combat multiple disadvantages that had a significant negative influence on children's life chances. Such services needed to be consistently targeted on under 4s where service provision had been persistently neglected and which was, as a result, fragmented and unevenly distributed geographically. Other factors found to be significant in the delivery of such services were the need to provide community-based services, to involve parents and provide family support at a high level. Developments also needed to be long term, sustainable, multi-disciplinary and culturally sensitive.

The influence of the US Head Start programme, which had been running since 1965, was also highly significant in the development of Sure Start. The Head Start programmes had been developed to support pre-school children from low-income families to improve educational attainments and general health and welfare. Early Head Start had been established in 1995 to extend the programme to children aged from birth to 3 and pregnant women. The development of SSLPs drew much from the structure and philosophy of Head Start, particularly the child-focused and multi-agency approach.

And so the SSLPs were born and with them the start of the government's later wide-ranging Sure Start initiative. Some of the key factors influencing policy development which resulted in the establishment of SSLPs, were:

▶ a newly elected government with a mandate to tackle social exclusion

▶ the decision to look at young children's needs across departments (the cross-cutting review)

▶ the review of research on 'what works' for young children

▶ the extensive involvement of agencies and practitioners in that review.

The commitment to SSLPs was significant, reflected in the growth of the number of programmes. Between the initial 250 established in 1999 and the sixth 'wave' in 2003, a total of 524 SSLPs were set up in the 20 per cent most disadvantaged wards in the country.

Continues

Continued

Evaluation of the SSLPs has been achieved through a six-year-long project, the National Evaluation of Sure Start (NESS). Earlier reports showed that there were mixed results with inconsistencies between SSLPs and some evidence that SSLPs may have failed to reach the most disadvantaged families they sought to support. Evidence showed positive developments in terms of involving parents but a more mixed and less successful set of outcomes for partnership between agencies. More recently, the NESS team reported that SSLPs had been successful in that:

▸ Parents of 3-year-old children showed less negative parenting while providing their children with a better home learning environment.

▸ Three-year-old children in SSLP areas had better social development with higher levels of positive social behaviour and independence/self-regulation than children in similar areas not having an SSLP.

▸ The SSLP effects for positive social behaviour appeared to be a consequence of the SSLP benefits upon parenting.

▸ Three-year-old children in SSLP areas had higher immunisation rates and fewer accidental injuries than children in similar areas not having an SSLP.

▸ Families living in SSLP areas used more child- and family-related services than those living elsewhere (adapted from NESS Research Team, 2008: 1).

Sure Start Children's Centres

After 2003, existing SSLPs and other existing provision such as neighbourhood nurseries and Early Excellence Centres were transformed into Sure Start Children's Centres, in response to further policy developments which sought to mainstream the types of provision developed through SSLPs. In 2002, the Sure Start Unit and Early Years and Childcare Unit merged to integrate Sure Start and government childcare strategies.

Children's Centres rolled out across the country, with one in every community (over 3,600) by 2011, fulfilling the policy goal to develop universal coverage from the previously targeted service, located mainly in deprived areas. The development of Children's Centres was placed firmly within local authorities, in that since 2004 they were responsible for 'co-ordinating local planning and carrying accountability for delivery' (Arnold, 2005: 7). In addition, developing leadership in Children's Centres was a key focus for ensuring effective change management, with the establishment of the National Professional Qualification in Integrated Centre Management (NPQICL) through the National College for School Leadership piloted in 2004 and rolled out to Children's Centre managers from 2005 onwards.

The development of Children's Centres was based on establishing holistic services for families and children under 5, aiming to provide:

▶ affordable, quality childcare and education

▶ health and family support services

▶ services for children and families with special needs

▶ co-located, integrated service provision to better meet the needs of all children and families and to provide early assessment and intervention for children with additional needs.

This can be seen as a particular example of the application of the principles associated with *Every Child Matters*, in that it should be possible for all children to be healthy, safe, enjoying achievement, making a positive contribution and achieving economic well-being. The aim in this case was to develop integrated mainstream services for all children, which will also better support the children and families most in need. In order to promote this, development work was done on mainstreaming Sure Start principles and practice through seven pilots running between 2002 and 2004. While the actual services provided varied, the pilots all focused on:

▶ developing parenting and family support

▶ training paraprofessionals (frontline workers such as early years practitioners) to provide services such as speech therapy

▶ co-locating and integrating service provision (including health)

▶ developing databases

▶ multi-disciplinary training (Sure Start, 2008).

The evaluation of the mainstreaming pilots provided feedback relevant for the development of Children's Centres:

▶ the use of existing local strategic networks, which was more effective than trying to build new ones

▶ the need for cross-agency steering groups, pilot co-ordinators and project managers to keep new developments on track

▶ feedback systems to monitor progress

▶ early planning and development of mainstreaming strategies

▸ time and resources for frontline staff

▸ regard for both national and local policy and priorities

▸ champions for mainstreaming Sure Start approaches and making the case for change (White et al., 2005).

One of the key arguments for moving from SSLPs focused on disadvantaged areas to universal Children's Centres was that some children and families with needs who lived outside Sure Start areas did not get a service. However, the development of Children's Centres led to a number of concerns about the loss of SSLPs as they stood (Glass, 2005). These concerns focused on several areas:

▸ Spending is now much lower per child as budgets are more thinly spread.

▸ Parental involvement and the role of the voluntary and community sectors were seen as under threat under local authority control.

▸ Services would be less focused on the most needy and would be more focused on childcare and parental employability.

▸ Prescriptive guidelines would lead to fewer local choices.

▸ Professionals from some other agencies, particularly health, were not employed by the Children's Centres and therefore it may be more difficult to secure effective services.

An evaluation of Children's Centres by the National Audit Office (NAO), published in 2006, found:

▸ most families were happy with the quality of services and centres were meeting the needs of some families

▸ fathers, ethnic minority groups (in areas where they were a smaller part of the population), families of children with disabilities and families with the highest level of difficulty were not yet having their needs met across the centres

▸ not all centres had developed effective working arrangements with health and employment services

▸ leadership challenges in developing effective inter-professional cooperation needed to be met

▸ difficulties in measuring the cost-effectiveness of services.

Similarly, Ofsted (2006a) found that Children's Centres were meeting children's needs and were generally well managed, but that measuring the outcomes of extended services posed a challenge as did short-term funding. They found that 'The most successful providers shaped the provision gradually to reflect their community's needs and wants in collaboration with other agencies' (Ofsted, 2006a: 3).

In early 2008, Ofsted reported again on the progress of Children's Centres, finding that:

▸ centres were generally successful in promoting the five *Every Child Matters* outcomes

▸ parents were positive about the childcare on offer and children using the centres were generally well-prepared for school.

However, although local authorities supported the setting up of centres, Ofsted (2008) found that they gave less support for monitoring and evaluation, and despite performance management guidance issued in late 2006 this continued to be an area for development for centres (DfES, 2006). The guidance aims to support clearer monitoring and evaluation to ensure that services also reach the most disadvantaged groups and that outcomes for children's achievement can be tracked.

The Office for Standards in Education also found that:

▸ services within centres are not always well coordinated and this may be affecting take-up

▸ not all types of families are using the centres fully, with ethnic minority groups and families with disabilities less likely to.

Since 2010, the Coalition government has started to change the focus of Sure Start Children's Centres (SSCCs) in line with its policy approach. Government cuts to local authority spending resulted in the closure of over 125 centres in 2010–2011. The Early Intervention Grant (agreed by the Spending Review, 2010) was sufficient to maintain SSCCs according to the government but in fact closures followed rapidly as did many mergers. The focus of SSCCs has shifted again to early intervention and targeted support for families in the greatest need, rather than the universal service Children's Centres had become.

Other changes planned at the time of writing are to introduce payment by results to SSCCs, currently being piloted, and to increase the use of evidence-based interventions. The introduction of increased voluntary and community sector involvement and local accountability are also planned. Further, there are plans to remove the requirement for both an EYPS and qualified teacher in SSCCs and to remove the necessity of having full day care in SSCCs in the most disadvantaged areas. The implication is that SSCCs are not seen as cost-effective in this administration, and that the wider policy agenda to focus early years services on the most disadvantaged in order to reduce costs will affect SSCCs in terms of numbers and purpose. There is also a possibility that these changes will result in a two-tier system of SSCCs and the further loss of centres. One of the reasons for making SSCCs a universal service was that many disadvantaged families did not live in the poorest wards where SSLPs were first introduced, and therefore the current closures may mean that many miss out.

Factors influencing early years policy development

As exemplified in the case study above, SSLPs (and later SSCCs) were established through the conjunction of a range of influences at a particular place and point in time. In the case study, one of the key factors was the complex interaction between political agendas, politicians, civil servants and the professional groups who became involved in the process of developing SSLPs. The election of the New Labour government in 1997 had resulted in a shift of political objectives and placed individuals with an interest in developing services for young children in positions of power. This provided a forum for the views of professional organizations such as the NCB and the Thomas Coram Foundation to become more influential. However, the development of SSLPs into SSCCs and the most recent changes to SSCCs are mainly the result of changing political agendas.

Factors influencing policy development do not operate independently, but form systems, which create policy unique to themselves. A system can be defined as a set of elements interacting to achieve a goal. The components of a system are the elements that are involved in the processes of the system, which can affect the system and may be affected by it (Levine and Fitzgerald, 1992). For example, in the development of SSLPs the elements involved in this process included the work of the cross-cutting review and the contributions of politicians, civil servants, practitioners, agencies and researchers (Figure 3.1). However, within systems theory there is a belief that in order to understand some events, we need not just see the elements contributing to an event but also the whole, recognizing patterns and interrelationships between the elements (Senge and Lannon-Kim, 1991). In the case study, the important feature of the policy development was not just who or which agencies were involved in the process, but the nature and quality of the interrelationships between these. A key feature of this development was the communication that took place between different elements, and the ways in which beliefs about how the needs of children and families could be best met were shaped by these communications. The development of SSLPs was not just based on ideas about how children's needs could be best met but also on perceived failures of previous policy.

As was said at the end of Chapter 2, it is important to remember that, nationally, governments determine the direction of early years policy and the ways in which other influences come to bear on government plans are complex. It is clear that the influence of factors such as lobbying by professional organizations and academic research may have no significant impact on policy development until it coincides with a political agenda. The ways in which political agendas are shaped and developed are discussed below.

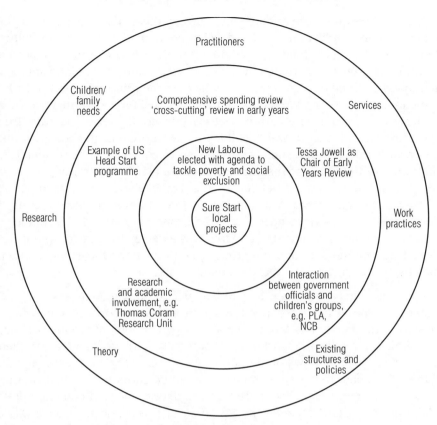

Figure 3.1 *Systems diagram of the development of Sure Start*

The social and cultural context of early years policy

One of the most significant influences on early years policy is the social and cultural context in which policy is made. Social and cultural changes over time shape views and attitudes towards how children and families should behave and be supported. One of the driving forces behind more recent policy in the early years has been changes in how childcare is seen in terms of its value to children and families and changes in attitudes towards working mothers.

Moss (2003) identifies three social norms which have influenced the development of childcare policy over time:

▸ individualized care of children within the family

▸ gender division of labour

▸ national economic survival.

The changing nature of the relationship between these norms has been significant in shaping early years policy development. In the UK, strong cultural beliefs in family responsibility for children and the privacy of the family as an institution have been punctuated by the state's assumption of responsibility for children where families are seen to have failed in their duty of care. Until 1997, this meant that care of children outside the home had for a long time been seen as a last resort – undesirable but necessary in some cases (Daycare Trust, 2005). However, attitudes towards childcare have more recently been reconfigured towards the view that such care is a positive contribution to all children's welfare, rather than a compensation for poor standards of parenting. This sea change in attitudes towards childcare has come about partly through the necessity of bringing women into a labour force hungry for new recruits in order to meet Moss's third norm: national economic survival. Acceptance of childcare as a universal benefit to children was aided by the integration of early years education and care and the growing belief that early learning is crucial to positive educational outcomes for children later on.

However, the belief that maternal care was best dominated early years policy for many decades. The concept of the superiority of one-to-one care of children within the family has largely hinged on perceptions of women's gender roles within the family and workforce. Historically, early years policy has been strongly influenced by views on the role of women and the 'best' care of young children. The belief that young children should be cared for by their mothers until school age was highly significant in the development of childcare policy throughout the period between the Second World War and the 1980s (Moss, 2003). For example, most of the day nurseries that opened during the Second World War to allow women to work while men fought, closed rapidly after the war finished as women were encouraged to return to their traditional roles, which included caring for children.

Even the Plowden Report (DES, 1967), which led to the expansion of nursery education through an increase in places, clearly stated that part-time places should be offered because they discouraged women from working, and children needed to be with their mothers at least part of the day. Only in an exceptional and limited number of cases where financial need overruled the objections to mother–child separation were full-time places considered. Although the report recognized the strong links between social class and educational success, it also emphasized the role of nurseries in compensating for disadvantage rather than as a universal service for all young children. The Plowden Report continued to influence nursery education until the 1990s by perpetuating the split between education and care; ignoring the under-3s; and ignoring the needs of working parents.

The principle that children were best off at home with their mothers was challenged by the steady rise in the numbers of women working from the 1970s onwards as, increasingly, women's wages became an essential part of the family income. In addition to individual families needing to increase their incomes, the changing roles of women driven by the women's movement throughout the 1970s and 1980s, and changing labour market needs have resulted in social changes around perceptions of women's gender roles. More recently, the need to fill gaps in the labour market with increased numbers of women workers has been a strong factor in policy development. Demographic changes have led to concerns relating to national survival in terms of meeting labour market needs and supporting the increasing proportion of older people in the UK. As Brannen and Moss (2003) point out, an increased focus on early years policy has been partly influenced by falling birth rates and an ageing population.

Although women continue to have the main responsibility for young children, large numbers are in the workforce. In the UK, 68 per cent of women with dependent children are in the workforce compared with 76 per cent of those without (Office for National Statistics, 2003). Women are more likely than men to work part-time, particularly if they have dependent children. Nearly 40 per cent of women with dependent children work part-time compared with 23 per cent of those without.

Women's changing role in the labour market has influenced the development of early years services as demand for childcare rose steadily through the 1980s onwards. In the absence of a coherent policy to support the growing need for childcare, the growth of private day nurseries filled some of this gap, but this has only met the needs of better-off families with well-paid jobs, as the costs of private day care have not been affordable for many parents. The introduction of tax benefits to reduce childcare costs to parents has improved this situation for some but the cost of childcare remains outside the reach of many families (Daycare Trust, 2005).

The availability and affordability of childcare places for less well-off families continues to be a thorny problem for many, despite the growth of places since the National Childcare Strategy and other subsequent childcare policies. Traditionally, families have relied on relatives to help out with childcare but there are fewer extended families and higher levels of geographical mobility now. As a result, fewer parents can rely on relatives to help out with childcare and their reliance on other forms of care has increased.

Other social trends have significance for the development of early years policy. Pugh (2001) identifies the increasing numbers of children on or below the poverty line in the last 25 years as one of four key issues influencing how children are growing up at the beginning of the 21st century. So why is child poverty such a significant issue at this point in time?

Child poverty grew in the UK between the late 1970s and through to the 1990s in response to market-driven economic strategies and low investment in education, health and welfare for children. This growth in child poverty was widespread, with one in three children living in poverty in 1998 as compared to one in ten in 1979. However, since 1999, when Blair announced his intention to eradicate child poverty, 600,000 children have been lifted out of poverty. Despite this significant improvement, 28 per cent of children in Britain continued to live in poverty (3.5 million children), making this one of the worst rates in the industrialized world (End Child Poverty, 2005). More recently, as the recession has taken its toll and the Coalition government has introduced austerity measures leading to higher unemployment (7.8 per cent in 2011), child poverty has risen yet again to 3.8 million in 2009–10, which amounts to 30 per cent of children in the UK (CPAG, 2012). Moreover, a reduction in child poverty is no longer a key element in current government policy.

Poverty was once most associated with a lack of work in families, but now 58 per cent of children living in poverty are in households with one adult working (CPAG, 2012). To avoid poverty, families need to have more than one adult working and/or in well-paid employment. The number of workers in low-paid jobs has doubled since 1977 with over 6 million people on low wages (one-fifth of the workforce) (End Child Poverty, 2005). Poverty is strongly linked to an inability to access well-paid work, with the gap between 'work rich' and 'work poor' families growing steadily. As part of the 'welfare to work' policy programme under New Labour, early years services were expanded to facilitate the return to work of more parents, particularly mothers. However, despite the Child Poverty Act being passed in 2010, the Child Poverty Strategy published in 2011 as a result of the legislation was described as 'weak' and 'empty of action' (End Child Poverty, 2011).

Poverty has an impact on many aspects of children's lives, including health and educational outcomes. It plays a key role in social exclusion and the 'cycle of deprivation' through which social exclusion impacts on children's lives from one generation to the next. The price of high levels of poverty is seen in high unemployment figures, high benefits bills, a poorly-skilled workforce and family breakdown. High levels of poverty are linked to high crime figures and anti-social behaviour among children and young people.

The outcomes of poverty are significant for children, with one-third of all children:

- not having three meals a day
- missing out on toys, activities and school trips
- lacking adequate clothing.

Poor children also have shorter lives, lower birth weight (associated with a higher chance of infant death and disease), lower achievement in school, fewer qualifications and more chance of death or injury from accidents or fires (End Child Poverty, 2005).

Activity

Think about the impact of poverty with reference to children you work with. You might consider some of the contrasting experiences of children who live in poverty and those who have access to a good number of resources. For example, access to a wide range of first-hand experiences such as holidays, day trips, and visiting friends and family may depend on whether the family can afford the costs. Make notes on the following questions:

▶ How does poverty affect some children?

▶ What is the impact of poverty on children's development and learning?

Discuss your ideas with colleagues or a mentor.

Political agendas

Prior to the election of the New Labour government in 1997, the long-term neglect of early years policy had resulted in early years services that were shaped as much through that neglect as by political intervention. For example, the provision of large-scale childcare by the state was seen as undesirable and thus before 1997 there was a reduction rather than expansion in local authority provision. Alongside this, there was a slow but escalating growth in the private and voluntary sector, with the development of adventure playgrounds and playschemes, mainly by voluntary bodies, the growth of registered childminding in some areas and a very slow growth in the number of private nurseries, which began to escalate in the early 1990s.

From 1997 to 2010, the central focus of social policy was the reduction of poverty, particularly child poverty, and early years policy came to the forefront as a key tool to drive poverty eradication and social inclusion. Tony Blair's Beveridge lecture (March 1999; reprinted in Walker, 1999) included a pledge to eradicate child poverty within 20 years, which was subsequently supported by a raft of new policies and legislation. Roberts (2001: 53) stated that these measures were designed to 'lift around 1.2 million children out of poverty'. However, by 2006 indicators showed that progress in eradicating poverty had reached a plateau and targets were unlikely to be met.

The political agenda New Labour rolled out between 1997 and 2010 was a multi-layered and complex set of strategies to reduce poverty, relieve pressure on the welfare state, raise standards in young children to improve outcomes for them as school-leavers, improve employability, reduce crime and increase social stability. This agenda was also shaped by a distinctive philosophy influencing policy development – the emphasis on 'joined-up solutions' was a central influence in shaping policy responses to eradicate poverty. This 'joined-up' philosophy was apparent in changes in the structure of children's services at national and local levels. One of the influences on this development in policy may have been studies by academics such as that by Peter Moss on the effectiveness of more universal early years services in other countries in meeting working parents' needs whilst raising educational standards. The benefits of universal early years services were the subject of campaigns and lobbying by organizations such as the Daycare Trust. In addition, studies such as the Effective Provision of Pre-School Education (EPPE) project have confirmed the value of early years care and education to young children in terms of benefits to their learning and development (Sylva et al., 2004).

A study by members and associates of the Centre for Analysis of Social Exclusion at the London School of Economics commented that the New Labour government's agenda to reduce poverty was both short-term cash and service benefits and long-term elements to improve life chances and standards for all children (Joseph Rowntree Foundation, 2005). This study also suggested that, in the short term, tax and benefits measures and reduction of unemployment were successful in reducing child poverty for about 1.3 million children.

The New Labour political agenda had its roots in the years spent in opposition to Conservative governments between 1979 and 1997. The Labour Party went through a period of bitter rivalry between right- and left-wing factions after their defeat in 1979, leading to a left-wing leadership win and the defection of the right-wing to a new party, the Social Democrats, in 1981. Failure to win the 1983 election led to reforms in the Labour Party's philosophy and policies, which became more marked after Tony Blair was elected party leader in 1994.

Effectively, the philosophy of the 'Third Way' (as it was initially called) was developed to ensure election success for the struggling Labour Party. The main theme was an economic strategy which sought to ameliorate the worst effects of laissez-faire economic policies on the most vulnerable groups. Within this broad approach, the expansion of childcare and other services for children and families has been seen in terms of its advantages to parents and the labour market, rather than in terms of children themselves. This is in contrast to other European countries where childcare is seen primarily as a service to children, reflected in state subsidy to ensure investment in high-quality staff.

Although the reduction of child poverty has driven a range of different social policy developments, the emphasis on improving conditions and outcomes for children has been a strong element of these. The trends in social development described above led to a focus on the early years after a long period of stagnant policy development and low levels of state involvement in strategic planning and development of the early years sector, as discussed in Chapter 2.

Developments included:

- increases in the number of childcare places to support working parents
- growth in the childcare workforce
- increased opportunities for training and gaining qualifications in the sector
- tax credits to support children and families, including those in low-paid employment
- extension of out-of-school care and extended school provision
- development of integrated service delivery.

One of the key initiatives, the National Childcare Strategy, introduced in 1998, has included a range of developments to support early years and wider policy goals. The National Childcare Strategy was also significant in flagging up the new centrality of early years in the political agenda after years of indifference. Thirty years of neglect at national policy level had left early years services in a fragmented and inadequate state, with:

- a poorly paid workforce, with limited access to training and career development for many practitioners
- service provision dominated by low levels of availability, lack of coherence between sectors and low levels of state investment
- an artificially created divide between care and education services, which meant many services failed to provide for the needs of children or parents.

The Coalition government came to power in 2010 and immediately introduced policies designed to reduce national debt as a key priority. The impact on early years has been significant in terms of the de-prioritization of policies aimed at supporting all families and the move away from reducing child poverty as a policy goal. Moreover, rising unemployment rates and an increase in families on low wages have placed more children in poverty than previously. Targeted services, deregulation and a focus on early intervention rather than universal services have changed the nature of early years policy and practice considerably. The closure of some SSCCs and the focus on family responsibility for children indicate a significant change in policy aims for young children.

Despite the extension of free half-day nursery places to 3-and 4-year-olds and the expansion of childcare places across the sectors, many working parents continue to struggle to find adequate day-long childcare that they can afford. The Childcare Act 2006 extended free places in nursery education to 15 hours a week for 38 weeks by 2010, a development which has been honoured by the

Coalition government, but this may still not resolve the issue of affordable childcare for all families as the development of full day care has remained largely in the private day nursery sector. Childminders continue to fill the gaps but numbers have fallen and childcare places for children under 3 remain fewer and more expensive.

For some children, sponsored day care in a day nursery or with a childminder is available. Such places are difficult to obtain and are normally reserved for families with children in need or at risk of abuse. Local authority day nursery places, originally intended for a wider range of children, were increasingly allocated to children where there was cause for concern throughout the 1970s onwards, based on the compensatory model discussed above. Such places are now rare, but children are still funded by social care services for day nursery and childminding places where such support is seen as preventing family breakdown or the necessity of admitting a child into care.

The net result is that, despite these developments, many children's care arrangements involve a number of different settings and individuals, are vulnerable to breakdown, and deny the child coherence and consistency of care. For example, a child may be childminded between 2 and 3 years old or go to a day nursery. He/she may then continue at day nursery or go to nursery school for half a day and be cared for by relatives, friends or a childminder for the rest of the day. In some areas, nursery schools provide extended care for which parents pay. Most private day nurseries provide free nursery education so that children remain in the same setting all day, but this can be an expensive option and one not available to less well-off families, despite tax credits. For many families, the options are bewildering and in choosing childcare it is no wonder that most parents do this on the basis of proximity and cost.

Under New Labour, supporting parents in their return to work was a key political agenda item. One of the main developments brought about by the New Labour government of 1997 was to bring all early years services, except those specifically to do with child welfare, within the auspices of the Department for Children, Schools and Families (DCSF), signalling a significant change in culture as regards government policy towards supporting working parents.

The publication of *Choice for Parents, the Best Start for Children: A Ten-year Strategy for Childcare* (HM Treasury et al., 2004) established the following objectives:

▸ choice and flexibility: parents to have greater choice about balancing work and family life

▸ availability: for all families with children aged up to 14 who need it, an affordable, flexible, high-quality childcare place that meets their circumstances

▸ quality: high-quality provision with a highly skilled childcare and early years workforce, among the best in the world

▸ affordability: families to be able to afford flexible, high-quality childcare that is appropriate for their needs.

Specific developments planned in the Strategy and implemented in some cases through the Childcare Act 2006 included:

▸ an increase in the limits of the childcare element of Working Tax Credit

▸ the current free entitlement for 3- and 4-year-olds to nursery education to be extended to 12.5 hours, 38 weeks a year from 2006 and 15 hours a week by 2010, with a long-term goal of 20 hours free early education and childcare a week

▸ a Sure Start Children's Centre in every community by 2010, offering access to integrated early years activities, childcare and family services

▸ extended schools to provide a range of services and, for primary school children, a guarantee of care out of school hours and during the holidays between 8 a.m. and 6 p.m.

▸ a new duty on local authorities to secure provision of childcare, complementing authorities' existing responsibilities in relation to early education.

Activity

Talk to some parents you know through work or as friends or neighbours and/or consider your own experience of parenting and work.

▸ What issues (if any) do parents face in balancing work and childcare?

▸ What do children and parents experience on a day-to-day basis in order for parents to work?

▸ What improvements do you think the ten-year strategy may make for these families?

▸ Do you think there are any negative aspects of the early years policy for children, parents and families?

These developments signalled another phase in the New Labour political agenda for early years policy. Policy was largely targeted on disadvantaged areas, anti-poverty strategies and 'welfare to work'. Later developments signalled a move towards universal (rather than targeted) early years services to meet the needs of a much wider range of children. In respect of the longer-term political agenda, these findings supported the development of universal good quality early years services for children as a way of reducing the intergenerational transmission of poverty and deprivation. As such, the development of early years services as outlined in the ten-year plan was central to the social inclusion agenda. However, social inclusion was dropped as a policy theme under the Coalition government and changes to benefits and support for parents have heralded a new approach in which the priority is to reduce benefit payments across the board as part of the wider austerity strategy to reduce national debt. For example, single parents will now have to be available for work once their youngest child is 5 years old, rather than 7 years old. Cuts have also been made to the Health in Pregnancy Grant, Sure Start Maternity Grant and Child Tax Credit for babies and toddlers. Child Benefit has also been frozen and cuts to Housing Benefit will affect many families, especially those in high-cost housing areas (Family Action, 2012).

Government bodies, professional organizations and other stakeholders

One of the influences on early years policy has been the role of government agencies and professional bodies in determining developments. For example, the transfer of responsibility for early years to the DfEE from the Department of Health in 1998 was significant in signalling that early years policies were to be dominated by education in the future. In addition, the transfer of responsibility for standards and regulation from directors of social care services to Ofsted's Early Years Directorate and the creation of new responsibilities for support services in education departments in 2001 firmly placed childcare in the remit of the educationalists. The role of the Department of Health and social care services within local authorities has become much less influential in shaping policy as a result.

The combined role of the DCSF, Ofsted and the QCA was to bring in widespread measures to standardize early years provision across the diverse sectors, with an emphasis on the educational aspects of early years provision. However, these developments did have complex outcomes for some providers. Numbers of childminders had been falling since the Children Act 1989 had introduced a stricter inspection regime, and this trend continued as pressure to join formal networks and gain qualifications, together with inspections by Ofsted, impacted on the childminder's role. Between 1997 and 2000, there was a 20 per cent reduction in the childminding workforce. Many pre-schools failed to compete successfully with other providers and folded in the same time period.

The role of individuals and organizations outside government has become significant in determining policy through the work of professional organizations such as the National Children's Bureau, the Thomas Coram Research Unit, the Pre-school Learning Alliance and the National Childminding Association, to name a few. A key factor for these organizations in finding a voice in early years policy has been their strong links with government agencies under New Labour, resulting in the joint writing of policy and guidelines and commissioning of research from professional organizations by the DCSF. So, for example, the 2001 paper *Childcare and Early Education: Investing in All Our Futures* was a set of guidelines for local authorities to develop successful early years provision, written by the Daycare Trust for the Local Government Association (LGA) within the auspices of the DfES (DfES/LGA, 2001). Further examples of this are found in the case study of SSLPs above.

Academic institutions have also found a steady voice in early years development through their role in developing aspects of policy, as well as the influence of research as discussed. For example, *Birth to Three Matters* was developed by Lesley Abbott and her colleagues at Manchester Metropolitan University as a DfES-funded project in 2002 (Sure Start Unit, 2002).

One of the features of the New Labour government of 1997–2010 was this increasing influence of professional organizations, academics and other stakeholders through their stronger links to civil servants and policy-makers. For example, the Daycare Trust has gained considerably in influence and hosts a forum for development and discussion that includes professionals, academics and policy-makers. This congruence of ideas and beliefs has been developed further through the last government's emphasis on evidence-based policy-making and systematic evaluation strategies for new policies. As such, academics, research organizations and professional bodies found a newly expanded role in policy development through government-funded research and evaluation projects. For example, the National Evaluation of Sure Start was conducted by a group of academics led by Edward Melhuish at the Institute for the Study of Children, Families and Social Issues at Birkbeck, University of London (Melhuish et al., 2005).

In early years education, studies such as the EPPE project have contributed to 'evidence-informed policy' in early years education and care (Sylva et al., 2004). The study explored the impact of pre-school care and education on the development of children from a range of backgrounds and identified key factors in quality settings. The outcomes supported the role of quality pre-schools in supporting all children's development and combating the impact of social disadvantage and special educational needs. The findings contributed significantly towards the debate on what characteristics make high-quality pre-school provision. Seven areas related to high quality were identified, relating to issues such as curriculum delivery, adult–child interactions, parental involvement and staff training and knowledge.

The Coalition government has to some extent continued with evidence-based approaches to policy-making affecting early years. The role of SSCCs is being evaluated under this regime as discussed above, and the introduction of evidence-based interventions is part of this change, aimed at reducing costs. However, as with all governments the evidence chosen is likely to be that which reflects the government's wider policy agendas and overall aims. For example, the influential Allen report (2011) on early intervention has been cited to support this as a key aim in early years policy development at present. Recommendations in the 2011 report have started to appear in current early years policy, such as in the assessment of pre-school children; a renewed focus on parenting programmes; early years education to focus on emotional and social development; more funding to Family Nurse Partnership schemes; and an emphasis on 'school readiness'.

Evidence-informed practice has been a significant development requiring individuals, organizations and policy-making bodies to support their decisions and practice with research findings. Evidence-informed findings and the outcomes of evaluation of projects are increasingly gaining a significant influence on policy development. However, it is necessary to be cautious of this approach as the contested nature of most research and the possibility of the selective use of findings can impact on the value of 'evidence' as a basis for change, as discussed further in Chapter 7. Although the increased influence and involvement is generally welcome, there is a concern that the overwhelming influence of government may stifle the independent voice of professional organizations, academics and other stakeholders in the early years.

Significant events

Significant events are those that focus attention on existing failures or flaws in policy and legislation or the quality of services provided. Although these flaws and failures may already be in the public domain or part of the professional debate, key events may have a disproportionate impact as catalysts of change. Key events often draw a disproportionate amount of media attention highlighting the need for change and shaping and directing public opinion. However, they must also resonate with government agendas in order to be influential. For example, the Utting Report (Department of Health/Welsh Office, 1997), drawing on research findings mainly from the voluntary organization associated with children in care, The Who Cares? Trust, determined that children 'looked after' by local authorities (children in public care) were likely to suffer dismal outcomes in terms of education, health, employment, mental health and risk of criminality, homelessness, drug and alcohol abuse. The report was commissioned in response to widespread concerns and public outrage at the series of revelations of abuse and mistreatment of children in the public care system. The policy response was rapid and broad, introducing the Quality Protects Strategy in 1998 (Department of Health, 1998), covering a range of measures to improve life chances for these children, including shorter waiting times for permanent placements, better monitoring of health and educational progress, and targets for improved educational achievements for children in care.

Another example was that the Green Paper *Every Child Matters* (DfES, 2003) (as discussed further in Chapter 4) was published in response to the recommendations of Lord Laming's inquiry report into the death of an 8-year-old girl called Victoria Climbié, who was killed by her aunt and aunt's boyfriend in 2001 (Laming, 2003). Victoria Climbié's death brought about a sustained focus on deficits in the existing legislation and guidelines to protect children from abuse and neglect. This single case highlighted existing flaws in the management of child welfare, deficits in communication between key responsible agencies, poor-quality training and the lack of ability of staff to work effectively in protecting children. The sustained media interest in the case and the particularly tragic circumstances of the child's death were significant in the role that her death would take in influencing policy change. However, the influence of the Laming Report on the timing and content of *Every Child Matters* was not a simple linear relationship. Existing developments and plans within government also determined the changes and no single factor can be seen as the sole determinant of policy change.

Subsequently, the death of 17-month-old Peter Connelly in 2007 once again highlighted flaws in the child protection system. This led to a further report by Lord Laming (2009) that found that many of the recommendations of his previous report encompassed in *Every Child Matters* had not been fully or effectively implemented in all local authorities. Steps to improve child protection services were subsequently outlined in the Munro review (2011), leading to increased numbers of children coming into care and earlier action to protect children (Cafcass, 2012). The report showed that 'since 2008 the number of children taken into care in England has risen by 62 per cent to more than 10,000 a year' (Bingham, 2012). The report also confirmed that in many cases, intervention was more timely and earlier. In this case, the links between the significant event and policy change are very clear.

International policy

In some ways, the influence of international policy development on UK policy is difficult to measure. However, there is no doubt that in recent years early years policy development in other European countries has been scrutinized and compared with that in the UK by academics such as Peter Moss and Helen

Penn. It is also true that at the present time there is a strongly Europhile influence in government. In this section, the influence of international policy on the early years is discussed in terms of its impact in the UK.

The adoption of the United Nations Convention on the Rights of the Child (UNCRC) in 1989 was a major step in establishing the rights of children as a key theme in policy development. However, within the EU there have been only limited developments in policy relating to young children, which have had only a small impact in the UK (Ruxton, 2001). This impact has partly been limited by resistance to the concept of EU intervention in the child and family policy field based on the persistent ideology of non-interventionism, which dominated UK child and family policy through the 1980s and 1990s, and by reluctance in most member states to extend the EU's influence in matters of social, as opposed to economic, policy. Areas where there has been an EU influence on family policy are in improving rights to maternity leave and restricting long hours of work. Both of these relate to economic affairs. However, Ruxton (2001: 69) argues that 'the EU has a very limited legal base for its action in relation to children'.

Despite this, there are common features of an agenda for early years policy in Europe. Moss (2001a: 28) identifies these as:

▶ a legal right to parental leave

▶ public support for the childcare needs of employed parents

▶ public support for at least two years' education for all children before they start compulsory schooling.

However, he also points out that in the UK there has only been a clear commitment to this agenda since 1997. More recently, there are indications that early years policy in the UK is coming increasingly under the influence of European developments, including the move towards universal early years services and integrated planning and services delivery.

Special educational needs: a case study of accumulative influences on early years policy

Special educational needs (SEN) policy provides a good example of how a number of the influences discussed above interact to shape policy and practice. In respect of SEN, key influences on policy include:

▶ social and cultural developments in terms of how children with learning difficulties are viewed

▶ government agendas such as increasing the level of social inclusion

▶ stakeholder views such as voluntary and parent associations

▶ international policy promoting the globalization of children's rights agendas.

Before the 1980s, children with SEN were defined through medical models of disability and it was believed that many of these children could not be educated. Following an enquiry into the educational needs of children with disabilities, the Warnock Report was published in 1978 and the Education Act in 1981, establishing the concept of integration (inclusion) by legislating that children with SEN should be educated in mainstream schools if this was at all possible and that educational objectives should be the same for all children (HM Government, 2006). A proportion of children identified as having learning difficulties are given a statement of SEN, which outlines the child's needs and how these will be met. At present, about 17.9 per cent of children in primary schools have SEN, and 1.4 per cent of children in primary schools have statements of SEN. Overall, two million children have SEN and/or a disability (DfE, 2011b).

Warnock (Warnock Committee, 1978) did not ignore the under-5s in the report, focusing on the following principles for supporting children in their early years with SEN:

▶ support for parents as their children's primary educators

▶ early identification and assessment of SEN and support for children under 2

▶ training for all professionals involved with young children to recognize early signs of special needs and the social basis of some of these needs

▶ prompt and sensitive disclosure of disability to parents and access to information about support at an early stage

▶ a named contact for parents to provide a focus for advice and support.

The Education Act 1981 was not at the time supported by additional funding and as such it became clear that statements of SEN were subject to resource-limitations from their inception, and this tension between entitlement and resource restrictions has continued as a factor, as the number of children identified with SEN has risen and many special schools have closed (Croll and Moses, 2000). Muncey (1988) also critiques the Act, suggesting that it had many loopholes through which local authorities (LAs) could choose not to make significant changes to their provision.

Additional pressures on the Warnock framework arose as testing within the National Curriculum, in 1988, created competition between schools, pressuring them to focus on the children who might get good results. Moreover, in mainstream schools, 'integration' may sometimes mean segregation within the school through a number of mechanisms including specialized units for children with disabilities, some of which are highly separate from the rest of the school (Dyson, 2005).

Continues

Continued

In the Warnock Report (1978), social deprivation was not identified as a cause of SEN. However, increasingly, clusters of children with SEN are found in particular schools, settings or areas as social disadvantage, poverty and class link to higher incidences of SEN as do gender (boys) and ethnicity (Dyson, 2005). Moreover, families with children with disabilities are more likely to experience poverty as they may have restricted access to employment because of the child's needs and there may be additional expenses associated with the child's disability. This clustering creates particular problems for schools, which struggle to 'improve' in terms of conventional measured outcomes whilst supporting the needs of high numbers of children with SEN. As more children are identified with SEN linked to social issues such as autistic spectrum disorders (ASD), the principles of inclusion are tested as settings and schools struggle to provide for children with high levels of need. Ofsted (2006b) found that the increase in the number of children statemented for behavioural, emotional and social difficulties (BESD) meant that these children were more likely to be excluded from schools and that their inclusion was the biggest challenge to schools and settings. In the early years, too many children with emerging BESD did not get a quality response.

The Warnock Report established the principle of parent partnership to better support children with SEN, which was eventually enshrined in the Special Educational Needs Code of Practice (1993, 2001). This is a set of detailed procedures for schools, early years settings and other agencies involved in assessing and providing for children with SEN. Although parents have consistently preferred their children with SEN to be educated in mainstream schools (apart from a small number where the child has severe/complex disabilities), it is also recognized that the limitations on resources could impact negatively on successful inclusion. The concept of parent partnership in SEN is supported by the right to appeal against statementing decisions, which has introduced a 'quasi-judicial element into provision for SEN' (Croll and Moses, 2000).

Since the Warnock Report, policy has continued to focus on inclusion agendas for children with learning difficulties, including children with disabilities. Policies in the UK have been influenced throughout by international developments, including the 'globalisation of rights and entitlements' for children with disabilities (Artiles and Dyson, 2005: 38). The United Nations Convention on the Rights of the Child (UNCRC) articles 12 and 23 address the rights of children with disabilities in mainstream education. However, the UNCRC has been criticized for not establishing a principle that access to services according to need for disabled children should be a right (Quinn and Degener, 2002, cited in Mittler, 2005).

The United Nations Educational, Scientific, and Cultural Organization (UNESCO) Salamanca Statement on Special Needs Education 1994, aligned the international inclusion agenda with children's rights campaigns and informed the 1997 Green Paper *Excellence for All Children: Meeting Special Educational Needs*, which linked policies in this country to international trends (Mittler, 2005).

Other policy and legislation includes:

▶ the SEN and Disability Act (SENDA) 2001, which provides some protection for disabled children against discrimination in schools and confirms their right to education in mainstream schools wherever possible

▶ Removing Barriers to Achievement (2004), which sets out the government agenda for children with SEN within the *Every Child Matters* policy agenda focusing on early intervention; partnership with parents; inclusion; and raising achievement through teacher training and monitoring progress

▶ Together from the Start (2003) and the Early Support programme, which focus on coordinating and raising standards for the youngest disabled children and delivering services to these children and their families through Children's Centres

▶ the Childcare Act 2006, which states that LAs will only be deemed to have met the childcare needs of parents if there is sufficient provision for disabled children.

More recently, the Warnock framework has been critiqued for no longer being able to meet the needs of children with SEN, not least by Warnock herself (Warnock, 2005). Key factors under debate are the impact of inclusion on special school closures, changed concepts of SEN now increasingly focused on social aspects of disability, and the impact of increased numbers of children with SEN in mainstream schools. In early years contexts, more children aged 3 and 4 have entered nursery education since the National Childcare Strategy started to promote increases in places in 1998. Earlier opportunity to assess young children's needs has led to many more children being identified as having SEN at an earlier stage, adding to the pressure on limited resources.

The *Statutory Assessment and Statements of SEN: In Need of Review?* (Audit Commission, 2002) suggested that statutory assessment is both slow and expensive, and ultimately may not ensure the child's needs are met due to poor levels of monitoring and geographical variations in the availability of resources. The report also found that parents struggled with statementing,

Continues

Continued

finding the process stressful to go through.

At the time of writing, plans to make changes to support for children with SEN have been published in the Green Paper *Support and Aspiration: A New Approach to Special Educational Needs and Disability* (DfE, 2011c). The rationale is that parents find the current system difficult to comprehend and to be involved in, with adversarial aspects when negotiating support. There is lack of parental choice, poor information and low expectations of children. Many special needs are identified too late and overall child and family needs are not always met (DfE, 2012a). The Green Paper recommends a multi-agency single assessment and Education, Health and Care Plan for each child with additional needs to replace existing statementing processes by 2014. Cognitive testing will be part of the planned 2-year-old assessment and 4,200 additional health visitors will be recruited to achieve this goal. The plan will include support arrangements from education, health and care services and will be regularly reviewed. It will have a similar legal status to current provision. Parents should also get better information on local services for children with SEN and disability, and personal budgets will be available as an option. Parents will get more choice of schools for their children, including an increased access to special schools by 'removing the bias towards inclusion'. In cases where special schools are under threat of closure, parent groups will have the option of taking them over (DfE, 2011b). These proposals are in line with Coalition government policy principles on enhancing the role of families, privatization and early intervention.

Five areas of change are identified: early identification and support; giving parents control; learning and achieving; preparing for adulthood; and services working together for families (DfE, 2011b). While early identification and parental control are key principles of Coalition government policy, it is interesting to see that working together remains a goal, as this has not been a major strand in current policy-making.

However, one of the goals of the changes, cited as the most significant in this area in 30 years, is to reduce the number of children identified as having SEN. At present, 17.9 per cent of children in primary schools are identified as needing School Action or School Action Plus, and it is believed that this identification is linked to low aspirations and expectations, leading to poorer outcomes for these children (O'Brien, 2011). This reduction may have implications for the levels of support some children may then receive, as under the present system, support is linked firmly to identification. Under the proposed system, children with SEN but who are not statemented may miss out compared to children with more severe needs, creating a two-tier system (Power, 2011). In addition, the inclusion of voluntary and community sector organizations in the plans may de-professionalize services for this group of children and reduce quality. Other concerns are about the levels of funding and training provision for relevant staff in the context of austerity policies and cuts to public spending.

The SEN policy agenda has been driven partly by international trends linked to children's rights movements and the need for government to better support all children to meet their potential and offset the high social cost of failing this group in terms of outcomes and life chances. These include higher chances of not being in education, employment or training than non-disabled young people and more likelihood of getting fewer or no qualifications. However, support for children with disabilities and SEN has also been the subject of a powerful lobby from disability charities and alliances, which support a clearer inclusion agenda with political and financial backing.

Summary

▸ The influences on early years policy are varied and have complex interrelationships, forming systems to create particular policy developments at certain points in time.

▸ That said, policy is essentially made by governments, and the receptivity of politicians and civil servants to different views and influences on early years policy development will depend on the prevailing political agenda.

▸ At the same time, political agendas are themselves influenced by social trends and developments, which will determine the context within which policy is framed.

Further reading

Pugh, G. and Duffy, B. (eds) (2010) *Contemporary Issues in the Early Years: Working Collaboratively for Children* (5th edn), London: Sage. Part 1 contains chapters on policy for early childhood services.

Eisenstadt, N. (2011) *Providing a Sure Start: How Government Discovered Early Childhood*, Bristol: The Policy Press.

Implementing Early Years Policy

Chapter 4

This chapter discusses several issues:

▶ what is expected of policy-makers in terms of approaches to development and implementation of policy, planning and communication of policy developments, and the type of research, monitoring and evaluation activities that best support effective policy-making

▶ the implementation of policy at national, local and individual setting levels

▶ some of the ways in which policy is implemented at the different levels and issues arising from this implementation (illustrated by an extended case study).

The implementation of policy involves a process through which the ideas, intentions, principles and practicalities of specific policy plans and developments are made real. At national level, this can be through the enactment of legislation, the development of new organizational structures or changes to existing organizations, and the transfer or alteration of responsibilities within or between local and national government. At local level, this can be through the development of new local authority structures or agencies, new ways of working, and new protocols for working arrangements between agencies and other bodies such as voluntary organizations. Policy implementation can also mean new jobs and careers, new conditions of service and qualification structures within the workforce. At setting level, implementing policy may be through new organizational structures, changed or new policies, different ways of working, job descriptions and arrangements with other agencies.

Often legislation is required to pave the way for significant policy changes, but other developments take place under existing law. In the simplest terms, new policy is the result of government activity in planning and delivering implementation strategies (including legislation) for policies developed by departments and agencies. However, the implementation of policy is complicated, reflecting interactions between a wide range of stakeholders in the early years, including those within and outside government.

Modern policy-making

There are certain features of policy-making at the beginning of the 21st century that are intended to promote effectiveness and value for money. Modern policy is expected to be efficient in terms of achieving planned outcomes in a cost-effective way and not delivering any unexpected side-effects that may render it ineffective or costly. Policy-making is increasingly influenced by evidence from research into the best way of achieving policy goals, and on evaluations of existing policy to determine its effectiveness. To this extent, modern policy is evidence informed and draws on lessons learned about the success or otherwise of previous policy (NAO, 2001). The government has promoted improvements in the quality of policy to try to develop long-term strategies and reduce both fragmentation in policy-making and the risks of policy either being ineffective in achieving its aims or having unforeseen negative and costly side-effects.

According to the National Audit Office, there are nine characteristics of modern policy-making. It should:

- ▶ be forward-looking
- ▶ be outward-looking
- ▶ be innovative and creative
- ▶ use evidence
- ▶ be inclusive
- ▶ be joined up
- ▶ evaluate
- ▶ review
- ▶ learn lessons (NAO, 2001).

In recent years, the central focus is on what policy actually achieves and this is supported by an expectation that there will be an evaluation of policy outcomes to ascertain whether policy goals have been met. This type of approach has become common in early years policy development, with evaluations being conducted by academics and/or professional organizations using government department or agency funding. For example, the National Evaluation of Children's Trusts (NECT) was commissioned in April 2004 by the DfES and the Department of Health to evaluate the pathfinder Children's Trusts established in 2003. In line with the development of stronger links between government departments, academics and professional organizations in terms of policy development (discussed in the previous chapter), the evaluation was commissioned by the DfES and the Department of Health and conducted by academics at the University of East Anglia in conjunction with the NCB (NECT, 2004). The evaluation of the 35 Children's Trust pathfinder projects was intended to inform policy implementation, giving early messages to practitioners involved in developing integrated service delivery. Such evaluations provide information about best implementation strategies for new or emerging policy developments and legitimize these in terms of the stakeholders involved. However, evaluation is not value-free and in itself is a political process, as what constitutes 'evidence' is contested. Similarly, evidence-based policy-making can make demands on evaluators to produce findings which fit with the remit of the political agenda (Taylor and Balloch, 2005).

Modern policy-making involves ensuring new policies are considered in terms of cost, impact, risks and priorities. Policy development now requires a consideration of a range of different options for achieving policy goals, and risk and cost analyses of these in order to determine the option most likely to succeed. There are also requirements to consult with stakeholders, pilot new policies and consider their impact before extending policy developments more widely. As such, departments are required to draw up implementation plans for policy developments. These plans can include:

- a timetable for delivering policy
- roles and responsibilities for those involved in delivery
- strategies for tackling barriers to policy development
- strategies for monitoring and reporting performance
- flexible approaches (listening, monitoring, reviewing) (NAO, 2001).

The ways in which implementation plans are developed in the field of early years policy is illustrated in the case study of *Every Child Matters* (ECM), discussed below.

Activity

Find out what decisions were made in your local authority about the first wave of Children's Centres. Select one of the centres in that first wave and ask someone in the centre itself or in the Early Years Service in the Children's Services Department the following questions:

- Why was that location chosen for a Children's Centre?
- How was the base for it selected?
- What difficulties and opportunities were encountered in getting the centre going?
- What arrangements are in place for monitoring and reviewing progress?

Two other issues have become central to modern policy-making. First, using the Internet to communicate information about proposed policies, to publish policy documents, to provide a forum for debate and to conduct consultations on proposed policy. The websites of government departments and agencies and professional organizations are now major vehicles used to communicate the details of policy implementation plans and, in the case of the latter, to debate and interpret the meaning of new policy on behalf of particular audiences. Research and evaluation study reports are published on government and other websites, providing extensive information about the reasoning behind particular developments and the effectiveness of these when put into practice. Timetables for introducing new policy are published, along with the consequences of policy implementation for different stakeholders including parents and children. For example, like many other policy developments since *Every Child Matters: Change for Children* (DfES, 2004b) was explained in a children's version on the ECM website, practitioners now have unprecedented opportunities to access information about early years policy developments and to view and take part in the critical debate that usually accompanies such developments. However, the opportunity to contribute to a consultation does not necessarily lead to making an impact on the shape that policy will take (see Barnardos, 2003).

The Useful Websites section at the end of the book gives details of the key websites for accessing this type of information in respect of early years policies and the debate around these. Individuals and organizations within the early years can use this information to keep up with policy developments in the field and to consider the impact of policy development at service delivery level within the context of their own role and/or agency.

A second issue concerns the way in which policies became increasingly developed as 'packages' in line with the New Labour government philosophy of 'joined-up' policy-making, as discussed in the previous chapter. Despite a change of government, policy-making continues to be increasingly focused on tackling linked issues through a range of interconnected policies. This is exemplified most recently in the sorts of policy 'packages' that have been developed to reduce costs of welfare and target more disadvantaged families, which were discussed in the previous chapter.

The case study discussed below illustrates how the concept of 'packages' of policies has been developed in the field of early years policy in order to tackle a range of interlinked policy goals. It also demonstrates many of the other features of modern policy-making, as discussed above, and in particular explores the ways in which the relationships and debates between stakeholders have become crucial in determining the shape of early years policy. However, first, the stages of policy implementation are discussed.

Stages of policy implementation

In Chapter 3, we looked at the influences on policy development and how they interact to determine policy goals. Once policy goals are determined, the government has the complex job of implementing these by directing and monitoring changes at national, local and individual practice levels. The success of policy depends on the ways in which implementation plans are introduced, communicated, debated and interpreted through practice.

Green Papers

New policy is often introduced through consultation documents, called Green Papers, published by the relevant government department or agency. Originally, these contained ideas and thoughts about how policy could be developed rather than specific proposals, although this is not now always the case (see the case study below) as Green Papers tend to contain more concrete and fully formed policy proposals than previously.

In early years policy-making, consultation is usually with local authorities and the broad range of voluntary sector organizations working with children and families and research institutes in the field. For example, there has been a recent consultation on the Green Paper *Support and Aspiration: A new approach to special educational needs and disability* which proposes radical changes to support for children with SEN and disabilities and a replacement of the current statementing process for children with SEN in schools (DfE, 2011c). Organizations and individuals will send their written responses to the relevant government department or agency, and such responses are usually published on the Internet by the organizations involved. The extent to which consultation responses influence government plans can vary and tends to depend on the confidence the government has in implementing their plans successfully, the extent to which there is general acceptance of those plans, the anticipated difficulties of implementing policy at local level and whether the proposed amendments will change the basic structure of new policy.

White Papers

Once the consultation process is completed, the government may draw up a more specific report containing concrete proposals for policy developments called a White Paper. White Papers 'signify a clear intention on the part of a government to pass new law' (TheyWorkForYou.com, 2005). A White Paper is not generally a consultation document although it may promote discussion about the detail of new legislation. A White Paper normally leads to the introduction of a bill, which is a draft new law. Not all policy requires legislation to implement it, as discussed in the case study below.

Effectively, a bill travels in a predetermined process through Parliament, as outlined in Figure 4.1. The stages of parliamentary process are designed to ensure that there is time for considered debate about all aspects of the legislation, for amendments to be tabled and discussed, agreed or disagreed, and for scrutiny by relevant bodies and committees to ensure that the legislation is robust and not fatally flawed. In the case of large, complex or very influential bills, progress through Parliament will be scrutinized by the media and concerned organizations.

Acts of Parliament

After the final stage, Royal Assent, when a bill becomes law it is known as an Act. There is a gap in time before the Act is implemented as it often requires changes in the way services are organized or delivered. For example, in the case of the Children Act 1989, implementation took place over a two-year period. This time is used to interpret the legislation at local and national levels and to put in place policies and structures, including financial measures, to ensure that the legislation can be successfully implemented.

The process may then involve intense activity on the part of government to issue guidelines and information about how to implement the policy or legislation at local level if this is required. This may include briefings and conferences, written advisory documents and meetings with key local government bodies. Within local authorities, information about expected changes will be disseminated through staff briefings, invitations to stakeholders to consult, and workshops to debate and plan with those stakeholders.

Implementing the proposals in *Every Child Matters*

The implementation of *Every Child Matters* is discussed as an extended case study of how policy affecting early years is put into practice at different levels. The discussion includes looking at the roles of different national and local organizations in ensuring implementation, how expectations are disseminated to local level, and the role of national and local government officers and professional bodies in developing and establishing implementation plans. Finally, the impact on different sectors of the workforce is discussed in the light of the range of changes to structures and work practices. *Every Child Matters* was chosen as an example because of its size and complexity as a policy agenda.

Understanding Early Years Policy

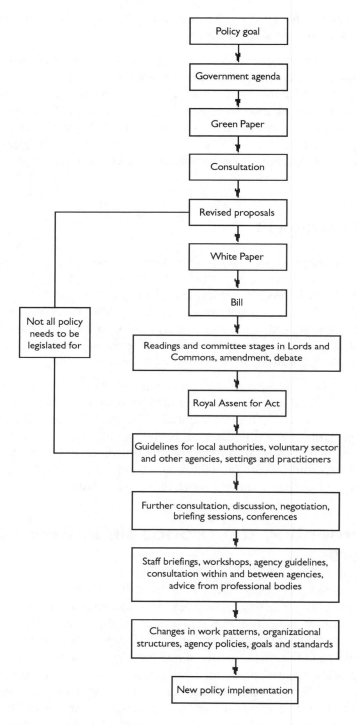

Figure 4.1 *Stages of policy implementation for the early years*

Implementation at national government level

The Green Paper *Every Child Matters* (DfES, 2003) incorporated a raft of policy proposals, which effectively extended and continued the drive towards integrated service planning and delivery for children and families. As discussed in Chapter 3, the impetus for this particular raft of policy developments came from the recommendations of the Laming Report into Victoria Climbié's death, although this single event acted as a catalyst for putting planned government policy into place rather than as the sole reason for policy change. To a large extent, the Green Paper was intended to extend existing policy plans further. However, new policy principles were also introduced, with a shift from focusing mainly on areas of disadvantage to include more emphasis on universal services to all children. As with a great deal of policy impacting on the early years, the recommendations of the Green Paper covered a wider range of policy areas, including family and youth justice. However, changes to how young children are supported and protected are key elements of the developments.

One of the key influences on the development of the Green Paper was the Inter-Agency Group (IAG). Formed in 2002 in response to issues arising from the Laming Report, the IAG is a group of representatives from key agencies in children's services, such as local authority directors' organizations in education and social services (for example, the Association of Directors of Education and Children's Services) and children's charities (for example, Barnardos, National Society for the Prevention of Cruelty to Children [NSPCC] and National Children's Home [NCH]). The group was originally convened by the President of the Association of Directors of Social Services (ADSS), and group members have met since 2002, becoming influential in their advice to government on issues arising from the Laming Report, including the Green Paper. One of the main outcomes of the group has been to bring together the views of the statutory and voluntary sectors and to convey these views to policy-makers in central government through their contacts with ministers, such as the Children's Minister, and senior civil servants in the DfES.

One of the main issues at national level was the need to 'join up Whitehall' and create much more cohesive planning for children's services between the DfES, the Department of Health and the Home Office (Waterman and Fowler, 2004). The Children's Minister post was established in mid-2003 along with a new sector within the DfES – the Children, Young People and Families Directorate – providing a focus for integrating children's and families' services within central government and bringing together responsibility for:

▶ children's social care

▶ childcare and pre-school support

‣ careers advice

‣ family support

‣ legal services (Waterman and Fowler, 2004).

In addition, the establishment of the Sure Start Unit within the DfES in 2002 was a significant step in establishing an integrated approach to policy development within the government. This is reflected in the confidence with which cross-departmental issues are handled within the proposals.

The Green Paper, published in September 2003, set out a range of recommendations for changes in the way that children's welfare and progress are supported. As already mentioned, a Green Paper is basically a consultation document, setting out intended changes and inviting comment on these. One definition of a Green Paper is a 'tentative report of British government proposals without any commitment to action' (TheyWorkForYou.com, 2005). However, this Green Paper varied from the norm in that there was little that was tentative about it. This is discussed in more detail below.

Key aims of the Green Paper included:

‣ linking child protection services to universal services for all children

‣ tackling chronic problems of poor communication and information sharing between services for children

‣ strengthening accountability and management of services to children

‣ developing a better trained children's workforce

‣ integrating efforts to support children's welfare with those to develop children's potential.

These aims were clearly placed in the context of existing government policy to tackle poverty and social exclusion for children and families. The Green Paper also stated that changes were to be focused on four key areas:

‣ supporting parents and carers

‣ early intervention and effective protection

‣ accountability and integration of services

‣ workforce reforms.

Key developments proposed were:

‣ creating Children's Centres across the country, initially in the 20 per cent most deprived wards

‣ promoting full-service extended schools

▸ funding to increase out-of-school activities

▸ funding to extend Child and Adolescent Mental Health Services (CAMHS)

▸ extending speech therapy services

▸ tackling homelessness

▸ reforming the youth justice system.

Within these proposals, some specific developments were identified that would bring about changes to early years service provision. One of the key themes within these proposed changes is that of integration of service delivery. In a sense, this concept came out of the perceived failure of different children's services to work effectively together to ensure children's safety and welfare.

This message was not new. Although it was a central finding of the Victoria Climbié inquiry, it was also a central finding of many previous child death inquiries, including those of Jasmine Beckford and Kimberley Carlile in the 1980s. Some of the specific developments proposed included:

▸ removing barriers to information sharing between services

▸ ensuring each child/family had a lead professional responsible for coordinating and monitoring service delivery

▸ developing schools and Children's Centres as delivery points for a wide range of services to improve the speed and efficiency of the response to identified need.

In order to achieve new levels of accountability and to integrate services, a number of structural changes at local authority level were proposed:

▸ new Directors of Children's Services for integrated education and children's social care services

▸ development of Children's Trusts to include some children's health services and other relevant agencies

▸ a lead council member for children

▸ the replacement of Area Child Protection Committees (ACPCs) with Local Safeguarding Children Boards.

At national level, proposals included:

▸ a Minister for Young People, Children and Families

▸ a Children's Commissioner

▸ workforce reform including a common qualifications framework and training routes for those working with children and a Children's Workforce Unit in the DfES.

The Green Paper was the subject of widespread attention among those involved in children's services and within the media, with a large number of organizations commenting on and publishing their response to the proposals. The breadth of the debate was described as 'unprecedented' in the follow-up document *Every Child Matters: Next Steps* (DfES, 2004a). The debate was supported and promoted through a series of regional conferences to brief stakeholders about the proposals and provide a forum for discussion. In addition to the Green Paper itself, a children's and young people's version was disseminated and consultation groups set up to get the views of a sample. Altogether, 1,500 adults and 3,100 young people responded to the consultation exercise. However, Barnardos queried whether the extensive consultation with children and young people actually influenced the outcomes at all (Barnardos, 2003).

In March 2004, the paper *Every Child Matters: Next Steps* was published, summarizing this response to the Green Paper and coinciding with the introduction into Parliament of the Children Bill. *Next Steps* included:

▸ an explanation of the proposals within the Children Bill

▸ an explanation of the aspects of change which did not require legislation

▸ the outcomes of the consultation process.

The consultation endorsed the government's proposals within the Green Paper to a great extent, both supporting the principles underpinning the changes and the practical measures suggested. However, there were a number of areas where concerns were expressed, particularly around the issues of resourcing the proposals, ensuring all stakeholders were fully involved and ensuring that local flexibility was maintained in delivering integrated services. More specifically, these included:

▸ the extent to which all stakeholders, especially voluntary and community sector organizations, were involved in the developments

▸ the lack of clarity about the role of the Director of Children's Services and Children's Trusts, and whether this model would be flexible enough to meet the requirements of all localities

▸ whether there would be sufficient funding and resources to support the developments in local authorities

▸ whether the role of the Children's Commissioner in England would be sufficiently robust.

The agencies expressing most concerns were voluntary sector organizations anxious to clarify their role in the new integrated local structures. Within the Green Paper, there was a lack of detail about how these agencies would be included in the new structures and whether they would be adequately represented in planning. Proposals to merge local authority departments clearly signalled the key role of local authorities in planning and service delivery but left some concerned that other agencies such as health and the police may be marginalized.

At local government level, the response to the Green Paper demonstrated some concerns about implementation strategies. The Local Government Association (LGA, 2004) urged that implementation of the Green Paper plans should take place within a framework of flexible options for structural changes within local authorities. The LGA emphasized that local authorities should have the flexibility and freedom to choose how they proceeded with integrating service planning and provision. This was echoed within debates about implementation within some local authorities. In particular, the emphasis on Children's Trusts as the only way forward was not accepted by all.

The Children's Commissioner role caused some particular concerns because it seemed to be couched in vague terms that left many questions about what the powers of the Commissioner in England might be. For example, the Commissioner has a role in involving children and gaining their views, but only a very restricted role in reviewing individual children's cases. This is in contrast to the Welsh Commissioner who has more extensive powers, for example to request and get information. The Children's Minister claimed that the vagueness surrounding the role in the Green Paper was because of the need for further consideration of the Children's Commissioner role. What is unclear is why the Commissioner for England's role still needed further consideration when the role of the Welsh Commissioner has been providing a model for several years.

The media focused to a considerable extent on plans to introduce a ban on smacking within the Children Bill. The long-running and periodically heated debate about banning smacking of children, in line with many other European countries, was resurrected by these proposals and this drew media attention more noticeably than any other aspect of the proposals. The strong pro-smacking lobby campaigned successfully to reduce the impact of the proposals, despite a rebellion by 47 Labour backbench Members of Parliament who voted for an outright ban.

The outcome was a compromise that satisfied neither the anti-smacking children's rights lobby nor the pro-smacking organizations. While the changes got rid of the contentious provision in previous legislation that some physical abuse of children could be defended on the grounds of 'reasonable chastisement', this does not constitute a total ban on smacking as lobbied for by organizations such as 'Children are Unbeatable!'. Instead, a compromise was pushed through that continued to allow mild forms of physical punishment within the law, but outlawed forms of punishment that caused visible bruising or mental harm to the child. The government has avoided addressing the smacking issue for a substantial time. It is likely that this is in response to its concerns about the possible electoral losses associated with a firm and outright ban.

The media also tapped into concerns about the ethics of the proposed electronic data sharing between agencies. These concerns focused on the need to review both the Human Rights Act and the Data Protection Act to allow for data sharing to take place. Lack of detail about the safeguards around privacy and confidentiality and concerns about the impact on children's rights were central to this debate.

Normally, the next step after a Green Paper would have been to publish a White Paper, as discussed earlier in this chapter. However, in this case the government at the time (New Labour, 1997–2010) took the unusual step of drawing up the Children Bill, missing out the White Paper stage. This decision may have been taken to ensure speed in implementing the policy developments, but in some senses it may have been because the *Every Child Matters* Green Paper was much more detailed and specific in its provisions than Green Papers usually are. There is also speculation from some quarters that the government's haste was due to concerns that further tragedies might occur before new policy was in place to protect children. The decision to miss out on a White Paper caused some unease in that there were fears that certain aspects of the proposals may be legislated on before they were fully developed, for example the role of the Children's Commissioner, as discussed above.

Although ostensibly a consultation document, *Every Child Matters* was largely a finished product, detailing proposed policy changes which have mainly survived the consultation stage with few amendments. It was clear that the government was determined to take forward its plans rapidly and with few concessions to those who were involved in the wider consultation. Despite the significant level of response to the Paper, no major changes were made to the original proposals, which raises questions about the purposes of the consultation process.

The provisions of the Children Bill were also outlined in *Every Child Matters: Next Steps* and discussed in relation to the outcomes of the consultation. The Children Bill included areas where policy change needed to be facilitated by legislative change. Not all aspects of policy change require legislation to implement, but where there are existing laws facilitating policy, legislation may be needed to allow change to take place. Some of the areas where legislation was needed to bring about the changes outlined in *Every Child Matters* are:

▸ introducing a Children's Commissioner for England responsible for promoting the views and interests of children within and outside Parliament

▸ outlining the functions of Children's Commissioners in Wales, Scotland and Northern Ireland

▶ requiring local authorities to make arrangements to work in partnership with other agencies, particularly with the voluntary and community sectors

▶ setting up Local Safeguarding Children Boards to monitor and direct multi-disciplinary child protection work

▶ establishing the role of Director of Children's Services within every local authority

▶ an integrated inspection regime covering a wide range of children's services headed by Ofsted

▶ a lead council member for children in each local authority.

Interestingly, although the bill contained clauses about encouraging and facilitating the development of Children's Trusts, the development of these was not made statutory. The Children Act 2004 included enabling clauses that laid down the legal basis for establishing Children's Trusts. As such, the role of Children's Trusts was clarified in terms of their key function of pooling budgets, staff, services and other resources to provide more integrated services but, despite the government's expectations that all authorities will eventually establish trusts, they are not specified as such in the Act. This meant that the provision of the Act allowed for more flexibility at local authority level as to how each would organize children's services than was initially anticipated (Ashrof, 2005).

The passage of the Children Bill through Parliament was turbulent, taking nine months, and being characterized by the tabling of amendments and re-amendments as a 'tug of war ' took place between the Lords and Commons over some of the more controversial parts of the bill. The main disappointments for children's charities and agencies were the compromises or decisions made about the information databases, the smacking ban and the role of the Children's Commissioner for England (*Community Care*, 2004).

The information database remained an issue after the Act was passed, partly because of initial lack of clarity about how it would work. It was decided that children who receive any mainstream services would be on the database, which effectively meant the majority of children, as most receive services from primary care trusts (PCTs). Concerns at the time included the replacement of the locally based Child Protection Registers with the national database (later named ContactPoint), which could lead to vital information about children who may be abused getting lost in a much bigger pool of information. The database was to include details such as name, address, gender, date of birth, parent details and information about professionals working with the child. Some concerns were based on the Civil Service's poor track record in introducing major information and communications technology (ICT) systems.

The Education Select Committee's inquiry into the government's child welfare reform strategy reported that the proposed database was too complicated and much too costly to be feasible. One expert witness, Richard Thomas, pointed out that a database of 11 million children could make it more, not less, difficult to identify problems and issues for individuals. This issue highlights some of the problems created by the volume and range of provisions within the Green Paper and the difficulties in progressing the strategy on a multitude of fronts simultaneously. Suspending the ongoing implementation of ContactPoint was one of the first policy changes in the field of children's welfare made by the Coalition government on coming to power in 2010.

As discussed above, the role of the Children's Commissioner, which had been questioned at the Green Paper stage particularly by voluntary sector organizations, was the cause of some of the turbulence. Children's rights groups such as the Children's Rights Alliance wanted the Children's Commissioner to have a role in supporting and developing children's rights issues and safeguarding children's rights. They wanted the Children's Commissioner to have a much wider remit to investigate cases, like the Commissioners in Wales, Scotland and Northern Ireland. However, there was strong opposition to this approach from Margaret Hodge, the then Children's Minister, and Baroness Ashton, Minister for Sure Start, and with a few minor concessions their view prevailed, despite an initial defeat in the House of Lords. This opposition to a rights-based role seemed to be based on the view that in such a role the Commissioner would get bogged down in individual cases (*Community Care*, 2004).

The outcome disappointed many children's agencies and children's rights groups, with concerns that the Children's Commissioner for England would have a weak role with fewer powers than his or her counterparts elsewhere in the UK and Europe. There were also concerns about the role of the Commissioner for England for non-devolved matters in Wales and reserved matters in Scotland, which could lead to confusion about responsibilities in some areas. In 2010, the Coalition government commissioned a review of the Children's Commissioner for England's role by Dr John Dunford, which concluded that the role had been 'disappointing' and was 'flawed'. He proposed that the new role should be now rights-based and that the Commissioner should report to Parliament and not be tied to the Department of Education. Dunford also recommended that the role of the Commissioner should also involve advising on new policy and its impact on children's rights, and that the Office of the Children's Commissioner and the Office of the Children's Rights Director should be merged. In line with current policy drivers, it was also recommended that the Children's Commissioner's advice and reports were evidence-based in future (Dunford, 2010). Most of these recommendations are in line with the original criticisms of the role by children's rights advocates.

The Children Bill became law as the Children Act 2004, paving the way for the changes outlined above. The key focus of the Act was enabling rather than prescribing change, allowing local authorities flexibility in how they implemented the proposals. Other changes that have not required legislation were detailed in *Every Child Matters: Change for Children* (DfES, 2004b), as discussed above.

Implementation at regional and local level

One thing that was clear from the start of the implementation of the *Every Child Matters* strategy was that local authorities were in line for the bulk of the structural and cultural change and that this would take place mainly within existing budgets. Although the strategy was influenced by and largely welcome to the Inter-Agency Group (IAG), representing key organizations involved in the implementation, this did not detract from the overwhelming scale of the task. Central government provided a massive amount of guidance and information to support this process.

One of the central features of the implementation of the Green Paper proposals was the extent of information made available to support the changes. The government website www.everychildmatters.gov.uk was a central resource for disseminating the ethos and principles of the reforms and detailing what was expected of local authorities and other key agencies to ensure the changes were made. Local authorities and other key agencies were advised by documents outlining their roles and the deadlines for achieving each phase of change under the general heading of *Every Child Matters: Change for Children*. This information was accompanied by a timetable for implementing changes, which included deadlines for the issue of guidelines and introduction of:

- a duty for agencies to cooperate with each other
- integrated services (Children's Trusts)
- an integrated Children's and Young Person's Plan
- a Director of Children's Services in each local authority
- a lead member for children's services in each local council
- an integrated inspection framework.

Support at regional level came largely through the appointment of regional change advisers to support local developments with a budget of £20 million. Change was initially particularly focused on the development of Children's Trusts and co-located teams. Typically, within local authorities there were staff briefings to provide information about the planned new structures, invitations to consult and workshops on inter-agency aspects of change. Bodies within local government involved in such discussions included ACPCs and strategic planning groups.

It may seem that the implementation of the strategy was well coordinated and informed, leading to smooth transitions. However, there were a number of major concerns about the implementation of the strategy at service provision level. Implementing large, complex policy packages like *Every Child Matters: Change for Children*, which requires significant structural and cultural changes across a range of professional groups and agencies, is a major challenge to local authorities. One issue, which is not uncommon in policy implementation of any sort, is the budget local authorities have had to bring about the changes. Local authorities were advised by Margaret Hodge to be smarter with their money when asking for more. The budget for change at local authority level was £22 million in 2006/07 and £63 million in 2007/08. This was not considered enough by local authorities and there was a view that it may limit the effectiveness of the implementation: 'Observers feared the limited funds meant that the Act would meet the same fate as the Children Act, 1989, which was regarded as a sound piece of legislation that didn't fulfil its expectations as a result of lack of funding' (Ashrof, 2005: 1).

Another issue is the range of problems associated with 'introducing innovative programmes into mainstream services' (Dawson, 2004: 24). Although local authorities had more flexibility to do this than initially anticipated, to achieve these changes required massive cultural and structural change. Local authorities had the responsibility of addressing structural change and how this would be achieved (a significant problem in itself), but there was very little said at central government level about the cultural change required to make integrated services work. It was anticipated that there would be both institutional and personal resistance to change among the workforce in the face of new regimes, new management structures, new ways of working and new cultures.

The emphasis on structural change may mask the need for cultural change as different workforces with their own ways of working, goals and motivations, philosophies and work practices come together. One concern was that the government simply failed to recognize the enormity of the transition required within local government to successfully integrate services. Multi-disciplinary teams were hardly a new concept, but evidence shows that many are left to cope with 'complex and unforeseen challenges', including different training, jargon, priorities, world views and working traditions (Rickford, 2005). Frost (2005) and his colleagues researched the work of several multi-agency teams to explore the issues and challenges in successful integration. He determined that teams faced challenges of the following kinds:

▸ structural

▶ ideological

▶ procedural

▶ inter-professional.

Frost found that teams either worked towards conflict resolution or conflict avoidance and that having another external agency (a common enemy?) to work against was effective in achieving better integration. He concluded that factors for success were:

▶ appropriate structures and systems, for example co-location

▶ shared professional beliefs and ideologies

▶ time for professional knowledge sharing

▶ active learning contexts.

The Children's Workforce Development Council (CWDC) was established to support workforce developments to achieve the goals of the *Every Child Matters: Change for Children* strategy. One of its roles was to ensure that a common culture between different sectors was developed. However, it is clear that to achieve cultural change takes time and effort and is not achievable through merely making structural changes. As Dame Denise Platt, Chair of the Commission for Social Care Inspection, said at the 2004 Inter-Agency Group Conference: 'In practice, integration too often means new boundaries around old behaviours' (Platt, 2004). The CWDC was decommissioned in 2012 by the Coalition Government.

Points for reflection 〰️

▶ Consider the last time you worked with or had contact with practitioners/professionals from another disciplinary background or agency.

▶ Were there any areas of difference in your view of the work you were doing, for example in the needs of a child and family?

▶ Did you focus on the same issues or have different ideas about what was important?

▶ Were your goals the same?

▶ Think about how comfortable you felt working with someone from a different professional background.

Cultural and structural change mean different things for different sections of the workforce. Social care service workers have been concerned that they will be overwhelmed by education and health as their separate departmental bases disappear. This view may be exacerbated by the continuing lead that education takes in the development of children's services. In 2005, 50 per cent of Directors of Children's Services took up their posts and 90 per cent of these were former Chief Education Officers (CEOs) rather than Directors of Social Services or other senior positions in children and family services (Hunter, 2005). It was widely acknowledged that ex-CEOs have a steep learning curve in areas normally firmly within the remit of children's social care services, such as providing statutory child protection services. Chief Education Officers generally lacked understanding or experience of safeguarding children and this lack could be dangerous for children (*Community Care*, 2005). Concerns focused around the possibility that changes that impacted more on social care services than on education underestimated the cultural differences between them. This in turn led to concerns about the destabilization of ongoing services to children and families during the transition period and whether child protection services would be at risk in the longer run (Waterman and Fowler, 2004; ADSS, 2005). Gillen (2008) evaluated progress towards Laming's recommendations five years on and among other findings suggested that introducing Directors of Children's Services had probably not improved accountability for safeguarding children. Concerns about the lack of child protection expertise of Directors of Children's Services was highlighted more recently in the Laming report (2009) into the death of Peter Connolly in 2007. Laming suggested that Directors of Children's Services should have child protection training and be made responsible to the General Social Care Council for child protection failures. He also stated that as most of the Directors were from education backgrounds and not social care services, that they should appoint a senior manager with this expertise.

Other concerns expressed by the Association of Directors of Social Services (ADSS) during the early stages of implementing Change for Children included the emphasis on co-location of staff and whether this had become a goal in itself rather than a means of delivering effective multi-agency services to children and families. Also, their report highlighted the fact that while other agencies had a duty to cooperate in the delivery of integrated services, Directors of Children's Services had no powers to make them fulfil this duty (ADSS, 2005).

It is clear that local authorities have had to find their own ways to implement the changes within the hard-won boundaries of flexibility agreed by central government and within the requirements of a rapid implementation timetable. This has meant that the changes have been implemented at different rates between local authorities, with some lagging behind and mixed progress (Jackson, 2005). Jackson highlights the different approaches to the development of pathfinder Children's Trusts within two authorities to demonstrate the diversity of approaches, and argues that the developments are not about 'bricks and mortar' but about finding ways of working in partnership that work within the particular context. There is no single approach to integration that will work in every context.

Concerns were expressed about the rate of progress overall in terms of the effectiveness of the ECM agenda. Lord Laming was reported as stating that good practice could have prevented child deaths subsequent to Victoria Climbié's, implying that this was not yet universal. The report suggested that the pace of change in putting Laming's recommendations into place was too slow in some areas (BBC, 2008a). The death of Peter Connolly sharply high-lighted that these concerns had considerable substance and Laming's (2009) report into his death highlighted that good safeguarding practice was not in place consistently across LAs and that 'working together' was still not fully operational across the board. The conclusion is inevitable – overcoming barri-ers between professionals trained to think their way of working is best takes time to achieve and involves massive cultural and structural change.

Implementing the Common Assessment Framework and Lead Professional Role

In this section of the extended case study, the introduction of specific strategies to support aspects of Change for Children is explored in order to examine some of the issues of implementation in more detail. A key element of the Every Child Matters: Change for Children agenda is ensuring that access to specific services for children with additional needs is embedded in universal services for all children.

The Laming report (2003) identified poor coordination between services, failure to share information and lack of professional cooperation as key elements contributing to the death of Victoria Climbié at the hands of her carers. However, other child death inquiries going back over several decades also identified similar aspects of multi-agency service provision as problematical in terms of effective safeguarding. Other vulnerable groups such as 'looked-after' children and children with disabilities have also experienced deficits in service delivery due to poor integration of different professional/agency involvement. In addition, many children have waited for unacceptable lengths of time for services to be provided as they went through serial assessments as a result of intra- or inter-agency referral. Children with disabilities, who may receive services from health, education, voluntary sector and social care services, were often particularly subject to multiple assessments and uncoordinated services.

Case study – Donny ⌐▱⌐

Donny was 6 years old when his school decided to explore the possibility that he had a specific learning disability, after a six-month period of discussions with his parents about their concerns, and in-class assessment by his teacher. Donny was assessed by an LA advice teacher three months later, who then referred him for assessment by an educational psychologist as she thought he might be dyslexic. Nine months later, Donny was assessed by the educational psychologist. However, in the meantime his parents had asked for a full paediatric assessment through children's health services because of the long wait and Donny's increasing frustration in school, which was affecting his behaviour. The educational psychologist identified that Donny was dyslexic a month before the full paediatric assessment confirmed this and suggested he was also dyspraxic. A year and a half after concerns about his learning ability had arisen (a quarter of his whole life and nearly two school years), Donny still had not received any services to support his learning or development.

The Common Assessment Framework (CAF) and lead professional and information sharing index (ContactPoint) were cornerstones of the strategy to embed safeguarding and support for children with additional needs within universal service provision. Key principles of the strategy were to:

▸ reduce the number of assessments children with additional needs are subject to, in order to simplify assessment, reduce stress on the child and family, make good use of resources and speed up the delivery of services to meet need

▸ ensure that services delivered by more than one professional agency to the same child/family are appropriately coordinated to reduce overlap and gaps in service provision and to improve accountability

▸ ensure that professionals are aware of other agencies involved with a child/family to improve the coordination of service delivery and to provide opportunities for professionals to share information about any concerns about a child with involved others.

The Common Assessment Framework

The CAF is an initial assessment process, which can be used by any frontline children's services professional, to provide an assessment of a child and family where additional needs are identified in terms of outcomes for the child. Assessment focuses on all aspects of the child's development, on the environment and on parenting capacity. It is positive in that it focuses on areas where need is met, as well as those where more support is required. For some children, specialist assessments will be needed in addition and the CAF may act as a referral for these.

The use of the CAF offers the opportunity to accelerate and simplify the assessment process so that children have fewer assessments and less waiting time for services to be introduced. The CAF is designed for use in consultation with families and children and, as it is a voluntary process, they can refuse to be assessed.

Common Assessment Frameworks are often introduced after a pre-assessment checklist has been used to identify the possibility of additional needs. Common Assessment Frameworks are not just used to assess – part of the process is to identify and secure relevant resources to improve outcomes for the child. However, CAFs do not replace safeguarding processes and procedures where child protection concerns are the key issue.

The initial introduction of the CAF was evaluated by Brandon et al. (2006) who found that:

▶ in general the CAF has been welcome, although the initial introduction took longer than expected

▶ the purpose of the CAF was sometimes misunderstood and sometimes it was just used as a referral tool rather than as an assessment

▶ the time that CAFs took to complete was seen as adding to workloads, and some professionals found the forms difficult to complete

▶ there were different levels of understanding of this type of assessment between professional groups, depending on previous experience, with health and social care staff more likely to understand holistic assessment than education staff

▶ parental involvement with the CAF was not always fully understood and staff were not always clear about parents' rights to refuse to be involved.

More recently, the CAF was found to provide better outcomes for children and young people. Using a futurising methodology which predicted outcomes if a CAF had not been done, the researchers also concluded that investing in early intervention, including CAFs, saved expenditure on specialist resources in the future (Easton et al., 2011).

The Lead Professional role

While the coordination of inter-agency services through one professional is not a new concept, the introduction of a lead professional (LP) has ensured a much more universal approach to this. The purposes of the role are to ensure that services are delivered effectively and efficiently to families, minimizing overlap and ensuring service provision is seamless. The lead professional may also reduce stress on families involved with a number of agencies by providing a single contact point for them. Sloper (2004) found that families with children with disabilities benefited from and welcomed having a single professional responsible for coordinating their often complex multi-agency services.

In their evaluation, Brandon et al. (2006) found that there were some concerns among professionals about performing this role, linked to lack of previous professional experience. These included:

▶ anxiety around taking on new roles

▶ concerns about the high level of responsibility in the role

▶ different concepts of the main purpose of the role.

Lead professionals need skills to work with families and other professionals, and these vary between different disciplines and levels of worker. Issues of whether particular staff are paid to take on this leadership role, whether they have appropriate skills and the time to do the role have been raised as the role has been introduced.

However, Brandon et al. (2006) identified a range of benefits to parents from introducing the lead professional role, including swifter outcomes for families and better communication between agencies and families.

The study also identified key factors for the successful implementation of the CAF and the lead professional including:

▶ enthusiasm at grass roots and managerial level

▶ a history of good multi-agency working and practice

▶ a clear structure for CAF/LP processes

▶ perceived benefits for families

▶ good support, training, supervision and guidance

▶ learning from others. (Brandon et al., 2006: 10)

And for poorer results:

▶ a mismatch between the 'vision' and the practice

▶ lack of agency join-up – conflicts of interest

▶ lack of professional trust

▶ anxiety about increased workload

▶ gaps in skill and confidence

▶ confusion and muddle about CAF/LP processes

▶ lack of support. (Brandon et al., 2006: 11)

Successful implementation could be achieved more effectively through a top-down approach, including a 'clear strategy' linked to local guidance and awareness raising, a phased roll-out and multi-agency training including managers, and an effective information technology (IT) system (adapted from Brandon et al., 2006: 11).

One of the main criticisms of the CAF and lead professional roll-out was that the training was not sufficient to ensure confidence in using CAFs and taking the lead professional role among all sectors of the children's workforce. Brandon et al. (2006) concluded that training needed to be ongoing rather than one-off and that more managers needed to be trained to ensure that new approaches to work required to effectively embed the CAF and lead professional were adopted.

The Information Sharing Index (ContactPoint)

The sharing of information between agencies involved with a child through a national database was recommended in the Laming report, leading to trailblazers in a number of authorities to test and evaluate the feasibility of such a database (2003). The resulting information sharing index, ContactPoint, linked up already established local databases and held basic information about children up to the age of 18, and, with their permission, care-leavers and children with learning difficulties, until they were 25. The information held was restricted by the Children Act 2004 and did not include any assessment information. The main additional information related to details of professionals and agencies involved with the child and family, including health and education services.

These details also included whether there was a lead professional and who this was, and whether a CAF had been completed in respect of the child.

The purpose of ContactPoint was for professionals involved with a child and family to be aware of other agencies and professionals who were also working with them. This was aimed at aiding rapid and effective inter-professional cooperation and ensuring better information sharing than previously. The resource implications were also outlined in terms of professional hours 'lost' in trying to track others involved with a child and family (ECM, 2008).

Reservations about the proposed database were voiced from rights groups and others from when the Children Bill was going through Parliament, focusing on concerns about privacy and rights, unauthorized access that could put children at more risk, the complexity and possible technical difficulties of a database this size, and a possible 'labelling' factor where contact with particular services could shape views of a child for years to come. The Association of Directors of Children's Services was reported to be concerned about the possibility of abusers getting access to the database because it was not clear who had responsibility for vetting the 330,000 authorized users. In addition, the fact that children of politicians and celebrities may be 'shielded' (their details guarded or left out) seemed to imply that the safety of the system couldn't be guaranteed (Elliott, 2007). This was supported by a DCSF-commissioned report published by Deloitte and Touche (2008) which 'identified "a significant risk" to ContactPoint from the security procedures of local councils and other organisations accessing the database' (BBC, 2008b). However, the proposed benefits of ContactPoint were largely supported by the evaluation of the local trailblazers, which found that the databases did link involved agencies more quickly and that this had a positive effect on the speed of intervention (Cleaver et al., 2004).

The introduction of the CAF and the lead professional, while generally welcome, has posed challenges in terms of implementation because of the new processes and ways of working demanded. Local authorities have been more effective where they have provided a clear lead on implementation as opposed to a less successful bottom-up approach. Training has been criticized where it has been seen as a 'one-off', rather than an ongoing process for all staff and managers. However, improvements and increasing use of the processes imply that early difficulties may be overcome if authorities can learn from each other's experience. The challenges of implementing ContactPoint were different, focusing on issues about the impact on children's rights in terms of privacy, technical problems and the safety of a national database accessed by a large number of users. ContactPoint was decommissioned in 2010 early on in the Coalition government's administration.

Summary ☐

The implementation of the *Every Child Matters: Change for Children* programme was part of much broader policy developments that included the aims of the National Health Framework and the provisions of the Childcare Act 2006, designed to make widespread changes to the ways that mainstream and specialist services are delivered to children.

The extended case study highlights the complex processes by which policy is developed and implemented and the key stages in this process. It also highlights the roles of different bodies and individuals, emphasizing that policy-making and implementation is essentially a human activity with all the unpredictability and flawed nature of human activities. Despite the apparently rational nature of the processes involved, policy plans are put into action by a process of negotiation between bodies with different levels of power and influence. In this case, government plans survived the process largely unscathed until a change of government in 2010 brought in new political agendas and changes of policy focus. While the Children Act 2004 remains, the term *Every Child Matters* is no longer in use in government documents and changes to aspects of early years policy have undone some of this agenda, as discussed above and elsewhere in this edition.

Key factors in implementing the strategy within *Every Child Matters: Change for Children* were:

▸ the role of key ministers and civil servants within newly integrated central government bodies, which reflected a strong commitment to improving children's welfare services

▸ the complex and ongoing interactions between these ministers and senior civil servants and representatives of the voluntary sector and local and regional bodies and bodies such as IAG

▸ the media role in highlighting particular issues for attention

▸ the government's success in defeating or reversing key amendments as the Children Bill passed through Parliament

▸ placing local authorities at the centre of implementation of the strategy.

Further reading

Waterman, C. and Fowler, J. (2004) *Plain Guide to the Children Act 2004*, Slough: NFER.

Contains an annotated copy of the Act with a useful preliminary discussion explaining aspects of the legislation and how it was developed. The annotations explain the meanings of different parts of the Act.

Keeping up to date with new early years policy means reading magazines such as *Nursery World* and *Community Care*, and newspapers such as *The Guardian* and *The Independent* – all of which can also be found online.

The main government websites for following early years policy developments and key documents are listed at the end of the book.

Chapter 5

Early Years Policy in Wales, Scotland and Northern Ireland: The Impact of Devolution

This chapter describes:

▶ the structure of devolved government that has developed in the UK since 1997

▶ the development of early years policy under the devolved regimes in Wales, Scotland and Northern Ireland

▶ the impact that devolution has had on the development of early years policy across the UK

▶ the potential value of comparisons of policy within the UK.

Devolution and policy-making

The UK is dominated in several senses by England, the country whose population constitutes more than 80 per cent of that of the kingdom as a whole and whose largest city, London, is the kingdom's capital. As Clark and Waller (2007) point out, commentators fall all too often into the error of making statements that purport to be about the UK, but are, in fact, only true of England. This chapter systematically examines early years policy in Wales, Scotland and Northern Ireland.

Some independent states have federal constitutions; some are much more centralized, although with local administrations that will always have some measure of autonomy. The UK is set up rather differently: 'neither unitary nor federal, but … a union state' (Pilkington, 2002: 7). England, Wales, Scotland and Northern Ireland each have a different relationship to the kingdom as a whole, a relationship determined by different histories. (The Channel Islands and the Isle of Man have constitutional positions that are different again. However, initiatives there have had less impact on the rest of the kingdom and for this reason we have left consideration of their position on one side.)

The UK is not unique in having various kinds of devolution. In Spain, the 'communities' that make up the state have different degrees of autonomy, with Catalonia and Euskadi (the Basque country) coming closest to complete home rule – and these arrangements were established in one brief period during the return to democracy in the late 1970s and early 1980s. The 'asymmetric' form of devolution in Spain has proved relatively stable and the same could prove to be true of the UK. However, differences in local powers can be seen as unfair and fuel debate as to whether there should be a more systematic approach (including devolution for England or for regions within England). The dynamic nature of devolution is exemplified by the current debate over Scottish independence and the possible outcomes of this as Scotland moves towards a referendum on the issue.

The support of young children has been one of the areas of policy most clearly under the control of the devolved governments in Wales, Scotland and Northern Ireland. It was also an area that had been comparatively neglected in these countries before devolution. One result of this has been that the devolved governments have often seen it as a sphere in which they could demonstrate their competence and progressive thinking. For example, in July 2001, when Northern Ireland began consultation on a strategy for children, Dermott Nesbitt, the Deputy First Minister, expressed the hope that the strategy would make his country a 'world leader' (*Nursery World*, 2001: 6). At the time of writing this edition, the consultation on the Early Years 0–6 Strategy in Northern Ireland was complete and the outcome report in progress. This strategy focuses on developing quality early years services, extending these to children aged 6 to provide better transitions and a more holistic approach to children's needs, equity of access to services and universal access to pre-school education (DENI, 2010).

The interest that many politicians in the three nations take in early years policy has been encouraged by lobbyists in England. It was already established practice there to compare the UK unfavourably with other countries, particularly with Spain, New Zealand, Denmark and the region of Reggio Emilia in Italy, all of which were said to provide models we should copy. Devolution has provided a new stick with which to beat those making policy for England. Thus, Bruce (2001) spoke warmly of her experience of early years work in Scotland (Rawstrone, 2001) and Lindon (2005) praised the Scottish guidance on the birth-to-3 curriculum, claiming that it was superior to similar moves in England. It is significant that it was in 2001 and 2002 that *Nursery World* provided unusually detailed coverage of developments in the devolved countries, since this was the period when policy there (on standards in childminding and the role of the Children's Commissioner) was more in tune with the thinking of a majority of early years practitioners than was policy in England.

Given the way in which developments in the three countries have been used in debate, it is worth pointing out that England is not always bottom of the league in terms of what the early years profession views as best practice. The scale of provision has often been better in England. England also took some steps to modify the artificial distinction in law and institutional arrangements between care and education before the other three nations. The NCH report *United for Children?* (2003) offers a more measured comparison of the four nations, although is still critical of developments in England.

Comparing Wales, Scotland and Northern Ireland

The next three sections of this chapter provide some basic information on early years policy in Wales, Scotland and Northern Ireland. Each country is considered in relation to five issues:

▶ the history of its devolved powers

▶ the integration of services for young children

▶ the expansion of early years services since 1997

▶ quality, curriculum development and regulation

▶ comparison with other parts of the UK.

Wales

Devolution

The gradual conquest of Wales by England in the Middle Ages led to absorption into England under the Tudors. In the 19th century, there was a systematic attempt to eliminate the Welsh language and children were punished for using it in school, even in the playground. It was not until 1907 that the first step was taken towards separate administration for Wales with the establishment of a Welsh Section in the Department of Education. In 1951, a Ministry of Welsh Affairs was set up under the Home Office (which then had a very wide remit). In 1957, responsibility for oversight of that ministry was transferred to Housing and Local Government. A Welsh Office was set up at Westminster in 1964. That body acquired responsibility for health in 1968 and for education in 1970. However, legislation continued for some time to be written for 'England and Wales' rather than for each country separately.

At the end of the 1970s, there was a half-hearted and unsuccessful attempt by the Labour government to establish a form of devolved government for Wales. Devolution was one of the commitments of the Labour Party when it won the General Election of 1997. The first Government of Wales Act was passed in 1998 and the first elections for the Welsh Assembly were held in 1999. Tony

Blair seemed to assume that Wales would be content with a minimal level of autonomy and initially the posts of First Secretary of the Assembly and the Secretary of State for Wales were held by the same person. Rebellion in the Welsh Labour Party led to an end to this arrangement and later to the Government of Wales Act 2006, which gave the Assembly primary jurisdiction over all its own domestic affairs. Developments in early years are seen as key to overall education policy. In particular, they have been seen as crucial to the success of attempts to promote the Welsh language, now spoken by an increasing number of people, especially the young.

Integration

Across the UK, there have been moves since 1997 to break down artificial divisions between care and education in services for very young children and to establish a more 'integrated' approach. Some have hoped that Children's Commissioners would have a key role to play in this process. Wales was the first country in the UK to show a strong interest in this idea, but the creation of a commissioner post was blocked by the Conservatives and, initially, by the 1997 Labour government. An inquiry into abuse in children's homes in Wales (Waterhouse, 2000) galvanized interest in the idea of a commissioner as well as in improvements in child protection. Legislation followed, creating for the first time anywhere in the UK a post of Children's Commissioner. This was also the first piece of legislation in the UK to make specific reference to the United Nations Convention on the Rights of the Child. Peter Clarke, the first Children's Commissioner for Wales, took up post in 2001. Development in the role of Children's Commissioner has been evident. For example, in 2011 the four UK Children's Commissioners released a joint report expressing their concern over poverty, the disproportional impact of spending cuts on the most disadvantaged and the need to ensure that 'all children's rights [are] fully understood and enjoyed across the UK' (p. 16). This highlights how a development that was first instigated in Wales led to change and coordination across the UK, and shows a significant change to the early debate on whether there should even be a role for a Children's Commissioner.

Expansion

Childcare was not well developed in Wales before devolution. As late as 1986, there was only one full day care setting throughout the country. The number of such settings in England would have been much lower then than it is now, but not as low as that. As recently as 2006, there was only one childcare place for every seven children under the age of 8 in Wales. Reliance on informal care by grandparents and others remained a strong factor (Clark and Waller, 2007). In 2001, the Assembly conducted a consultation of the public on its overall 'Plan for Wales' which dealt with priorities in childcare, education and health. The Assembly government was already committed to ensuring that early education was available to all children whose parents sought it and that out-of-school care was similarly available to all by 2010. Subsidized childcare is one of the key aspects of the Genesis Project (part funded by the European Union) which was set up to reduce barriers faced by parents returning to work. A larger-scale investment began with the 'Flying Start' programme (2005–08) under which £46 million was spent on children and families in deprived areas on childcare and various forms of family support. As a result of these and other initiatives, there has been a significant increase in the number of places available (nearly 19,000 in the first five years of the Assembly's operation). As in other parts of the UK, promotion of childcare has been seen by the Labour Party as a means of encouraging parents back to work, at least as much as it has been seen in terms of the needs of children. The 'Flying Start' evaluation found that advances have been made in multi-agency working although parents felt this had had varied impacts. However, children who had benefited from the programme were showing advances in school and this tallies with the positive evaluation of parental support and home learning. Overall, the programme succeeded in widening access to health-visiting services but further evaluation is needed to know if and how this improves outcomes for children and parents (Ipsos MORI, 2011).

Quality, curriculum development and regulation

Even before devolution, there was a separate approach in Wales to quality and the curriculum, partly because of the increasing readiness of Westminster to allow some concessions to the Welsh language in the education system. This was strengthened by the decisions taken in 1996 on the Welsh equivalent of the framework for desirable learning outcomes in pre-school education. From the start, the Welsh framework was seen as superior to the English one, with a stronger focus on the child as learner and an open-minded approach to the value of play. This has been a source of considerable pride in Wales. The powers of the Welsh Assembly include control over curriculum issues. In 2003, a new Foundation Phase was proposed and a revised version of that guidance was produced in January 2008. In comparison with the new Foundation Stage guidance that came into force in England in September 2008 and which makes only a slight dent in the barrier between pre-school and school education in the child's fifth year, the Welsh Foundation Phase led to the abolition of Key Stage 1 in 2010 and is bound to impact significantly on Key Stage 2. It also continues the Welsh traditions of heavy emphasis on the role of play and of ascribing value to Welsh. (Among other things, it identifies a seventh area of learning in addition to the six originally devised for England and Wales – one that focuses on cultural diversity, a development of the original focus on bilingualism.) Moreover, the new phase was introduced with even greater care than its English equivalent, with a formal pilot in 41 settings monitored by a team led by Iram Siraj-Blatchford and Kathy Sylva. The final version was presented in October 2007 and full implementation took place in 2011.

Related initiatives include:

▶ the pioneering role played by the Welsh Assembly government in the development of new approaches to the safeguarding of children, moves which pre-dated and influenced the 2004 Children Act

▶ the launch of a National Play Strategy in 2006

▶ changes in the system of initial teacher education and training

▶ a common inspection framework applying to all settings, introduced in 2008

▶ the *Good Practice Guidance for Out-of-Classroom Learning* issued by the Assembly government at the end of 2007 (Welsh Assembly government, 2007)

▶ ongoing investment in the 'Flying Start' programme.

Wales and the rest of the UK

Many of these developments have strong parallels with those in the rest of the UK. Wales has moved towards closer integration of services and seen childcare to a large extent in terms of getting parents off benefits and back to work. Part of the explanation for these similarities is that the Labour Party has been the dominant party in Wales, as it has in the UK as a whole. However, there are some strong points of contrast, among them:

▶ the energy with which the Welsh Assembly has tackled this issue, typified in its determination to secure a Children's Commissioner

▶ the emphasis on play

▶ the more radical approach to the question of when formal schooling should begin

▶ the approach to cultural diversity that follows from the commitment to promoting the Welsh language.

There are, however, areas where Welsh and English policy are still very similar. For example, the Welsh Code of Practice for special needs is clearly based on the English one, although this is likely to alter when the Green Paper consultation on special educational needs is enacted in England later in the parliamentary session (DfE, 2011b).

Scotland

Devolution

Unlike Wales, Scotland remained independent of England until the beginning of the 18th century. When the two countries were first united (in the early 17th century), it was on the basis of having the same monarch (James I and VI) rather than because Scotland had been conquered or absorbed in some way. Scotland had its own Parliament until 1707. Divisions between different parts of the country were at that time as important politically as any division between Scotland and England. After the unification of the two Parliaments, differences remained in the legal and educational systems. A separate Scottish Office was established in Westminster as early as 1885.

When the Labour Party attempted to introduce devolution in Wales in 1979, a similar attempt was made for Scotland, one that was also unsuccessful. Margaret Thatcher was deeply opposed to devolution. However, once in power, Tony Blair moved rapidly to set up a new form of government for Scotland and in 1998 the Scotland Act laid the basis for a Scottish Parliament with its own Executive (later re-named the Scottish Government). The areas under the control of the Scottish Parliament include all those relevant to early years policy. Like Wales, Scotland continues to send MPs to the Westminster Parliament and the UK government retains control over significant areas of policy, including defence and foreign affairs. Initially at any rate, the Scottish Parliament had wider powers than the equivalent Assembly in Wales. Devolution (rather than full independence or full union with England) appears to have the support of a large section of the Scottish people (Bromley et al., 2006). In 2007, the Scottish National Party (SNP) emerged as the largest party in elections to the Scottish Government, although without an absolute majority. The SNP formed the new government, which included Scotland's first Minister for Children and Early Years – Adam Ingram – who spoke of his ambitions for young children. However, this was a matter of detail and emphasis rather than outright conflict between the parties. As the Chief Executive of the Scottish Out of School Care Network said, 'all the major parties seem to agree on putting money into childcare' (Marcus, 2007: 5).

At the time of writing, there are plans for a referendum on Scottish independence in 2014.

Integration

Scotland has pursued the concept of integrated services for young children with some eagerness and has won the admiration of many in England as a result. The first integrated service for young children in the UK was established in Strathclyde in the 1980s, well before local authorities in England were legally obliged to go in that direction in 2001, and ahead of those pioneering authorities in England that set up such services in the 1990s. In some respects, until recently integration has gone less far in Scotland than in England. For example, there were still separate systems for regulation and inspection of childcare and early education. Nevertheless, there had been significant moves towards integration, including:

▸ the New Community Schools programme launched in 1998

▸ the early establishment of a post of Children's Commissioner

▸ the policy document *For Scotland's Children* (Scottish Executive, 2001), which laid down an overall approach to integration

▸ the establishment of local Childcare Partnerships, similar to the EYDCPs in England, but held by some to have been more successful

▸ joint inspection of child protection services

▸ the development of a new BA degree for integrated services developed by a partnership of James Watt College and the University of Strathclyde

▸ the new framework for qualifications and professional development introduced by the Scottish Social Services Council in late 2007.

In 2008, efforts to increase integration were taken forward significantly by the introduction of the umbrella policy *Getting it Right for Every Child (GIRFEC)* (Scottish Government, 2008). Rose (2012) suggests that developing effective multi-agency services is crucial in achieving Scottish early years policy goals of 'prevention, early identification of concerns and structured interventions' (p. 155). *GIRFEC* is based on principles of coordinated service delivery but more importantly involves 'whole-systems' changes to ensure effective service provision. The focus is on developing existing universal services such as health and education to work better together through changes to 'culture, systems and practice' (p. 156).

One of the key elements to this policy is the introduction of the role of the 'named person' to provide a point of contact for agencies and families in terms of any concerns about the child. This would be a professional from either health or education, depending on the age of the child, and is universal to all children. In respect of children with additional needs where more than one service is involved, there will also be a lead professional to coordinate multi-agency planning. In many ways, this parallels the role of the 'lead professional' in English policy, where a child who is being assessed within the Common Assessment Framework has a specific person to lead the multi-professional 'team around the child'. Similarly, the National Practice Model is a single or multi-agency assessment and planning tool with parallels to the English Common Assessment Framework (CAF). The principle underpinning this model is 'one child, one plan' and although the details differ, the approach has the same goals as the English CAF, which is to reduce assessments and complex planning for children and families to a single multi-agency assessment and child plan. The National Practice Model, however, focuses very clearly on the participation of children and young people in assessment and decision-making processes (Rose, 2012). The Early Years Framework was introduced in 2008, covering pre-birth to age 8. The Framework focuses on developing better early intervention rather than 'crisis management', aiming to achieve 10 changes over 10 years to improve the lives of young children. These include improvements in services and in multi-professional collaboration to achieve better outcomes for children and families. However, the Framework is being implemented in a restrictive economic climate with some emphasis on the aim to reduce costs in respect of later interventions (Scottish Government/COSLA, 2008).

Expansion

In the period since devolution, there has been significant expansion in early years services, particularly in after-school care and integrated pre-school centres. At times, this has been seen as threatening maintained provision (partly because it has happened at a time of falling birth rates that already placed some maintained settings at risk). When it formed the new government in 2007, the SNP had a long-standing commitment to provide funding to support childcare and early education, and took a number of initiatives. These included the decision to provide £15 million to extend free pre-school education from 33 to 38 weeks as part of a set of major funding proposals for education as a whole, building on plans already formulated in 2006.

Legislation is planned for 2013 to increase free early education and childcare from 475 to 600 hours each year as part of the Children and Young People Bill, which is based on strengthening children's rights in Scotland and providing cohesive support for all children.

Quality, curriculum development and regulation

The system of education in Scotland has always differed from that in England in several respects. Neither the National Curriculum nor standard assessment tests (SATs), nor the literacy and numeracy hours were ever imposed north of the border. Devolution has encouraged further change. As in Wales, ideas on the earliest phase of the curriculum are integral to plans for schooling as a whole. Thus, the work being conducted early in 2008 on curriculum guidance was concerned with the age range of 3–18 years rather than birth to 5, as in England. The Curriculum for Excellence was introduced with four key capacities 'to enable each child or young person to be a successful learner, a confident individual, a responsible citizen and an effective contributor' (Education Scotland, 2012). The focus is on a comprehensive lifelong-learning approach to curriculum development which differed from the more fragmented approach to early years curricula in England until recently.

In 2007, the Scottish Social Services Council published new regulations on the qualifications of managers in all early years settings. In 2008, the Scottish Care Commission announced a number of changes in the inspection system, including a new grading system and a greater use of self-assessment in the inspection process. Scotland has also pioneered the further development of outdoor play. The first completely outdoor nursery in the UK was established in Fife and in early 2008 there were new funding initiatives to support outdoor play by the Scottish Government and by Aberdeenshire Council.

Scotland and the rest of the UK

The excellent work that has been done on some aspects of curriculum development in Scotland and the pioneering initiatives taken even before devolution on the integration of early years services have won praise in England for Scottish achievements. This may sometimes give a misleading impression of the contrast. The integration of inspection in the area of child protection can divert attention from the fact that Scotland still has systems for the regulation of early years childcare and education services that are separate in a way that they no longer are in England. The fact that the country has a single set of curriculum guidance for ages 3 to 18 can divert attention from the fact that the guidance for children under 3 remains quite separate.

Plans to increase the hours of free nursery places for 3–4-year-olds to over 600 a year when the Children and Young People Bill becomes legislation in 2013 will mean higher levels of nursery provision in Scotland than in England and the 'best free nursery package in the UK' (Henry, 2012: 1). This provision will also be available to 2-year-olds in care.

GIRFEC (2008) and the Early Years Framework (2008) have in some ways paralleled some of the developments within the Every Child Matters policy framework, but the emphasis on early intervention is echoed by recent policy shifts in England under the Coalition government (Scottish Government/COSLA, 2008).

Northern Ireland

Devolution

If there was violence in the history of England's relationships with Wales and Scotland, that fact was largely forgotten in modern times – at least in England. Both Scotland and Wales have political parties that are seeking full independence from the UK and the process of devolution has been marked by bitter argument. Nevertheless, devolution itself has been implemented with nothing much worse than the odd shouting match. The history of Northern Ireland is different. It has entailed not only wars in the distant past, but rebellion in the early 20th century and armed conflict for much of the last part of that century. Previous forms of devolution have foundered on conflict within the province. Whereas the choice in Wales and Scotland has been between full union, full independence or a form of devolved government, the choices in Northern Ireland have been between full union with the UK, full union with the Irish Republic or a form of devolution that represents some kind of compromise between those two national identities.

It now seems that the re-established system of devolved government achieved in 2007 has a solid chance of continuing to make progress rather than of breaking down as other attempts have done, especially as it is based on agreement between the two bodies that had been seen as representing extremes of opinion – the Democratic Unionist Party (DUP) and Sinn Fein (the Irish nationalist party).

Well-deserved praise in both the Republic of Ireland and the USA has been heaped on Tony Blair and others who managed to broker this unexpected deal. However, mediators cannot magic agreement out of thin air. It seems likely that it was exhaustion after years of conflict, the economic prizes offered by peace, the increasing secularization of the Republic of Ireland that assuaged Protestant fears of the Catholic Church and the dawning realization on both sides in Northern Ireland that England and its politicians were relatively neutral on the future of the province rather than being committed to the union that, together, created the context in which real peace could be established. The DUP and Sinn Fein have shown themselves capable of working together on bread-and-butter social and economic issues, including early years policy. Sinn Fein, in particular, has a strong commitment to education – something it has in common with other forms of late 19th-century republicanism, but which the party itself would relate to the illegal 'hedge schools' provided for the Catholic population during the long struggle for independence. A major feature of the new regime is increased cooperation with the Republic of Ireland, which has manifested itself in joint action to develop better child protection systems and the establishment of an all-Ireland service for children with autistic disorders.

Integration

There is still an institutional division in Northern Ireland between the care and education of young children, a division that may have been aggravated by the fact that social services in the province have institutional arrangements with many similarities to those in the Republic of Ireland, while education has more in common with England. The division manifests itself largely in a separation of childcare for the under-3s and pre-school education for 3- and 4-year-olds. This is, of course, similar to the situation in Scotland. Just as in England some see a tension between the demands of the National Curriculum at Key Stage 1 and the implications of the curriculum guidance for the Foundation Stage, so in Northern Ireland there is seen to be a degree of tension between the demands of the revised National Curriculum and the play-based 'Enriched Curriculum' for younger children piloted in 120 schools across the province from 2001 to 2006 and now part of the new National Curriculum. Before the current agreement on devolution, the Department of Education had attempted to protect pre-school settings by restricting the provision of reception class places, measures that came into effect in September 2007. (Again, there are parallels with Scotland.) Northern Ireland has also promoted a new integrated approach to children's services with the creation of posts of Children's Commissioner and, later, Children's Minister, and greater cooperation between agencies at local level. In 2007, the Department for Education in Northern Ireland (DENI) assumed responsibility for the province's Sure Start programmes, the first stage in its acquisition of central responsibility for all children's services that was announced in 2006.

The next step is the implementation of the Early Years (0–6) Strategy which sets out to make links between existing early years services for 0–4-year-olds and the Foundation Stage in primary schools 'a comprehensive early years strategy that focuses on the development and well-being of each child, including affordable access to high quality early years provision for families living in areas of disadvantage and poverty in urban and rural areas' (DENI, 2010: 2.5). The strategy aims to improve transitions between early years services, pre-school and school, to improve quality in early years services and to improve integration of services. However, the strategy will not come with new resources attached despite chronic underfunding of the sector and existing inequalities in early years provision across Northern Ireland. Moreover, the ongoing fragmentation of early education and care is an issue that remains problematic in terms of equality in service provision and within the sector (CiNI, 2010).

Expansion

Even before the general election of 1997, Northern Ireland had taken steps towards the promotion of early years services with the establishment of inter-agency early years committees in each Health and Social Services area (as in the Republic of Ireland, Northern Ireland has a unified structure for the delivery of both health and social services through regional boards). After 1997, two reports were published from Westminster outlining plans for the development of early years learning and childcare services, plans similar to those being developed for England. By 2004, many of the targets set in those two reports had been met or surpassed. However, as discussed above, the current situation is that developments in the early years sector within the Early Years Strategy are expected to take place with no new resource commitment.

Quality, curriculum development and regulation

The quality of staff involved in early years services has been a major issue and it is only in the recent past that cooperation with the Republic of Ireland and with the rest of the UK has led to the development of something like adequate vetting procedures. Criticisms of the over-formality of teaching in Year 1 of primary education suggest the need for further work on training and qualifications. However, considerable work has been undertaken on curriculum development. There has been a review of the Special Needs Code of Practice (largely borrowed from England). The EPPE project in England has been mirrored in a similar study in Northern Ireland (EPPNI) under the direction of Professor Edward Melhuish. Northern Ireland, often in close cooperation with agencies in the Republic of Ireland, is pioneering some interesting work in the field of special needs. One of the province's largely unnoticed achievements over the last 40 years has been the research work undertaken at the University of Ulster on cognitive development in the early years, especially where that is affected by visual and hearing impairments. Regulatory regimes have been less well developed in some respects than in England, but a new Education and Skills Authority was established in 2008 to bring together the work of several existing bodies and this should lead to improvements in this sphere. The authority is being asked to tackle not just the issue of inter-professional coordination, but the much more tricky issue of cooperation across the sectarian divide.

Northern Ireland and the rest of the UK

Wales and Scotland have both had significant contacts with regions in other countries that have achieved a significant measure of devolved power in recognition of their separate national identities. In particular, both the Scottish Labour Party and the SNP have had continuing contacts with the major parties in Catalonia in Spain where interesting initiatives in early years services have occurred. There have been similar moves on the part of the Labour Party in Wales and Plaid Cymru, both of which have been interested in the 'normalization' of the Catalan language and the implications for Welsh.

Northern Ireland is unique among the countries of the UK in having a special relationship (underpinned by a growing number of institutional arrangements) with a completely independent state, the Republic of Ireland. As fears among the Unionist/Protestant community about the implications of this contact slowly diminish, these contacts could begin to prove especially fruitful and introduce new elements into the internal debate in the UK on early years services.

The introduction of the Early Years (0–6) Strategy appears to indicate that early years policy in Northern Ireland is following similar basic principles and policy aims of the other UK countries, with a similar emphasis on improving quality provision, improved integration and smoother transitions between stages of education. However, different social and structural issues may mean that implementation takes a different form to similar policies in the rest of the UK.

Activity

Imagine a child born in a UK country you are familiar with.

Define the child's social and economic situation in general terms. (Are his/her parents rich or poor or middle income? Does the family live in an urban or rural area? Are they part of the majority population or from a minority ethnic group? And so on.) Again, you should bear in mind the kind of situation with which you are most familiar.

▶ Describe the child's likely experiences of childcare and education services up to the age of 7.

▶ Do you think things would have been different if the child had been born in similar social circumstances, but in another UK country?

The impact of devolution

This chapter has highlighted both similarities and differences between the countries comprising the UK and the ways in which they have influenced each other in the development of early years services.

At times, there has been a kind of competition between them with lobbyists urging their own countries to emulate what they see as best practice in one or more of the other countries. Among the reasons have been:

▶ genuine concern about the well-being of young children

▶ the fact that there was a lack of development before devolution, so that there was a lot of catching up to do

▶ the lead offered by the New Labour (1997–2010) government in London

▶ the new opportunities created by devolution.

However, it seems likely that a perfectly natural wish to do visibly better than England, the dominant partner in the union, comes into the equation.

The fact that contrasts are often made between what happens in Westminster and the initiatives taking place under devolved governments sometimes over-shadows other and equally interesting comparisons. There are, for example, many similarities between Scotland and Northern Ireland and between those two countries and France, a country whose early years policy is rarely afforded consideration in the UK. Closer attention to comparisons between the countries with devolved powers, rather than between them and England, probably has some interesting lessons to reveal.

More attention might also be paid to issues of national identity and culture. The place of Welsh in the education system has been a very live issue in Wales. However, overall there is very little evidence to suggest that Wales, Scotland and Northern Ireland are developing specifically 'national' solutions to the needs of young children. This might have been expected. In Spain, the significant developments in education and social welfare policies that have taken place in Catalonia and Euskadi have been built on what has been seen as the best professional practice from abroad rather than on aspects of national identity. Indeed, some in the UK have argued strongly that the needs of children are universal and that, therefore, there should be very few differences, if any, between policies in different parts of the UK (for example, Kullas, 2000). This is an issue that could become increasingly contentious not just in the context of devolution, but in the context of allegations that 'multiculturalism' has failed.

Points for reflection

There are some who argue that all parts of the UK should have essentially the same standards in early years services because the needs of young children remain essentially the same wherever they are.

Others argue that different developments in different parts of the UK are helpful because:

▶ they facilitate experimentation

▶ they can reflect differences in national identity

▶ they can reflect different demands from the public in different places.

Outline what you think are the main arguments that can be made for or against the differences in policy to which devolution has led.

Summary

This chapter has shown how:

▶ there are a number of differences between early years policies in the four major parts of the UK

▶ devolution has created new opportunities to develop early childcare and education

▶ devolution has also, to some extent, created competition in a way that has probably helped to speed up developments in this sphere.

Further reading

Clark, M. and Waller, T. (eds) (2007) *Early Childhood Education and Care*, London: Sage.

Offers an excellent description of early years policy in each of the four major parts of the UK (and in the Republic of Ireland). It provides much greater detail than has been possible in this chapter and has case studies that help the reader understand the impact of policy on individual children.

Pilkington, C. (2002) *Devolution in Britain Today*, Manchester: Manchester University Press.

Good on the early development of devolved powers.

Rose, W. (2012) Incorporating safeguarding and well-being in universal services: developments in early years multi-agency practice in Scotland. In Miller, L. and Hevey, D. (eds), *Policy Issues in the Early Years*, London: Sage.

Welsh, F. (2002) *The Four Nations: A History of the UK*, London: HarperCollins.

Offers a useful introduction to the broad historical context.

The International Dimension of Policy-making

International agreements

The UK is an independent state. It is only subject to the authority of others to the extent that it has signed up to international agreements. Even in such cases, any country ratifying an agreement may abstain from ratifying a particular aspect of it. Agreements form the basis of international law. Few of the existing ones relate directly to the early years.

The *UN Convention on the Rights of the Child* (Office of the United Nations High Commissioner for Human Rights, 1989) is probably the one that is best known to early years practitioners here. It was agreed in 1989 and ratified by the UK in 1991, although with a number of reservations, some of which were withdrawn in 2008. The Convention has not determined law and policy in this country. However, it has often been invoked – for example, in the debate on whether England should have a Children's Commissioner.

In March 1990, an international gathering at Jomtien (Thailand) arrived at an agreement on *Education for All* (UNESCO, 1990). This laid down a framework for action, but left it to each national government to set its own goals within that framework. The first Declaration was supplemented at a conference in Dakar (Senegal) in the year 2000 (World Education Forum, 2000). Among the features of the declarations that might be noted are that:

▶ the emphasis is on the quality of learning rather than simply on the number of people accessing education

▶ the first of six 'dimensions' outlined in the declarations is an expansion of pre-school services.

Jomtien and Dakar have received comparatively little attention in the UK, presumably because of an assumption that the basic objectives have already been achieved.

As a member of the European Union, the UK is bound by EU decisions in several respects. The treaties that underpin the EU are specifically concerned with economics rather than social policy. However, the boundary line between these two cannot be absolutely clear. When early childhood services are established in the interests of children, that is a matter of social policy. If, on the other hand, it is suggested that better childcare facilities are needed to release more women for the workplace, that is a matter of economic policy and the EU does have a say in it.

In March 2002, the European Council meeting in Barcelona published an agreement that member states would seek to provide childcare for at least 90 per cent of children between their third birthday and the official school starting age, and for at least 33 per cent of children under 3 by the year 2010. Nothing was said about the quality of settings or the means of provision. There has been little interest in the *Barcelona Objectives* in this country. However, the UK has trailed behind several other states in meeting them.

Influences from abroad

International conventions and declarations are not the only ways in which early childhood policies in any one country can be influenced. The ideas of Froebel, Montessori, Piaget and Vygotsky have had a significant impact here. The launch of OMEP (*Organisation Mondiale pour l'Éducation PréScolaire*) in 1948 was only the first of a number of initiatives to foster exchange between practitioners that have generated a growing, though still far from complete, consensus among early childhood specialists across the world.

Most international exchange has been in the field of pedagogy. Recent innovative approaches to the curriculum have been partially shaped by ideas from abroad, such as Headstart (developed in the USA), the approach associated with Reggio Emilia in Italy and the Te Whāriki curriculum in New Zealand. Although it does not come from a single source, it is also worth mentioning the influence of the forest schools movement in Northern Europe in securing a more positive approach to outdoor learning in England. (Scotland was already noted by English pioneers, such as Wilderspoon, to be more imaginative in the use of outdoor play than England. That contrast has stayed in place. Recent work on the curriculum in Wales and northern Ireland has also been important in this field. There are, however, signs of greater interest in outdoor play among English practitioners and there are reasons to hope that policy makers will follow these trends.

There is always a risk that contact with foreign models will be used to generate 'recipes' for new practice without an understanding of the local circumstances that produced them. Certainly, Johnson (1999) is critical of what he sees as a raiding of the Reggio Emilia experience to produce nothing more in the English-speaking countries than ill-digested ideas torn out of context.

There is another issue – the fact that there has been less attention paid in Britain to potential lessons from abroad on what government policy might be. Reggio Emilia provides an example. At the end of the 1980s in a period of financial constraint in Italy, there were moves to limit the responsibilities of local authorities for pre-school services. With widespread approval in the community, the local government in Reggio Emilia confirmed its continuing role in the field. This example of popular support for early childhood services in a situation of budget cuts is at least as interesting as the innovations in curriculum for which Reggio Emilia is better known.

However, it is clear that politicians of all parties are inclined to look abroad mainly for models that confirm the validity of their own approaches, rather than to examine what is happening elsewhere in ways that might challenge their preconceptions. Surveys conducted by international bodies, such as UNESCO, UNICEF, the OECD and the World Bank, have not been used as intelligently as they might have been. The two surveys published by the Organisation for Economic Cooperation and Development under the general title *Starting Strong* (OECD, 2001, 2006) are among the better-known studies of policy in different countries.

Case study 🗁

Happy Days Nursery is a setting managed by its proprietor. The market town where it is situated is twinned with a comparable town in Spain. Under these arrangements, two of the staff have been invited to participate in a visit to the twin town in Spain and, in particular, to spend a couple of days at a local authority-run pre-school for 3–6-year-olds. One of the two staff going is reasonably competent in Spanish, although she has never had contact with early childhood services there.

At a Happy Days staff meeting, the forthcoming visit is a major agenda item. It becomes clear that some colleagues are dubious about the value of the trip. The only material the two staff going have to prepare for the visit is an advertising leaflet addressed to local parents from the setting they are visiting.

What can they do to prepare adequately for their visit and make the best of it? What sources of information might be available? Which aspects of the setting they are visiting should they plan to investigate most thoroughly? What might go into an information package on their own setting that they can take to Spain? What differences might they expect to see between their own setting and the one they are visiting? What can they do (before and after the visit) to persuade their colleagues that the contact was worthwhile?

Comparing countries

For the rest of this chapter, we offer introductions to early years policy in six different countries. There are reasons for our choices, but we make no pretence that they represent the full range of experience among the couple of hundred nations in the world. Each country has its own characteristics and the attempt to learn from what they have done must be based on an appreciation of that fact (Glass, 2001).

In choosing countries to consider, we had two principles in mind:

▶ We wanted to avoid repeating material found easily elsewhere on well-known examples of policy and practice abroad.

▶ It seemed a good idea to cover a wide geographical range.

We decided to have examples from economically developed countries in both Western and Eastern Europe. After careful consideration, we decided to pick France, which has a very different tradition in the approach to early years policy from the UK, and the Netherlands where ideas being entertained by the new Coalition government for England have been put into practice with mixed results. The Czech Republic was chosen as being broadly representative of the more economically advanced parts of Eastern Europe.

The principle of going for a geographical spread led us to select one country each from Latin America, Sub-Saharan Africa and Asia.

There were several interesting choices in Latin America. Uruguay has the advantage of being relatively compact (in comparison with, say, Brazil). Kenya, for all its problems, has a reputation for very progressive policies in education. China is a country of obviously growing importance in world affairs.

We chose two issues: (1) the administrative integration of different services for young children and (2) inclusion in its widest sense, to make comparison with policy in the UK. The limited survey undertaken here also demonstrates the significance of the issue of how much money is invested in the supply side (i.e. how much money the government invests in provision, either directly by the state or by commissioning work by other organizations) and the demand side (i.e. how much money the government invests in financially supporting parents to place their children in settings of their choice). This is clearly a major policy issue that needs further investigation, including international comparisons.

Activity

You may have an interest in a country that does not appear among those below and want to learn something about early childhood services there. Some pointers on using the Internet for this are as follows:

▶ Use your usual search engine to seek information on 'children's day care in …' or 'pre-school education in …' followed by the name of the country. If you are interested in a particular topic, you could search for 'inclusion in …', etc.

▶ Bear in mind that if French or Spanish is one of the official languages of the country you want to research, you are likely to find that most documents are in that language, so your ability to understand it will be crucial. However, if the main national language is other than French, Spanish or English, you are likely to come across documents in English translation because writers in those countries want to reach as wide an audience as possible.

▶ Be aware that even in competent translations into English, there can be problems with jargon. In Latin America, terms such as 'childcare' and 'child protection' are often used to cover all services designed to promote the interests of children, including health and education, as well as having the more focused, social work related, meaning they have here. The word 'kindergarten' may be used to refer to all early years settings in a country or to a particular type. A word in another language whose strict meaning is 'childcarer' may be translated as 'childminder', although it is 'nursery nurse' that is meant.

▶ Use some of the documents your search unearths to look for others. For example, if a document about early childhood policy in general suggests the importance of a particular individual in that country, search for information on that person.

France

For most of the 19th century and the first half of the 20th century, people in Britain who wanted to further the cause of early childhood services looked to France for inspiration. When political backing for such services went into a steep decline in the UK in the 1950s and 1960s, interest in the French model diminished. When there was renewed pressure for better services from the 1970s onwards, it was to other European examples that people here usually turned. In more recent years, there has been a new interest in France's commitment to childcare (Frean, 1997; Martin, 2010).

France has led the field in many ways in government support for services. Crèches to allow mothers to seek paid employment were pioneered in the 1840s. In 1862, the French government began to subsidize such initiatives, recognizing them officially in 1869 as being of *utilité publique*. In the 20th century, a book by Norvez (1990) aroused fears that France might face a declining birth rate and ageing population, although it was not until 2003 that an increase in the birth rate became an official policy objective. Such concerns encouraged the idea that the state should facilitate early years services to make it easier for families to raise children. One consequence was a new emphasis on day care settings, most of them run by local authorities. This included the *halte-garderies* that were originally set up to help mothers deal with emergencies but have come to be used by many women working part-time or outside the standard working week. It is striking that – apart from a number of workplace nurseries – the private sector has played little role in the provision of day care in France.

Childminding has also been supported (Algave and Rualt, 2003). In 1990, a new legal framework was introduced (with further measures in 1992). Registered childminders (*assistantes maternelles*) now enjoy most of the protections offered to other employees. Their qualification requirements are stricter than in the UK, although in other respects they are less closely regulated than they are here. Day care and childminding are services employed principally for the care of the under-3s, and the numbers remain relatively low in their case with 64 per cent of children in that age group cared for by a parent rather than anyone else at the beginning of this century (DREES, 2002).

Pre-school education has an even stronger position than day care. In the early 19th century, philanthropists developed a type of infant school for the children of the poor called the *salle d'asile*. Such schools were made subject to the *ministère de l'instruction publique* as early as 1836. In 1881, the term *école maternelle* was officially adopted for these settings. Teacher training colleges began to recruit students who intended to work specifically with the youngest children from 1884. The law of 30 October 1886 made *écoles maternelles* part of the state school system, with a decree the following year laying down a basic curriculum and rules on the training and qualification of staff. In 1910, a system of inspection (drastically revised in 1972) was established. The law of 11 July 1975 gave every 5-year-old whose parents wanted it the right to attend an *école maternelle* (or a primary school if a local *école maternelle* was not yet established). The overwhelming majority of children over 3 now attend these schools. So much do primary schools rely on this fact that special 'transition initiatives' (*actions passerelles*) have been put in place to assist children who have missed out on pre-school education.

The 2002 curriculum guidelines for pre-school education lay down five curriculum areas – language development, living together, self-expression, discovering the world, and creativity. The English EYFS (in its 2000 and 2008 versions) was very different in emphasis, but the Tickell Review in 2011 suggested something more like the French approach. A less obvious, but also significant contrast with England lies in the way in which pre-school education enjoyed official backing from a much earlier stage than it did in Britain. One of the key figures in the development of early childhood pedagogy in France is Pauline Kergomard who was (from 1879 to 1917) the *inspectrice générale de l'école maternelle*. Both in her work as a civil servant and in her publications, she argued cogently for the relevance of the new science of child development and the importance of learning through play, and helped bring about a much closer linkage between professional opinion and political decision-making than has ever been enjoyed in this country (Plaisance, 1996).

As well as day care and pre-school education, there are a number of other early childhood services that are well established, including:

▶ various forms of playwork settings known under the general heading of *acceuil collectif de minuers*

▶ toy libraries (*ludothèques*), which are often free-standing and have their own national association

▶ regulated agencies that provide care workers of various kinds, including nannies, operating in the homes of clients

▶ *lieux d'acceuil parents–enfants* (LAEP) centres (similar to Sure Start centres), which provide supportive services to parents in group settings

▶ *maisons d'assistantes maternelles* – a recent development where registered childminders work together outside their own homes

▶ a website giving detailed information on early childhood services. This went into full operation in 2010 and won an international prize (see www.mon-enfant.fr/web/guest/accueil).

As well as investing heavily in the supply of early childhood services, the French state has developed an extensive system of financial assistance to parents. A complex collection of different mechanisms was replaced in 2004 by the *Prestation d'Acceuil de Jeune Enfant* (PAJE) which reduced the existing system to two complementary benefits – one to offset the costs of early childhood services, the other to support either parent in taking up to three years off work to care for a young child.

State commitment to early childhood services has had the intended effect of making it easier for parents, especially mothers, to afford to have children. Even before an increase in the birth rate was set as a formal policy objective by the government, France had seen:

▸ a reduction in the rate of poverty among two-parent families (although with a lower success rate for single-parent families)

▸ a major increase in the birth rate – which is unusual among the wealthier European nations (OECD, 2004).

This has won approval from some, but questions have also been raised as to whether the care system has benefited employers, who now have a more flexible workforce, more than it has children (Fagnani, 2009).

In terms of sheer provision of early childhood services, France has achieved more than the UK. Progress towards the integration of services has been less of a preoccupation there than it has here. Pre-school care and education are separated at every level from that of local settings to that of central government. In addition, playcare activities for children below school age are closely linked to similar services for older children and come under the aegis of the Ministry for Youth, Sport and Social Life. Moreover, the principal national playwork qualification – the *brevet d'aptitude aux fonctions d'animateurs* (BAFA) – is at a much lower level than those of the professional staff in day care and pre-school education. The promotion of LAEPs by social workers rather than staff working in other early childhood settings has been a further complication.

On the other hand, more recently there have been several initiatives to encourage closer coordination of day care and education for children under 6.

▸ Since the late 1980s, many local authorities have employed staff to coordinate the work of different kinds of early childhood settings (Baudelot and Rayna, 2000). Some areas, such as the city of Nantes, have developed their own overall plans for early childhood.

▸ Since 2000, each day care setting has had to have a set of policies and procedures that, among other things, spell out the pedagogical aspects of the work undertaken.

▸ In 2001, there was legislation to strengthen the educational content of playcare activities.

▸ In 2002, each *département* (the largest unit of local administration) has had to establish a commission to bring together different interests in early childhood provision in order to generate greater coherence in provision.

▸ There are now many *établissments multi-acceuil* – multi-functional settings where different kinds of service operate on the same premises.

Another contrast with the UK is in the way in which policies on inclusion have developed. In the 18th and 19th centuries, France was the world's leading country in the development of education designed to meet the needs of the visually and hearing impaired and of children with learning disabilities. In more recent times, it has made the inclusion of children with special educational needs a key element in the policy manuals of day nurseries. However, the central concept has remained – that of 'special needs' rather than 'inclusion' – and there has been no real effort to take other possible sources of disadvantage in the educational system into account. On the contrary, the focus that has been in place since the late 19th century on education as an area where French identity is emphasized and differences of faith and culture downplayed has discouraged the development of any wider sense of inclusion.

There are, therefore, significant differences between France and the UK. It is also worth noting the fact that recent developments have placed the educational aspect of such services in greater question than before. Worries about the effectiveness of the primary school system generated criticisms that the *écoles maternelles* were doing too little to make children school-ready (*Haut Conseil de l'Éducation,* 2007). This led to an official report in 2008 suggesting that school-readiness should become a much more central focus for preschool education. Soon after that, Darcos, the Minister of Education, queried whether there might not be too many highly qualified staff among those working in the *écoles maternelles*. He denied that he wanted to close the settings themselves but his remarks were seen as supporting the proposals published a few weeks earlier by Dazay, a schools inspector, that this was precisely what should happen, that the age of formal education should be lowered and something like the English reception class system introduced. The hostile reaction of the teachers' unions and of many parents caused the government to back off, but the recession brought the issue back on to the agenda.

The Netherlands

A major reason for examining early childhood policy in the Netherlands lies in the close similarities between that country and our own. Both are constitutional monarchies with a strong tradition of liberal democracy. Both have aging populations that are a potential source of economic and social difficulty. Both have large black and minority ethnic groups (BME) and have experienced controversies over multiculturalism.

There are also some political similarities. The 'Polder Model', adopted by recent governments, is similar to the concept of 'partnership' as the key to a 'third way' in politics that was advanced under New Labour. The Dutch new-style policy agreements in various areas – the *Bestuursaccorden Nieuwe Stijl* (BANS) – and the decentralization of aspects of social policy that went with it have some parallels with the Local Area Agreements introduced by Blair. However, the move towards decentralization in the Netherlands has been more wholehearted. The development of childcare is one of the fields in which local authorities have gained greater freedom of action.

There are also parallels in early childhood services. The Netherlands is one of the few countries where the UK's playgroup movement has been widely imitated with the *peuterspeelzaal* (playgroup) forming part of local provision. More important similarities lie in the long-established institutional differences between care and education services for young children in both countries and in the reliance in both governments on demand-side initiatives to promote early childhood services.

A reluctance to see the mothers of young children in paid employment has been a feature of public opinion in many European countries for some time and this has been particularly true of the Netherlands. As late as 1997, survey evidence showed that 20 per cent of the Dutch population disapproved of working mothers and 50 per cent particularly disapproved of placing children in day nurseries (van Praag and Niphuis-Neil, cited in Ministry of Health, Welfare and Sport and Ministry of Education, Culture and Science, 2000: 24). What is striking about this is that these figures were taken to demonstrate a strong shift in the 1990s *towards approval* of working mothers and day nursery care.

It was economic pressures that began to alter attitudes from the mid-1980s when new policies were first devised to encourage women into paid employment to make up what was seen as a potential shortage of workers. The early 1990s saw 'stimulative measures' designed to encourage the development of some 49,000 new childcare places.

In the 21st century, there was a decisive shift towards reliance on subsidizing demand rather than supply in Dutch childcare services. The key event was the passing of the Childcare Act (*Wet Kinderopvang*) of 2005. Although there had been a considerable increase in provision, there was still unmet need and at the same time many facilities were under-occupied (Diemet, 2009).

▸ The Childcare Act established a system under which payment for childcare was shared by parents (at a level that depended on family income), the national government and employers, although the employer's contribution was in the end voluntary. The subsidies were only available to families if both parents were employed (or the parent in a one-parent family was in work).

▸ Government subsidies were available for childcare costs up to a maximum level. (It was, of course, open to parents to purchase more expensive childcare if they could afford it.)

▸ Subsidized childcare fell within new regulations. These included childminders (*gastouders*) who had to be linked to approved agencies. Grandparents or others caring for children to whom they were related could, however, be subsidized if they registered as childminders.

▸ A previously existing system of regulations on quality (mainly relating to health and safety) was replaced by a new simplified system with area health authorities made responsible for inspection and enforcement (much like the system in England and Wales from 1948 to 1971).

The system introduced in 2005 entailed a number of difficulties:

▸ While employers were often willing to subsidize the childcare costs of skilled employees in order to secure their services, they were reluctant to subsidize the childcare of the unskilled and low-paid.

▸ The cost of childcare subsidies rose far more significantly than had been anticipated. It became clear that a very significant part of the increase was due to grandparents registering as childminders. In other words, the policy of funding the demand side was not leading to a major increase in services, but to a large subsidy going into a type of informal care that was already there (Lloyd, 2008).

▸ There were fears expressed by *MOgroep*, the Dutch childcare providers association, and the *Belangenvereniging van ouders in de kinderopvang* (BOINK), a national organization for parents, that the new system was attracting the unwanted attentions of foreign investors (especially in the field of out-of-school care). They might see a way of making easy money and might be less concerned about the maintenance of quality, especially at a time when the Dutch government was committed to de-regulation in this as in other spheres. It is not yet clear how justified these fears are.

The Dutch government was not especially exercised over the third of those problems, but did tackle the other two which were both costing it a considerable amount of money. In 2007, the rights of employers to back out of childcare subsidies were curtailed. In 2011, changes were introduced that severely restricted the ability of parents to secure subsidies for the use of grandparents as carers. All registered childminders had to be willing to take children other than those to whom they were related and had to secure a diploma in care at Level 2. Trying to deal with the childcare issue by funding the demand side had backfired badly.

Pre-school education was also in the process of development. As long ago as 1985, the Dutch government ended the provision of separate nursery schools and integrated those that existed with primary schools, which now cater for children aged 4–12 years. Hence, there is no official pre-school service, although there are many playgroups that fall under the aegis of the Ministry of Education, Culture and Science rather than forming part of the welfare system. Out-of-school playcare services also fall within the ambit of the Ministry of Education. Such services have an important role to play in childcare since the Dutch school system entails a long break in the early afternoon – something that poses a particular problem for parents in employment. The extended school (*brede school*) is now an important aspect of the primary school system and schools (whether state-provided or the equivalent of our grant-maintained schools) are obliged by law to provide out-of-school-hours care.

As in the UK, systems of day care and early education have developed quite separately, and in many respects the integration of nursery and primary schools in the 1980s has reinforced this separation. The integration of care and education is not high on anyone's agenda. However, the *Onderwijs Raad* (Education Council), an advisory body, has been pressing for more attention to pedagogy in childcare settings and has even begun to use the term *leeropvang*, equivalent to the British 'educare'. The BANS for children and young people lays particular emphasis on cooperation between different agencies providing services for families with children aged 0–6 years. However, the clear separation of day care and education inhibits such moves. The authors of an official report on early childhood services in the Netherlands noted that some believe that pre-school playgroups have an important pedagogical function, but would not commit themselves to adopting this point of view (Ministry of Health and Ministry of Education, 2000: 70).

The fact that the care and education systems are so separate has also probably had an impact on the progress of inclusion in early childhood services. The Netherlands is committed to inclusion in schools, a policy that takes the needs of BME communities as well as those of children with disabilities into account. In recent years, an increasing number of children with special needs have been included in mainstream schools (Muskens and Peters, 2009). However, this has not had much impact on childcare services. The regulations (being mainly concerned with health and safety) have little to say on the kind of pedagogical practice that might support inclusion. There has even been in the *Samenspel* ('playing together') programme a tendency to provide separately for the children of recent immigrants.

There are significant ways in which early childhood services in the Netherlands differ from those in the UK:

- ▶ the specific demands made of employers in the childcare subsidy system

- ▶ the much greater commitment to extended schools

- ▶ the greater success of childminding

- ▶ the relative lack of regulation in childcare.

On the other hand, early childhood services in both countries have been shaped significantly by:

- ▶ continuing controversy as to whether mothers of young children should be in paid employment

- ▶ the continuing distinction between care and education

▸ the reliance in the recent past on demand-side rather than supply-side policies in the promotion of early childhood services.

The Czech Republic

For most of the 20th century, the Czech lands formed part of Czechoslovakia. In 1993, Slovakia gained its independence and the Czech Republic was formed.

The Communist regime that was in power from the end of the Second World War until 1989 had wanted to encourage mothers back into the workplace, partly to support economic development, partly to promote gender equality. A widespread system of local authority *jesle* (crèches) formed a critical part of this policy. When the regime fell, antagonism towards the Communists helped to reinforce traditional ideas about the family (Valentova, 2009). Most of the municipal *jesle* were closed. They were not replaced on any significant scale by day care services run by the voluntary or commercial sectors. By 2006, fewer than 0.5 per cent of children under 3 were in day care and childminding has not really developed as an occupation in the Republic. However, 16.7 per cent of women with children under 3 were in some form of paid employment (OECD, 2006). Their children were normally cared for by a relative or by a *chůva* (the Czech word covers nannies, baby-sitters and au pairs). The employment of nannies is expensive and restricted to the affluent, but the number of families doing this appears to be increasing. Nannies are often secured through professional agencies, but there is no obligation to do this and neither agencies nor independent nannies are subject to any specific regulation. Although pre-schools are not intended to provide a care service for children under 3, about a quarter of the children in that age group attend their local *mateřská školā* at least part of the time. The extent to which this is a way of getting round the lack of group day care or is a practice of parents who wish to see their children get an early start in their education is unclear. Many primary schools also have their own *školni družina* (after-school club).

The principal form of pre-school education is provided by the *mateřská školā*, for children aged 3 to 6. Most are run by local authorities, a few by voluntary organizations, even fewer by private companies. A majority of children attend these pre-schools for at least part of the time before compulsory schooling starts at 6 (often in the last year before school age), but the rate of participation is lower than it is in France or Spain. These settings fall under the Ministry of Education, Youth and Sport (as opposed to *jesle* which come under the Ministry of Health in most cases, but under the Ministry of Social Affairs in the case of those that have an explicit 'therapeutic' function). The great majority of practitioners in pre-schools have qualifications from a four-year secondary-level course offered at 18 vocational schools across the country. This training has in the past been significantly focused on creative activity and sport rather than on the foundations of literacy and numeracy or knowledge and understanding of the world. Most of the teaching staff are low-paid, their salaries being equivalent to three-quarters of the average wage for all full-time employees in the Republic. Those that are graduates are rather better paid. A new set of curriculum guidelines issued in 2001 extended the range of skills expected of children leaving pre-schools for primary education, with emphasis on interpersonal skills (OECD, 2006). The guidance is cast in fairly general terms, leaving scope for different approaches, especially in the voluntary sector. This has facilitated the development of pre-schools following the Waldorf–Steiner and Montessori patterns and more individual settings, such as the *Detsky Klub Šárynka*, an innovative forest school.

The children's day care and pre-school education systems are quite clearly separated in the Czech Republic from the level of central government downwards. The question of how far care and education can be integrated in early childhood services has, however, barely arisen because day care services are so little developed. Now that the Republic has to a large extent shrugged off its Communist past and Czechs are becoming more aware of early childhood services in other countries, the idea that the state should keep out of family affairs unless forced to intervene because parents cannot meet their responsibilities is beginning to gain acceptance.

The Czech Republic has long had a network of special schools for children with various disabilities. In response to influences from abroad, there have been recent moves towards including more children with disabilities in mainstream schools. The policy of seeking greater inclusion in the mainstream has been mainly directed at children with identified disabilities. However, it could have wider implications since the Republic is one of the East European states that was accused by the European Monitoring Centre on Racism and Xenophobia of over-readiness to identify Roma children as having learning disabilities and sending them to special schools on the basis of faulty diagnoses. Similar accusations led to a successful case being taken to the European Court of Human Rights in 2007 (Devrove, 2009). However, many educationists in the Republic support the idea of special provision for Roma children because of the difficulties they are seen to encounter and present in mainstream schools.

Controversies about early childhood services have been and remain an issue in the Czech Republic. This illustrates how the ways in which services are organized tend to reflect recent history and raise questions about the values of a society.

Uruguay

After an 11-year period of military rule, the Latin American republic of Uruguay returned to civilian government in 1984. For some time after that power was contested, mainly between two right-wing parties, but in 2004 the *Frente*

Amplio (Broad Front), an alliance of communists, socialists and progressively-minded Catholics won the election. Tabarè Vázquez, the new head of government, initiated a wide-ranging programme of economic and social reform. When he retired in 2010, he had an 80 per cent approval rating in the opinion polls. (Recent British prime ministers might well feel envious.) The *Frente Amplio* won the election that year and, although there were some changes of key personnel in the government, social policies (including those relating to early childhood) were continued.

Uruguay already had a number of early childhood services. One unusual feature of the country was that the lack of services was greatest in urban rather than rural areas (Llambi et al., 2009: 4). The reverse is normally the case, whatever the level of development of the country in question. To a significant extent, this was because of the uncontrolled influx of families into the capital Montevideo, which now has about half the population of the entire country. As in Britain under New Labour, the provision of childcare was seen largely in terms of helping women, especially single mothers, into work. It was a way of tackling child poverty (Llambi et al., 2009; Perera and Llambi, 2010).

The action that has been taken in relation to early childhood services has had several defining features:

▸ *The policy has been the clear responsibility of the central government.* More specifically, it has been the responsibility of the *Instituto del Ninõ y Adolescente del Uruguay* (INAU), a government agency under the direction of the *Ministerio de Desarrollo Social* (MIDES), which was created by the Vásquez government in 2005 as a key part of its social and economic strategy. INAU's strapline is *Nos importan todos los niños* (which could be translated as 'Every Child Matters'!) Responsibility for pedagogical aspects of children's services rests with the *Ministerio de Educaćión y Cultura* (MES) and a civil service agency, the *Administración Nacional de Educación Pública* (ANEP).

▸ *Work on early childhood services and, in particular, day care for children under 3 forms part of ENIA (Estrategia Nacional para la Infancia y Adolescencia), a general plan for advancing the interests of children,* first put forward in 2008. The Plan incorporates childcare, family support, health, education and child protection and relates initiatives in all these areas to each other. Uruguay has also taken the lead in developing SIPI (*Sistema de Información para la Infancia*), a software system designed to support safeguarding activity that has now been adopted by several Latin American countries. ENIA was originally intended to run to 2015. It has now been extended to 2030, by which year it is intended that childcare should be available to all children whose parents want it.

▸ *Although MIDES and ENIA control the strategy, a good deal of the work of supporting children (including day care and pre-school education) is pro-vided by centres for the care of children and their families (Centros de Atención a la Infancia y la Familia – CAIFs),* which are run by voluntary (usually Catholic) and commercial bodies. The principal feature of early childhood policy is the development of such bodies. In other words, the expansion of children's day care and early education has been based on increasing supply rather than on assisting parents to meet the costs of services set up on other kinds of initiative.

▸ *Uruguay has adopted a policy of close coordination of early childhood services, but – unlike Britain – has not done so by giving education the lead role.*

ENIA has led to a significant increase in the number of children able to attend day care centres and pre-schools, although the number of places is still inadequate. By 2009, 40 per cent of children under 3 were in day care. Research is ongoing as to how far this has helped mothers into paid employment and whether other initiatives are needed to assist them with this. The emphasis has been on expansion. There is some evidence that the services for younger children that existed in 2004 had a positive effect later on in the school system (Berlinski et al., 2006). This suggests that there was quality of practice at that stage. There is less evidence as to whether quality has survived or even thrived in the period of expansion since then.

It is clear that the care and education services provided for young children are well integrated in Uruguay, at least at the level of central policy-making and planning. The intention is that they should also be closely integrated within the local CAIFs. A commitment to inclusion has gone along with this.

What has happened in Uruguay is an impressive example of services for pre-school children being driven forward by a government committed to them and to seeing them as a full and integral part of its social policy. The *Frente Amplio* has also developed a supply-side strategy for expansion while still leaving room for action by voluntary and private institutions in the provision of early childhood settings and other related services.

It remains to be seen whether the national plan for early childhood services will survive the impact of the world recession on the country and whether expansion will facilitate developments in pedagogy and overall quality or be achieved only at their expense. The example of Uruguay is, however, one that merits more attention than it has received so far in Britain.

Kenya

Kenya faces the challenge of all previously colonized countries of finding a way of combining the best of traditional and European ideas on early childhood services and has achieved a great deal in this respect (Adams and Swadener, 2010). The matter is complicated by the fact that Kenya itself is made up of many different ethnic groups that are sometimes in conflict. The lead role in early childhood services has been played by education, specifically by the Ministry of Education, Science and Technology (MOEST). This emphasis dates back to the Ominde Commission Report of 1964, published soon after independence from Britain, which spoke of the significance of education in the building of a new nation. Kenya has what may be the most highly developed education system in sub-Saharan Africa. Early childhood services are a part of this and the extension of provision and improvements in the quality of this sector formed a key part of the Education Sector Strategic Plan for 2003–7.

Formal primary education begins at the age of 6. It has been free since 2003, but is not compulsory. This reinforces the tendency for poorer families not to use early childhood services, since they now wait until free education begins. Another consequence is that girls are often kept away from school to provide care for their younger siblings while their parents work. Thus, free primary education has benefited boys much more than girls. Those who purchase pre-school education are often the better off and more ambitious and such parents frequently demand 'proper education', that is to say formal teaching of literacy, as early as possible – a demand that conflicts with the views of more experienced practitioners. This is, of course, a familiar situation, but one that appears to be particularly acute in Kenya. There is also a high drop-out rate among staff that has undermined the efforts of the World Bank and others to invest in their training.

The coordination of early childhood services in Kenya is the responsibility of a project management support group chaired by the deputy director of primary education in MOEST and involving high-level representatives from MOEST itself, the Teacher Service Commission, the Ministry of Finance, the Ministry of Health and Kenyatta University.

MOEST recognizes seven types of early childhood setting:

▶ nursery schools

▶ pre-unit classes – these are similar to British reception classes

▶ kindergartens – this term is not very clearly defined, but usually refers to settings that have both care and educational objectives

▶ day nurseries – such settings have limited pedagogic aims; they are often run by faith or other voluntary agencies for children from families facing particular difficulties

▶ playgroups – Kenya has a number of playgroups based on the British model

▶ madrassas or Islamic schools

▶ home-based care centres – these are parent support settings rather than agencies focused primarily on children.

In some ways, this range of services reflects the models derived from the former colonial power or from international bodies such as the Bernard Van Leer Foundation, the Christian Children's Fund, the Aga Khan Foundation, UNICEF and the World Bank, which have been active in the promotion of pre-school education in Kenya. There are a number of other initiatives that reflect more local traditions and concerns:

▶ Many communities in Kenya still follow a pastoral nomadic style of life that does not fit well with attendance at schools or early childhood settings in fixed premises. This has had a significant impact on the participation in schooling of the Masai people, among others (Phillips and Bhavnagu, 2002). One particularly interesting and highly influential approach to this issue was developed by staff from a number of international agencies and the Kenya Institute of Education in the Samburu District of Northern Kenya. Believing that existing work on pre-school education in the area had been too focused on the training of staff and on fixed premises, they looked at traditional ways of caring for young children. Older women provided young children with care and education (especially in the form of traditional story telling) usually in shady outdoor enclosures (*loipis*) while their parents worked. In return, parents supplied the older women with many of their necessities. More than 80 new centres based on the Loipi model were set up in the district. Health personnel worked alongside the women to provide better physical care (including immunization). Parents were helped to create toys that had an educational function for their own Loipi settings (instead of the charities supplying Western-made equipment of this sort). By 2008, although Samburu is the second poorest district in Kenya, it had the highest proportion of children in pre-school education. The model was taken up by other nomadic peoples in Kenya and by neighbouring African states (Bosire, 2006; Van de Linde and Lenaiyasa, 2006).

▶ Another innovative development that seeks to blend traditional and Western approaches is the *Mwana Mwende* programme run by Anne Njenga. (The name of the programme means 'the child that is loved'.) This was launched in 1997 by a number of local voluntary organizations concerned about the welfare of children under 3 and of teenage mothers. The objective has been to raise the self-esteem, commitment and abilities of the young women for their own sake and that of their children. It has attempted to blend care (including health care) and education concerns and worked through the mothers of the children concerned rather than trying simply to rescue the children in some way. A key feature has been work on the inclusion of children with disabilities. The American Beth

Blue Swadener and her colleagues have argued that *Mwana Mwende* represents a significant turn to more collaborative approaches to early childhood services between Africans and those from more economically developed countries (Swadener et al., 2000; Kabiru et al., 2003).

▸ A third example of blending local and Western approaches is provided by the work of the Aga Khan Foundation in establishing pre-schools in areas with large Moslem populations, following a more 'holistic' approach than some of the longer established madrassas or Islamic schools.

Experiments such as these have gone alongside a programme to develop the training of early childhood practitioners in ways that link education and care together closely and link both of those to more general community development. For some time, the National Centre for Early Childhood Education (NACECE) has encouraged local adaptation of their national guidelines by their district counterparts to ensure the relevance of the work undertaken. In general, pre-school education has been a carefully considered part of both NACECE's capacity-building programme and the political commitment to the Kenya Education Sector Support Programme (KESSP), which is one of the fast-track programmes devised in just nine countries under the Education For All (EFA) project. A key role in all this has been played by Henry Manani (2005, 2007), the coordinator of NACECE and deputy director of the Kenya Institute of Education.

Like Uruguay, Kenya has seen a government-led programme of expansion and innovation in early childhood services in recent years. There is still much to be done, but it provides an interesting example of what can be achieved.

China

One reason for examining early childhood services in China is the sheer importance of the country. It also offers an opportunity to reflect on the innovation that may come from the interaction of Western and other approaches to such services.

Mutual learning is particularly relevant in the development of the early childhood curriculum. Two examples may be given:

▸ In the early stages of primary school, Chinese children are taught techniques of drawing in a way that contrasts vividly with the approach to creativity in the UK. The American Ellen Winner, who first reported this in the West, has developed an interesting approach that learns from and develops what has happened in China (Winner, 1989, 1993).

▸ Music played a significant role in Confucian (ethical teaching system) ideas on moral development and still has a major role in schools and pre-schools in China today (Yim and Ebbeck, 2009). Some settings in the UK

– such as the Ellesmere Children's Centre in Sheffield – that have had contact with those in China have picked up on and implemented Chinese approaches successfully.

As China began its unusually swift economic development, a new emphasis on day care for young children began to appear. More and more parents needed such services and also valued pre-school education as a way of helping to ensure their children's success in later life. The well-established policy of pushing couples into having only one child has added to the reasons for seeking access to childcare and education services. It is seen as a way of giving the single child the experience of living with peers and as essential to prevent 'spoiling'. Initially, it was the state that provided early childhood services. The more recent past has seen the development of private enterprise in this field. This includes not only large Chinese companies (such as the Shanghai-based Xiehe chain with its 30 pre-school settings) but also foreign companies, such as the American Family Box chain, which opened its first kindergarten in China in 2009. Now less than a quarter of day care centres across the country are run by the state (Luo et al., 2009: 13).

Access to day care and early education is a major problem. The primary contrast is that between rural and urban areas, as is the case in most of the world. Even where they exist, early years settings in rural areas are often poorly staffed and equipped. Only 12 per cent of the staff in the rural settings studied by Luo et al. (2009) were considered by the authors of the report to be fully qualified. Where services are set up in rural areas, it is often close to production zones. There are frequently serious dangers to health and safety associated with them. The lack of pre-school provision in rural areas and the poor quality of some of what does exist makes for longer-term problems. There is evidence that of the six dimensions on the scale of school-readiness devised by Dr Ou (a scheme that has been widely used, although it does not have official backing), most children in rural areas are only ready for school in terms of their gross motor skills (Luo et al., 2009: 14–15).

However, the key issue is not so much the contrast between rural and urban areas but between the poor and the wealthy. Early in 2010, the Western press covered the story of a single father in a large city who could only keep his young child safe while he worked by chaining him to a piece of street furniture and leaving him with food. Less anecdotally, Qinshua et al. (2005) found that low-income families in the capital Beijing faced serious childcare problems in terms of availability and price. It can now cost parents in China more to send a child to pre-school than to university! Many low-income parents in cities are recent migrants who have come to improve their standard of living and make use of grandparents in their original rural homes to care for their children. As in other countries, there is little support for grandparents playing that role (Nyland et al., 2009).

Wealthier families also face such problems and often find it difficult with long working hours to make use even of those pre-school services they can afford. Residential nurseries which were once (as they were in the UK in the first half of the 20th century) largely a resource for children whose low-income parents were incapable of providing care are now more often used by affluent parents (Tobin et al., 2009: 33). Many couples have opted for the expensive, but convenient option of having a live-in *ayi* ('nanny'). These are often very young women with little or nothing in the way of training, but who do at least provide some continuity of care as well as cover when parents are working late. Parents who cannot afford this option sometimes send younger school children to settings which offer after-school tutoring. They may be thinking, not only of their children's education, but also of the solution these after-school settings offer to childcare problems towards the end of the working day.

A major issue in pre-school settings has been the demand of ambitious parents that their children should be made to learn formally (Zhu and Zhang, 2008). Tobin et al. (2009: 91) argue that the growth of the private sector (especially in the major coastal cities) is likely to make settings more open to such demands. There have, however, been a number of developments in the pre-school curriculum in recent years.

In 1989, the first regulations for early years settings in China were issued (although Hong Kong, still then a British colony, had produced guidelines for kindergarten practice in 1981). The guidelines were considered by Carter et al. (2007) to have 'consolidated progressive influences'. However, they also felt that serious difficulties had been encountered in translating the principles of the 1989 regulations into practice. In 2001, the Ministry of Education issued further guidelines for pre-school education on a trial basis, with a plan to evaluate their effectiveness. This was followed by a plan for early childhood settings for the period 2003–7.

There is some evidence that official guidelines are influencing practice. At the very least, there are indications of a growing acceptance by more senior staff of the kind of pedagogical ideas that are widespread among practitioners and theorists elsewhere (Hsueh and Tobin, 2003; Jiaxiong and Nianli, 2005). Yu and Pine (2006) report on an action/research project they conducted in the major cities of Nanjing and Beijing. Up until 2001, pre-school practitioners had been forbidden to do anything about literacy. This was changed by the new guidelines, but little was done to assist practitioners to develop the relevant skills. The researchers introduced practitioners to ways of encouraging 'emergent literacy'. They found that, not only were these techniques successful with the children, but the staff gained enormously in self-confidence and interest in their work.

In the fast-changing early years scene in China, some of the principal concerns of early years practitioners in the UK seem less important than they do to us.

Outside Hong Kong, where the colonial Board of Education recommended the 'unification' of pre-school services provided by the Education and Social Welfare Departments in 1994 (Curriculum Development Institute, 1996), the integration of care and education services has barely been an issue in China – primarily because of the poor development of day care services. The more important issue has seemed to be the need to improve the training of teaching and classroom assistant staff (*baoyuyuan*) in pre-schools.

The issue of inclusion has also failed to get very high up the agenda of many practitioners, although both provision for special educational needs and the principle of inclusion have had official backing since the National Education Committee issued its *Educational Guidelines for People with Disabilities* in 1994. There are continuing difficulties caused by the widespread prejudice against children with disabilities (Gargiulo and Piao, 1996). The early years curriculum guidelines drafted in 2001 made 'recognition of individual differences' a key aspect by which early years pedagogy was to be assessed, but the shortage of facilities as well as prejudice continued to inhibit the development of inclusive practice even in the major cities where at least some settings have adopted an active policy in this respect (Hu and Szente, 2010). Apart from disability, there are issues relating to other aspects of inclusion. The Communist Party has been committed from the start to gender equality, but low-income parents, especially in rural areas, still tend to see the education of boys as being more important than that of girls (Carter et al., 2007: 17–18). At the same time, worries about separatist movements have hampered the development of teaching in minority languages.

The provision of early childhood education and care has been strongly affected by recent economic growth. The heavy reliance on the market to meet demand (to the point where many local authority settings have been privatized) has had a serious impact, not only on the availability of services, but on the nature of the services themselves. There has been some progress in the improvement of premises and general health and safety, but not as much as might have been expected and many settings have staff groups that are small and poorly qualified. Practitioners are often unaware of developments elsewhere (in relation to behaviour management, inclusive practice and the foundations of formal learning) that might help them achieve greater competence and self-esteem. There has been some recent recognition of this problem. In November 2010, the government said that pre-schools constituted the weakest part of the education system. It blamed local authorities for much of this (perhaps unfairly). The State Council agreed to make more money available for early childhood services and new guidelines on the funding and management of pre-schools were issued in 2011.

These are all signs of a slight shift from demand-led policies to a new attention to provision. Beyond that, there is the possibility that has only just begun to be recognized – that China has a great deal to teach as well as to learn about pre-school care and education, something that Chinese achievements in the fields of art and music already indicate.

Lessons from different countries

Although there were reasons for selecting the countries featured here, there is inevitably an element of arbitrariness about the choice and there has not been enough space to go into much detail about even those that were chosen. Nevertheless, a few conclusions are possible:

▶ There is nothing inevitable about the way that early childhood services operate in our country. There are important differences between the policies of different nation states and this fact alone demonstrates that it is possible to do things differently.

▶ At the same time, we should be careful about making over-simplified use of this kind of material. We need to get beyond statements that other countries are higher up some kind of league table of provision than we are or borrowing ideas from abroad for our own curriculum recipe book.

▶ This is because the policies shaping early childhood services are deeply influenced by views on the nature of the family, on the form of the state and on economic development that vary widely from country to country.

There are, however, some lessons on policy that do appear to emerge from the evidence.

▶ One is that the view that has become more or less orthodox among early years specialists in this country – that the organizational integration of various services for young children is crucial to the success of those services and that the education profession should have the leading role – is far from inevitable. A majority of countries have retained institutional distinctions between care and education and those that have gone for close integration have often – like Uruguay – chosen a different institutional route to achieve this.

▶ The principal lesson is that if you want to make early childhood settings more available to more families, then focus on supporting the demand side (by tax credits or subsidies to parents) is going to work significantly less well than investment in the supply side (by the provision of settings directly by the national or local state or by other agencies working under contract to the state). This argument has secured government support in many countries (although not in England) since newly emerging states often see education as a having a critical role to play in nation-building.

▸ It is also important that we recognize what we have to learn from countries outside Europe. There is still a lingering tendency to ignore the lessons we may have to learn from Latin America, Africa and Asia. Innovative approaches there to both provision and the curriculum are relevant to the 'developed' world.

Points for reflection 〰

▸ You can think about this on your own or make it the topic of a group discussion with colleagues or fellow students.
▸ What are the most important things we might expect to learn from early childhood services abroad in terms of both daily practice and pedagogy on the one hand, and policy and organizational arrangements on the other?
▸ How far is it possible to get to grips with what is happening in another country on the basis of written information alone?
▸ What are the factors bringing about differences between countries that you need to take into account when judging what we have to learn from them?

Summary

▸ Policy on early childhood services is determined within each nation state. Only formal conventions and similar documents can bind a nation state and relatively few of those have immediate relevance to early childhood services.

▸ Nevertheless, the international dimension of policy development is important. The communication of ideas about such services between different countries entails views on policy as well as pedagogy.

▸ Examination of the early childhood policies of several countries shows how much variation there is, suggests some of the reasons for this variation and, therefore, helps us to a critical understanding of our own circumstances.

Further reading

Nursery World magazine and various academic journals frequently include articles covering early childhood services in other countries.

The most comprehensive surveys available are the two volumes (so far) in the OECD's *Starting Strong* series of reports on different countries. Bear in mind when they were published and that policies in this field – as in other areas of social policy – may change significantly over time.

Some shorter pieces that can be recommended:

- Penn (2009) 'A Mother's Place is in the Home' looks at differences between different European states on the role of day care for young children.

- Waller (2009) 'International Perspectives' deals, like this chapter, with the international dimension of early childhood services but with emphasis on pedagogy and the curriculum rather than on policy.

- White (2009) 'Explaining differences in child care policy development' provides a useful analytical framework.

The Impact of Policy

Chapter 4 provided an overview of how policy is devised and clearly highlighted how the raft of policies within early years has led to a significant expansion of service provision. On one level this can be welcomed, as it would seem likely that this would lead to improvements for children and families. Nonetheless, it is necessary to explore the likely impact of the diverse policies on different stakeholders.

This chapter:

▶ explores how policy developments impact on three key groups – practitioners, children and parents

▶ aims to show how policy can offer potential benefits for one or more of the groups but at the same time may also create tensions.

Since 1997, there have been some major shifts in early years policy. In many respects, as discussed in earlier chapters, the National Childcare Strategy provided an impetus that has led to significant changes in early years services, and the Children and Families Bill (2012) suggests this will continue. Over the past few years, expectations from government, local authorities, other services and parents in regard to early years services have increased and there has been a massive increase in provision, including part-time funded places for 3-year-olds (DCSF, 2007) and the intended expansion of places for 2-year-olds in deprived areas (HM Treasury, 2011). There is a much greater focus on having practitioners with professional qualifications, a more rigorous inspection process to drive up quality throughout the sector and an expectation that future service provision will work in partnership not only with parents but also with a range of other services drawn from health and social care as well as education. Overall, these changes seem positive, but to understand the impact on practitioners, children and parents requires more in-depth consideration.

Practitioners

The early years workforce is diverse, in terms of the qualifications and experience it holds. However, there are some areas where this diversity is not evident, for example in age, where around a third of the workforce is below the age of 25. It is also significant that approximately 98 per cent of early years practitioners are women, few are from ethnic minorities, few have disabilities and the majority hold a qualification at or below Level 3 (for example, Modern Diploma, BTEC National Diploma). Another significant difference is that almost half work in the profit sector, compared with less than 10 per cent of teachers, although there has been a fall in the number of private providers and a rise in the number of voluntary providers (DfE, 2011a). One reason for these differences, which has been discussed in previous chapters, is the division of responsibility between care and education. The term 'early years care and education' is often now used, with the aim of breaking down artificial barriers between care and education as the boundaries between each are generally unclear and young children need both, not one or the other. This is also reflected in local authorities with the merger of child social services and education departments and the creation of Director of Children's Services posts to lead the formed departments. Nonetheless, even when account is taken of these developments, care has often been seen as inferior to education and this is reflected in the qualification level, perception, training opportunities and salary level of practitioners: with those practitioners within the early years sector who are not qualified teachers being seen with less regard than those with qualified teacher status. In terms of conditions of employment as well as low pay, this often entails working longer hours and an absence of other benefits such as sick pay and time/funding for professional development (Osgood, 2004). The Nutbrown review of qualifications and standing of early years as a profession confirms that many of these issues persist (Nutbrown, 2012).

When this is seen in the context of government plans for workforce expansion and professionalization, it raises fundamental questions. The ten-year strategy, released by the previous government, set out plans for early years services, identifying the importance of the early years workforce in achieving the ambitious strategies of the plan (HM Treasury et al., 2004). These points have been reiterated in recent government plans aimed at increasing provision for funded places for 2-year-olds (albeit in targeted areas) and the new Statutory Framework for the Early Years Foundation Stage (HM Treasury, 2011; DfE, 2012b). Although both these polices are aimed at children and families, they have a significant impact on practitioners. They stress the importance of practitioners having the appropriate qualifications and skills to work with children. This shows the interrelatedness of policy: documents are produced by government on the basis of manifestos, political ideologies, expert reports or even public opinion. However, for successful implementation, turning the policy into practice will at least require alterations to practice and possibly a fundamental overhaul of practice. The basis of this is a simple realization, but it is important to acknowledge that the quality of early years settings is clearly integrated with the quality of practitioners. The EPPE project (Sylva et al., 2004, 2012), which has tracked outcomes for over 3,000 children who have experienced various types of day care (for example, LEA-run nurseries, community playgroups and integrated centres), found that:

▸ the higher the qualification level of practitioners, particularly the leaders in each setting, the better the quality of the setting and the outcomes for children, particularly those with a poor early years home learning environment

▸ settings led by graduates were particularly effective and this has to be seen in light of the current situation where qualification levels are low

▸ access to training was variable in a significant number of settings, particularly those in the profit sector where there is an extremely high turnover of staff, which creates inconsistency and difficulties in sustaining a workforce that is able to continue their professional development over time.

Based on government plans for child and family services, this presents significant challenges in achieving many of the ambitious targets in two main areas: leadership of early years settings and creating a sustainable workforce.

Leadership in the early years workforce has not received the same level of attention as in other sectors of education, particularly school. One difficulty for the early years sector is the fragmented range of services that make up provision. This ranges from multiple-site private nursery chains to integrated centres that provide a range of health, social and educational services to community-run playgroups (which in some areas, such as rural areas, may be the only provision available). In expanding services, the Labour government, in its attempt to keep a central hold on developments, took a managerialist approach to funding and provision, which has led to a range of demands on setting leaders, including increased administration, a range of targets to achieve and complicated requirements to attract and maintain funding (Osgood, 2004). This raises issues about the balance between the complexity of centrally imposed management requirements and the demands on each type of provider. For example, a large Children's Centre may be able to respond to a broader range of requirements than a childminder working independently and offering provision for a group of children at varied times during the week. This is not meant to suggest that large-scale private provision is better or more effective. In fact, some of the most successful provision, previously designated as Early Excellence Centres (these would now mainly fall under the umbrella term of Children's Centres, many of which also evolved from Neighbourhood Nurseries and Sure Start Local Programmes), started as locally-based voluntary sector provision (Osgood, 2004). Within these settings, there was an emphasis on collaborative and cooperative working at the same time as responding to the government's agenda of reducing social exclusion. For policy development and implementation, this emphasizes the need to consider further developments carefully and ensure that account is taken of the need to develop collaborative practice, rather than simply assume that policy alone can achieve this.

As part of its ten-year strategy for childcare, the government signalled a commitment to increase the number of Children's Centres to 3,500 by 2010 (by mid 2012, there were 3,600 centres although the numbers have declined since 2010). These centres provide an integrated range of services to meet the social, health and educational requirements of children and families. The diverse range of services that children's services aims to provide will require leadership from appropriately qualified and skilled practitioners if the full potential of the policy for integrated services is to be realized. In response to this, the government, for the first time, has acknowledged the need for a range of skilled practitioners, including graduates in early years (HM Treasury et al., 2004), and the need for highly qualified practitioners has been consistently confirmed from varied sources (e.g. Sylva et al., 2004, 2012; Siraj-Blatchford et al., 2008; DfE, 2012b). This move is welcome as there is a large body of evidence that shows the need for effective leadership in education, although less on leadership in early years (Muijs et al., 2004; Close and Wainwright, 2010). Kagan and Hallmark (2001) argue that leadership in early years encompasses a number of roles:

▸ administrative skills

▸ pedagogical leadership

▸ an ability to lead community services and initiatives

▸ the ability to act as an advocate for groups and show political awareness.

This highlights the need for effective education up to degree level and effective leadership training. Leadership is complex and to be effective leaders, practitioners need to develop the characteristics associated with a leadership identity (Woodrow, 2008). Other groups, such as universities providing Early Childhood Studies courses, children's organizations and sectors of the academic community have argued the need for this for several years. A positive development was the announcement of the Graduate Leader Fund (DCSF, 2008a). The fund, which replaced the transformation fund, was allocated to local authorities and the Children's Workforce Development Council (CWDC) aimed to raise standards and enhance quality through the provision of graduates in settings. The fund was intended to provide scope to attract new graduates into the sector and provide resources to enable practitioners already within the sector to train to graduate level. A welcome development with this fund was the commitment to provide resources through this channel until at least 2015, which was designed to enable local authorities and early years settings to plan on a more long-term basis rather than from year to year. In addition, the fund was primarily focused on the private, voluntary and independent (PVI) sector where only 3 per cent of the workforce, compared with over 40 per cent in the maintained sector, are graduates. The two main graduate opportunities available within the sector are the Early Years Professional Status (EYPS) and the National Professional Qualification in Integrated Centre Leadership (NPQICL). These routes offer either graduate or postgraduate training for practitioners. With EYPS, which the CWDC see as having equivalency to qualified teacher status, practitioners are trained to take a lead role in planning and delivering the curriculum. With NPQICL, which is similar in nature to the National Professional Qualification for Headship (NPQH), holders generally take a management and leadership role. There is an expectation that Children's Centre managers will attain this qualification and it has relevance across education, health and social care (National College for School Leadership, 2008). However, due to government spending restrictions the fund was withdrawn in April 2011 and the early intervention grant (a funding stream for early education settings) contained no specific allocation to replace this. The full impact of this will become clear over time but evidence has shown that the presence of graduate leaders with Early Years Professional Status leads to significant quality improvements within a setting (Mathers et al., 2011). A review of the NPQICL is also under way and in the current funding climate it is likely that this will lead to reduced rather than enhanced funding. This is a clear example of how policy decisions are made on the basis of multiple factors and of how changes in direction do not always reflect the evidence of positive impacts.

In addition to having good leaders in the early years sector, in order to achieve the ambitious expansion plans and targets set in policy documents, a systematic overhaul of the early years workforce will be needed. As well as the importance of the early years workforce in terms of sustainability, there is a clear link between the skill level of the workforce and quality (DCSF, 2007; Tickell, 2011; DfE, 2012b). At present, early years practitioners cover a continuum of experience and qualifications. This ranges from little past experience and no formal qualifications to Level 3 qualifications, such as CACHE diplomas or BTEC Early Years qualifications, to degrees, such as Early Childhood Studies or qualified teacher status (Nutbrown, 2012). For those with qualified teacher status, who usually work in school environments, either within maintained nurseries, reception classes or foundation units, their terms and conditions of service are set within national agreements or are guided by these. But, as stated earlier, for the majority of practitioners within early years, the level of reward, working conditions and opportunities for development and progression do not match those of practitioners with qualified teacher status and the majority are not covered by national agreements on pay and conditions. To address this situation, there will need to be a radical rethink of how policy can take account of and be applied to the fragmented range of early years services. This will need to explore how best to support and develop the workforce to ensure that early years care and education services are of high quality, sustainable and take account of the expectations of children and parents. An Integrated Qualifications Framework (IQF) was under development but the emphasis on this was lost with the disbanding of the CWDC in 2012. Within early years, practitioners cross a number of traditional professional boundaries. In addition, there has been an exponential increase over the past two decades in the range of qualifications for early education and childcare (from less than 20 in 1990 to approximately 160 in 2010), and the challenges of developing a coherent, fit-for-purpose qualification framework to ensure appropriate training and progression opportunities for the early years workforce continue (Nutbrown, 2012).

In 2004, a National Audit Office report of early years services identified three key issues to creating sustainable provision: the lack of premises, the lack of a trained workforce and the withdrawal of start-up funding (NAO, 2004), and the latter two still clearly exist. The report drew attention to the importance of not only creating places, but of also sustaining them. One of the greatest challenges in terms of sustainability could arguably be ensuring an adequate supply of appropriately qualified practitioners for expanding early years services and ensuring there are processes in place that value and reward these people once they are in post.

Activity

Think about each of the following and, if possible, talk to practitioners with different experiences to gain their perspective:

- ▶ What level of qualification should early years practitioners have? Explain why you think this.
- ▶ Is there a need for some/all practitioners within early years to be educated to degree level? Explain why you think this.
- ▶ What may be the barriers to attracting people to work in early years services?
- ▶ What measures are needed to keep practitioners within early years services?
- ▶ Is there a clear career pathway for practitioners in early years? If not, what would need to be done to establish one?

When thinking about each of these points, an important consideration should be the diversity of early years services. Unlike schools, which generally have a similar pattern of organization (but do not necessarily offer the same experience for children), early years services span a range of providers. For example, there are childminders who may work predominantly in isolation in local communities; private organizations with multiple sites; Children's Centres, which may be voluntary or local authority operated and provide a diverse array of educational, social and health support services. What is clear from an accumulating body of evidence is that the higher the overall qualification of practitioners, the greater the quality of early years care and education they offer (Brind et al., 2011; DfE, 2012b; Nutbrown, 2012). Arguably, the workforce issue and, up to a point, the issue of providing more consistent frameworks for developing practitioners has been tackled but several years on, even in light of the Childcare Act 2006 which set out expectations of training for practitioners, significant challenges remain. However, to achieve the ambitious plans previously outlined, future policy will require far more than simply putting graduates into the workplace. Moss (2004) draws attention to Target 26 set by the European Commission Childcare Network in 1995 which set the ambitious aim, for the UK at least, of ensuring that a minimum of 60 per cent of practitioners working with children have completed at least three years of post-18 training (for example, degree level) and that the remainder of staff without this should have access to it either at training institutions or through continuous professional development. Even so, increased training levels alone are not enough. To value practitioners with increased levels of training, there also needs to be a rethink of salary levels, clearer progression routes and a career framework that makes this possible (HM Treasury et al., 2004; Nutbrown, 2012), and over the past few years there has been little progress in these areas. The government outlined a commitment to addressing these issues, but it remains to be seen how great an impact this will have on creating a sustainable workforce (Hill, 2005). The CWDC had primary responsibility for creating an appropriately qualified and trained workforce to effectively meet the needs of children and young people (DCSF, 2008b). In 2012, the Teaching Agency was formed with two main aims in relation to early years provision: (1) the supply and retention of the workforce and (2) the provision of a quality workforce. However, given the ongoing reviews of qualifications and the short period of time the agency has existed, it is still too early to evaluate progress.

Since the election of the Coalition government in 2010, there has been a renewed emphasis on providing integrated early years services, but the current set-up of services in many ways makes this difficult to achieve. Evidence of this can be provided by exploring two different examples. For a number of years, there has been a decline in the number of registered childminders and this continues (Brind et al., 2011). To provide integrated services, it is necessary for practitioners to work in partnership with a range of stakeholders. For childminders, this can involve working with the local authority, the NCMA and parents. Although this may seem unproblematic, when it is considered alongside other aspects of their role, such as meeting the expectations of the Early Years Foundation Stage (DfE, 2012b), marketing their service, attending training and managing finances, this shows the complex nature of the role and potentially highlights how the mismatch between expectations and reward has led to a significant reduction in numbers. In response to this, a number of authorities have appointed childminder coordinators within local authorities to provide support for childminders. The role of the support childminders is to work with a small group of new childminders and offer them guidance and advice on different aspects of the role over the first year. However, there has been a decrease in the number of childminders from 71,500 in 2006 to 57,900 in 2010 (Brind et al., 2011), and as expectations increase, which is likely to be the case with the new curriculum, this may be exacerbated and have a negative impact on provision and parental choice.

With the change in service organization and integration, it seems an ideal time to consider the roles of those who work within early years services. Questions exist about whether the current division of roles is appropriate to meet the demands that current and planned early years policies will place on providers and practitioners. Again, the previous government acknowledged this in its ten-year childcare strategy by stating that a new profession, combining learning and care, is needed that will exist alongside teachers (HM Treasury et al., 2004). Moss (2004) draws attention to the need for such a role, often described as a pedagogue and similar to that seen in many European countries. The role of a pedagogue needs to be seen as different to that of a teacher and to have its own clear identity. Pedagogues will take a holistic approach to each child and family member and encompass a number of skills that will enable them to take account of the individual social, emotional and cultural identity of each person they work with. Similarities are likely to exist in terms of the training they receive, as they will be educated to degree level. Graduates from Early Childhood Studies degrees have followed courses focusing on the holistic needs of children and families, but in employment these skills are often not fully utilized, which is partly attributable to the lack of appropriate professional roles. In a number of European countries, a pedagogue role exists, which encompasses supporting children's education and care and spans health, social care and educational contexts (Fitzgerald and Kay, 2008). The Early Years Professional role covers aspects of this position but it is heavily focused on leading the curriculum in early years settings, and in the move to multi-agency working it may not help to achieve this. Anning (2004) refers to the need to develop 'a community of practice' within early years where knowledge is used in action and developed in ways acceptable to the community. This raises issues for integration and emphasizes the need for practitioners with a high level of skill in different aspects of early years care and education, as well as a high standard education, and could be seen as further support for the role of pedagogues who are able to use their skills and knowledge to engage in and make decisions to benefit children and families without over-dominance from the managerialist style that is often indirectly enforced through current arrangements and funding from the DCSF. The debate around workforce structure and roles continues. The Children and Families Bill, which will be laid before parliament in 2012–13, addresses the need for better working between health, social care and education practitioners. While there seems to be no intention in this legislation to introduce radical changes in roles, the fact that increased integrated working is still an aim after many years, past legislation and significant organizational change, it raises questions about whether the current roles and professional boundaries within the early years sector are fit for purpose. The Nutbrown review (2012) acknowledges these variations and challenges in the interim report.

Children

The significant expansion of early years services now means that there are large numbers of children who experience some type of early years care and education. This may be in the form of one to two sessions per week in a pre-school setting, to five funded sessions in a nursery, or a mixture of provision from different providers on a full-time basis. When considering the impact of the many policy changes, it is important that the implications for children are considered. For example:

- ▶ Is increased provision appropriate for all children?
- ▶ Is the curriculum offered appropriate to the needs of children?
- ▶ Do practitioners have the necessary qualifications, experience and access to training?
- ▶ Is there support in place to meet the diverse developmental needs of each child?

When considering these issues, it is unlikely that there will be a simple yes or no answer. It is also important to understand that policy alone cannot be blamed for failures or praised for success. To make an evaluation of the provision for children, it is necessary to evaluate if policies have laid the basis for high-quality and appropriate provision.

For children, one of the most significant changes in early years care and education has been the introduction of a unified Statutory Framework for the Early Years Foundation Stage (EYFS) (DfE, 2012b), which brought together *Birth to Three Matters* (Sure Start Unit, 2002) for children aged from birth to 3 and the *Statutory Framework for the Early Years Foundation Stage* (DfES, 2007a). Over the past decade, the Foundation Stage has received much greater attention and is now seen as being as relevant as other key stages, which has led to positive changes both within early years settings and schools. This has included the appointment of Foundation Stage coordinators who are often members of school management teams, access to additional training for teachers in appropriate pedagogy for early years, a greater focus on outdoor play and more flexible and child-directed activities. But there are still concerns with provision in the Foundation Stage, particularly in some reception classes. For example, the qualifications of many practitioners may not be specific to early years, there are often low levels of support staff and some schools have mixed Foundation and Key Stage 1 classes (Aubrey, 2004), which can lead to an inappropriate curriculum for young children. This remains an issue in a number of schools, particularly smaller schools. A number of settings also have very limited outdoor space that children are able to access freely. It could be argued that many of these concerns cannot be attributed to policy failings, but new policy has not necessarily brought improvements.

Points for reflection

Think about the issues above and any other possible concerns that you have seen or discussed relating to foundation provision and jot them down. Then answer the following questions:

▶ Which of the issues can be linked to potential policy shortfalls and which may have other origins?

▶ Are there any that have multiple causes or are difficult to place in one list or the other?

In terms of structural issues, such as the building or outdoor space, it can be argued that new policy developments which focus on appropriate pedagogy for early years cannot be linked with inopportune building design. With other issues, such as practitioner qualifications and training, it is more difficult to separate them. In many respects, introducing a curriculum appropriate to the needs of young children is a positive step, but it would not be difficult to envisage that practitioners would be likely to need significant support and training to implement this policy to its full positive effect. The decision to have a separate curriculum for children from birth to 5+ and then in Key Stage 1, could also be seen as continuing with poor policy, as it does nothing to reduce the issue of fragmentation in early years care and education provision and the start of formal schooling for younger children, nor does it introduce a coordinated approach to learning. This also links to the current policy on school starting age that many criticize as too young and inappropriate for children (Dowling, 1999; Sharp, 2003). The provision of curriculum documents alone is also not the complete solution as there are still clear requirements on practitioners to promote and sustain interactions between children and ensure that activities provided are appropriately matched to children's levels of development (Siraj-

Blatchford and Sylva, 2004; Siraj-Blatchford et al., 2008; Sylva et al., 2012).

Since the National Curriculum was introduced, there has been increasing criticism of the impact it has had on reducing the place of creativity within education. This was particularly acute for children in Key Stage 1 and reception classes, where the didactic approach of the Numeracy and Literacy Strategies was (and still may be for children in Key Stage 1) experienced on a daily basis. In comparison, the child-centred pedagogical approach advocated in the Foundation Stage curriculum guidance, which has been further developed in the reviewed EYFS (DfE, 2012b), was welcomed as a positive step forward and was seen as more likely to lead to child-initiated activities, sustained and extended by interaction between practitioners and children, and this positive step has been further developed in the new EYFS curriculum. The provision of the new document alone will not guarantee this, but the approach advocated throughout it (for example, giving children time to explore, gain understanding, problem-solve and make discoveries) is clearly in line with effective early years practice. However, this is not meant to suggest that direct teaching is wrong. As Siraj-Blatchford and Sylva (2004: 726) highlight, 'Direct instruction is not harmful; it is the balance that is important', which again highlights the need for skilled practitioners. Interestingly, though, the move to embedding creativity as a key component of early years education took many years. Plowden (DES, 1967) highlighted the need for appropriate early years provision but in terms of acquiring knowledge and skills, whereas the Rumbold Report (DES, 1990) emphasized the need for a creative approach to ensure a greater coherence between education and care and to provide effectively for all aspects of children's development. It is only several years later, though, that this has been partially realized for children up to the age of 5.

Another important consideration for children is whether there is a holistic policy approach to meet the emotional, social, health and physical aspects of development as well as the educational aspects. Kurtz (2003) identifies a wide-reaching policy approach to promote the health and well-being of children, not least through the Sure Start initiative, which placed health at the centre of its agenda through the aim to tackle and reduce the impact of poverty and the links this has with low educational standards (Glass, 2001). Since 2000, there have been reductions in poverty, infant/child mortality and accidental injury rates, which suggests a successful policy agenda, as discussed further in Chapter 8. However, different interpretations can be made from the same data based on the definition of poverty used (Lister, 2004). In terms of absolute poverty (when a family lacks enough money to meet basic needs), progress has been made, but in terms of relative poverty (when a family lacks resources to have a good diet, participate in society and have access to amenities that are seen as customary in society) progress is more debatable. This is significant though as the central aim of Sure Start was to promote inclusion and participation of disenfranchised families. The introduction of the National Service Framework for Children, Young People and Maternity Services, which sets ambitious health and treatment targets for all children, also confirms that there is a wide-ranging policy agenda to support all aspects of children's development (Department of Health/DfES, 2004). The National Service Framework has made advances; however the ambitious targets set for all children continue to present a clear challenge to find ways to implement the policy across boundaries between networks of public, private and voluntary service providers (Masterson et al., 2004). It still remains to be seen whether the challenges this presents can be overcome in the Children and Families Bill (2012–2013).

Parents

The issue of partnership between providers and parents has become more significant over the past few years and there is now a clear expectation, and rightly so, that providers need to work in a way that acknowledges the contribution parents make and values and respects their opinions. But the issue of partnership is often misunderstood and the term may be bandied about without full acknowledgement of the needs of parents (Fitzgerald, 2012). As the complexity of early years services has increased, this has raised a number of issues for parents. To work effectively with parents requires policies that are joined up and responsive, which cannot be achieved through the provision of services alone. Services need to be available at times when parents require them, and must be accessible, affordable and integrated to provide consistency.

There is a variety of ways that practitioners can work in partnership with parents. Swap (1993) describes a continuum of partnership models that can be used by early years care and education settings but which also provides a basis for other services, to assess their level of partnership working with parents:

▶ *The protective model* – this operates along the lines of a business and requires parents to delegate responsibility for education to the setting, as the aims of home and the setting and the roles of practitioners and parents are different.

▶ *The school-to-home transmission model* – this recognizes the importance of the family but only places an emphasis on one-directional communication – from the setting to the home – and assumes a level of parental agreement with decisions taken by the setting. In this model, there is likely to be little sharing of ideas between the setting and the community.

▶ *The curriculum enrichment model* – this recognizes the benefits of collaborative learning between practitioners, parents and children, and integrates knowledge from families and the community into the curriculum and learning. There is a focus on the curriculum as this is seen as an important vehicle for impacting on learning.

▸ *The partnership model* – this is built on long-term commitment, mutual respect and widespread involvement of families and practitioners at different levels, such as joint planning and shared decision-making. It reflects the fact that children are embedded in and influenced by the home, the setting and the community.

Activity

Think about each stage of the model and settings that you have worked in or been on placement at.

▸ What examples have you seen of partnership working and which stage of the model would you place them at?

▸ Have you seen any particularly effective or poor examples of partnership working? What was it that made them effective or poor?

▸ Think about one aspect of partnership working with parents (you could base this on something you have seen in practice) and write a brief outline of it.

▸ Identify where on the model you would place the setting.

▸ Draw up an action plan to work out how you would develop partnership working to the next stage of the partnership model. Compare the strategies you have identified with a partner.

The introduction of policies can lay the basis for partnership working with parents (and between professionals), but policy alone cannot ensure that this will be achieved. To achieve high levels of partnership working requires practitioners and families to work together in an open and respectful way. This requires practitioners to communicate effectively with families and each other, which can be challenging, particularly when services are delivered by a number of agencies. In this respect, the challenges ahead for practitioners from different disciplines to work effectively with parents are significant.

The availability and accessibility of services is another key issue for parents. There is clearly a body of data to show that there have been significant increases in early years provision (DfE, 2011a), but it cannot be taken for granted that this equates with good levels of availability and accessibility for all children and families. To think about this more analytically, a number of questions have to be asked:

▸ Are services available equally in all areas (for example, urban and rural areas)?

▶ Are services affordable for all families?

▶ Are services available when families require them?

▶ If children attend more than one setting, are the different providers coordinated to ensure smooth transitions between them?

▶ Are there adequate transport facilities available for families to access the different providers they may need?

▶ Is the full range of services required by families provided in the same location?

Families living in rural areas still often face significant challenges in accessing appropriate and affordable services and this is likely to exacerbate with the introduction of funded places for 2-year-olds. This may be because there is simply a shortage of provision or that what is provided is either not able to offer early years care and education for the required amount of time or not at affordable rates, but this is not confined to rural areas alone. The government has acknowledged this and has expressed a commitment to enhance the level of wraparound provision to assist parents by providing integrated provision (DCSF, 2007). A clear challenge in achieving this aim, though, will be moving the policy on extended school provision and reversing the decline in the number of childminders ceasing practice. Another challenge faced by parents is organizing the daily family routine around early years care and education provision, and this becomes particularly challenging when there are children of different ages within the family (especially if there is a child below statutory school age and a child above). To access the different range of providers and fit this in with work and other family commitments can involve the family in negotiating complex plans, making numerous journeys and still often having to rely on informal care networks throughout the week (Skinner, 2003; Truss, 2012).

In terms of accessibility, there has been success in government policy in attracting parents to services that previously may not have been affordable. The Neighbourhood Nurseries Initiative (NNI), which expanded childcare provision in the 20 per cent most disadvantaged wards in England by providing start-up funding to support new provision, was partially successful. Bell and La Valle (2005) found that:

▶ two-thirds of families using Neighbourhood Nursery provision had not previously used childcare facilities

▶ the provision was used by over half of parents in the early morning and late afternoon

▶ the level of satisfaction with the provision was generally high and that almost a fifth of parents had been able to enter work since accessing the nursery.

More recently, the increase in childcare provision has continued but differences have been seen in the distribution between the more and less deprived areas.

Notably 73 per cent of full day care in Children's Centres and 58 per cent of nursery schools were located in the 30 per cent most deprived areas. In contrast, 19 per cent of both sessional care and childminders were located there (DfE, 2011a). When this is contrasted with the evidence from Bell and La Valle (2005), it confirms that increased provision created by the NNI still seems to be evident where much of the cost of provision is covered (e.g. nursery schools). In contrast, provision which is more usually paid by parents (e.g. sessional care) is disproportionally located away from more deprived areas. This raises concerns when seen alongside the recent reduction in the number of Children's Centres and highlights the importance of funding to ensure equality of access. With the removal of ring-fenced funding, it may also mean less use of early education among more deprived families, which is contrary to the aims of the government as set out in the spending review (HM Treasury, 2011).

Another factor that can impact on participation in service provision is the attitude of current users. The aim of many Children's Centres is to attract 'hard to reach' families, but practitioners need to be aware of how the attitude of current users may impact on potential new users so that cliques do not stop potential new users feeling excluded. This can be a particular concern if a setting is located in a catchment area that draws families from varied socio-economic backgrounds (Sheppard et al., 2008). The Family Parenting Institute argue that there is a need for an overarching family policy to include often excluded groups from services, for example children with disabilities or parents with mental health problems. The number of policies that impact on families is vast and they generally develop in a piecemeal way across many government departments, and each needs to be 'family proofed'. A particular issue that still requires much more detailed attention is the level of support that is provided to families in the first 12 months after the birth of a child (Family and Parenting Institute, 2005). There have been limited advances in this area with the introduction of the Parenting Fund, which has provided two rounds of funding for promoting good practice for family and parent support services (Family and Parenting Institute, 2008). To address this, a much more sustained effort will need to be made to support all parents, as well as targeting those in disadvantaged areas, if the outcomes for all children are to be raised.

The government agenda of reducing disadvantage and social exclusion is often tied to the success of policies that provide childcare places and enable parents, who previously were not employed, to return to work. This may be one method of judging the success of policy developments, but other issues need to be considered for parents. The issue of work–life balance has developed momentum over recent years and is particularly significant to families with young children (DTI, 2004). In response to this, the government announced improvements to the length of maternity and adoption leave and financial benefits to 39 weeks in 2008 (DTI, 2005), and this has now increased to 52 weeks. There have also been positive moves towards allowing parents of young children to ask their employers to consider adopting a flexible approach to working hours and the introduction, albeit minimal, of paid paternity leave. These issues highlight the need for policies to address a range of issues and to be focused on more than simply moving parents back into the employment market. The emphasis placed on the move from welfare to work by government is to some degree understandable as there is a correlation between being employed, the number of adults in a family and levels of poverty. Caution is still needed if new issues, such as reliance on a variety of providers for childcare and increased family stress levels, are not addressed in the developments. There is little point in formulating policies that move parents into work and simply replace one set of difficulties with another. To avoid this, policy-makers need to consider the holistic needs of families and ensure that policies are able to respond effectively to the diverse needs of each family.

Activity

You have been asked to write a short evaluative account of the impact of the Early Years Foundation Stage curriculum over the past decade as part of a review of early years provision for the Teaching Agency. The account will be read by a range of providers, government departments and parents.

When planning your account, it would be useful to think about the impact in terms of practitioners, children and parents. This will help to ensure that the response takes account of the impact on the key stakeholders and is more likely to identify the benefits of and any difficulties in the curriculum.

An important aspect of any written response to this type of activity is to support all claims with relevant evidence. This could come from a range of sources, including other reports, policy documents, academic papers, research studies and other relevant texts, such as books on child development. What would be your key headline points?

Your response is likely to have included a range of positive impacts and some drawbacks. There is a broad range of information that you could have drawn on. You may also have identified other relevant stakeholders that you feel should be considered. For example, the practitioner group could include people with very varied experiences. It may include individual practitioners who work in a large voluntary setting, an individual childminder or an owner/manager of a private nursery. This diversity within the initial groups may seem challenging. However, considering the perspective of a range of interested stakeholders and responding to this, particularly where it is supported by evidence, will include the quality and level of analysis within your response. The points below summarize some of the issues you may have considered for each group.

Practitioners

▸ The commitment to have at least one graduate in every setting, to deliver the curriculum, is likely to offer significant opportunities for practitioners to engage in continuing professional development.

▸ The curriculum draws together and builds on information from a range of sources to show development over time (for example, *Birth to Three Matters*, *Curriculum Guidance for the Foundation Stage*, primary national curricula) and may lead to a more coherent and less bureaucratic burden for practitioners.

▸ It places the role of practitioners in supporting children's development and welfare as central and this could help to professionalize the workforce.

▸ The demands of the curriculum will have different impacts. For example, for childminders it could add significantly to what is expected of them and they may not have access to appropriate support and training, or the resource implications of gaining this could be prohibitive.

▸ Linked to previous points, the increased expectations and development opportunities need to be formally recognized and a career structure is likely to aid progression and retention of practitioners (to achieve the stated government aim of having a world-class workforce).

▸ It could aid inter-agency working, as all registered practitioners and settings will be working to the same unified and coherent curriculum.

▸ It emphasizes the need to have well-trained practitioners and leaders (e.g. an EYP) to lead the curriculum.

Children

▸ It has a coordinated and joined-up curriculum.

▸ It has a play-based curriculum, which is appropriate to supporting children's development.

▸ It takes a holistic approach, which places equal value on social, emotional, physical and cognitive development.

▸ It takes careful account of children's welfare needs.

▸ It emphasizes that children develop at different rates and that this is part of expected development.

▸ It provides a consistent approach across all settings, which will be particularly beneficial for children attending more than one setting.

▸ It promotes equality for all children and recognition of diversity.

▸ It views all children, from birth, as competent learners and sees them as capable.

▶ Children are encouraged to participate in their own learning, which is in line with the principles of the UNCRC.

▶ The appropriate approach to learning advocated by the curriculum is in stark contrast to the Key Stage 1 curriculum and children may find the transition point difficult.

Parents

▶ It sees parents at the heart of supporting their child's learning and development.

▶ It sets out clearly what parents can expect from early years care and education providers.

▶ For young children, particularly if parents are not familiar with early years care and education, the approach may seem very formal.

▶ The documented approach to early years care and education may be interpreted by parents as being superior to the care they, or family members, can provide.

▶ It lays the foundation for the inclusion of all children.

Your response to this activity may also include points which, although not directly related to the introduction of the statutory curriculum, are closely interlinked with it. This highlights both the challenges and fascination of gaining a clear insight into how policy has a widespread impact on practice and all those linked with it. What we hope is clear is that it is not possible to have a full understanding of how practice impacts on all stakeholders without at least some understanding of the policy that has led to current provision.

Summary ☐

▶ This chapter has explored the impact of policy on different stakeholders by examining each group in turn, but in many respects the divide is artificial.

▶ The purpose of this approach, however, was to show that it is important to consider how one policy can have both positive and negative impacts on different stakeholders.

▶ When presented with any policy, it is important to think carefully about these issues but also to consider how the policy as a whole fits with other policies and services.

▶ It is only through careful analysis that those to whom the policy applies will be able to take a more central role in the shaping of future policy as well as in the implementation of current policy.

Further reading

To understand the impact of policy on practitioners, children and parents, it is helpful to read documents and reports that may be aimed at each of these groups. A number of government publications, particularly from the Sure Start Unit, are relevant and their websites are listed at the end of the book. In addition, the following publications may be of interest:

Department of Health/Department for Education and Skills (DfES) (2004) *National Service Framework for Children, Young People and Maternity Services: Executive Summary*, London: Department of Health/DfES.

Lays out plans for health. See also below.

HM Treasury/Department for Education and Skills/Department for Work and Pensions/Department of Trade and Industry (2004) *Choice for Parents, the Best Start for Children: A Ten-year Strategy for Childcare*, London: HMSO.

Provides a comprehensive overview of the intended direction of future policy in early years care and education and will be useful to readers. This document will assist in a critique of current policy as it sets out a number of intended outcomes, many of which still reflect policy of the current government.

It is important, though, for readers to be aware that these are government intentions and they do not engage in a critical debate of the issues covered.

Sylva, K., Melhuish, E., Sammons, P., Siraj-Blatchford, I. and Taggart, B. (2012) *Effective Pre-school, Primary and Secondary Education 3–14 Project (EPPSE 3–14) – Final Report from the Key Stage 3 Phase: Influences on Students' Development From Age 11–14* London: DfE.

The EPPE project has been a significant piece of research since it began in 1997 and is likely to continue to be as it follows a large cohort of children through their primary education years. There are a number of publications from this project that will be useful to readers, but particularly the findings from the first phase, which tracked children through to the end of Key Stage 1. This paper outlines how EPPE investigated practice and identified how improvements could be achieved. It includes an in-depth discussion of the qualitative findings from settings identified as providing high standards of practice.

Chapter 8

Analysing the Impact of Policy

This chapter explains :

▶ a number of approaches that can be taken to analyse policy, including examples drawn from current policies to set this in a practice context and to promote an understanding of how drawing on research evidence and comparison with other countries can assist in this analysis

▶ how analysis and many of the questions posed would apply equally to the range of policies in early years services.

When analysing the potential impact of any policy, it is important to look broadly. It can help to think about this in terms of completing a jigsaw puzzle. At the start, you connect the edges. This gives an outline shape and some information about what the finished puzzle will look like, but it does not provide the whole picture. Over time, you try different pieces together, move them around and gradually the whole picture starts to fall into place. By the time the puzzle is complete, it is likely that you will have handled each of the pieces several times and will have thought carefully about how they fit together, and referred frequently to the box to compare the emerging puzzle and complete picture. Analysis is very similar to this. The pieces of the puzzle can be seen as representing policies. To gain a more in-depth understanding of different policies is difficult, but there are a number of approaches that you can take to help achieve this. Analysing policies is about looking at how they fit with current policies and practice, looking at how different parts of the policy impact on different stakeholders and how all this fits together in providing appropriate and responsive services for children, families and the wider community.

To analyse policy, you can contrast current approaches with historical evidence, consider how policy impacts on varied stakeholders, consider themes running through different policies or contrast the approach in the countries of the UK with that of other countries. By drawing on one or more of these methods, it is likely that you will be able to identify benefits and areas for development within policies and begin to gain a more analytical view of the impact of policy on the lives of children, parents and practitioners.

Why analyse policies?

Policy formation and implementation is a complex process that can take a considerable amount of time. A challenge for all policies is reconciling different priorities between those whom the policy will affect, such as practitioners, parents and children (National Audit Office, 2001). A number of different elements also need to be considered, including the implementation costs, the ability of services and service providers to deliver the policy aims, potential benefits, impact on different stakeholders and sustainability. Many policies aimed at children and families can cover a broad remit. For example, Children's Centres (many of which were former Sure Start local projects) bring together health, social services, education and voluntary services to respond to the requirements of individual families or sections of the community. It is also likely that the broader a policy, i.e. one which covers many policies in the area of children and family services, the more likely it is to impact not only on other people but also on other policies. A potential risk with this broad approach is that the policy may not benefit all those whom it is intended to benefit. Sanderson (2003) contrasts the approach of evidence-based practice and the belief in government departments that 'what counts is what works'. At a simple level, this does not seem problematic. In the context of complex policies, though, it is likely that an approach to analysis that simply aims to say whether a policy is working or not working will not capture the true impact of the policy, which is likely to include positive and negative elements. Sanderson (2003) highlights other problems with this approach. What is meant by the term 'what works'? Just because a policy is working for a parent does not mean it works for a child, or a policy that works in one area will work in another. There is also a heavy government focus on measuring outcomes, usually through targets, but not everything is easily measurable or attributable to one specific policy. Since the change of prime minister, there have been signals that a broader approach to measuring policy/service outcomes, rather than service outcomes alone, will be implemented. However, this remains to be seen across service providers. To overcome this, it is important to take a systematic and detailed approach to analysing the impact of policies that may provide the means to:

▶ decide if the information is accurate and how it will impact on practice

▶ argue why some aspects of policy are preferable to others

▶ identify aspects of good practice

▶ identify where there are shortcomings

▶ ensure high-quality services

▶ identify gaps in policy and service provision

▶ highlight how policy is meeting the requirements of different stakeholders

▶ offer a critical appraisal of a new approach to service delivery

▶ offer a critical appraisal of a local, regional, national or international policy.

Since 1997, a number of policies have been introduced into children and family services. The election of the Coalition government in 2010 signalled continued change; however the change has focused more on effective use of reduced funding, such as on moving towards targeted rather than universal services, removing ring fencing for varied early years grants and increasing the role of the private, voluntary and independent sector to compete for tenders (Sylva et al., 2012). The National Childcare Strategy set out the government's intention to increase provision across the maintained, voluntary and private sectors through a number of initiatives. Children's Trusts, which were implemented in most areas by 2006, aim to integrate locally based education, social services and some health services for children and young people (DfES/Department of Health, 2004). The Children's National Service Framework set out long-term plans for sustained improvement in health from birth through to adulthood (Department of Health/DfES, 2004). In 2007, the Children's Plan (DCSF, 2007) set out intentions to enhance the role of Children's Trusts, place schools at the centre of the community and integrate service provision; all with the aim of improving outcomes for children and families. The Coalition government has not set out a dramatically different policy direction, although it has commissioned a number of reviews, which have the potential to have a significant impact on the provision of services, and on children and families and pratitioners (e.g. the review into the role of the Children's Commissioner in England; the Nutbrown review of the early years workforce, status and qualifications; consultation on and the subsequent publication of the 2012 Children and Families Bill). Consequently, when analysing the impact of these policies, it will be necessary to explore which objectives have been met, which have not and if all those intended to benefit from the policy have done or are likely to do so.

Levels of policy

Policies can be designed and implemented at different levels. National policies, which set out detailed arrangements, are often formulated in response to legislation. For example, the Children and Families Bill 2012 will lead to policies being implemented that will impact on the organization of children's services; the relationship between education, health and social care services; strategies to improve the well-being of all children; and support to address the diverse needs of looked-after children. In response to this, organizations, local authority service providers and early years care and education settings may amend existing local policies or implement new ones to ensure that working practices take account of new expectations, and potentially new legislation. Analysis can be carried out on policy at each of these levels. This approach can provide valuable information in seeing how far a policy is meeting the stated aims and objectives, and if the statements and philosophies of the policies are evident in practice (Fitzgerald, 2004).

Approaches to analysing the impact of policy

As seen in earlier chapters, policies can impact on different aspects of service provision and take time to become embedded. Policies can also be analysed at different stages – from initial design, at implementation, through to ongoing maintenance of the policy (NAO, 2001). Glass (2001) argues that when analysing what works, it is necessary to think broadly. For example, when looking at poverty, policies that link to housing, the quality of public services and the urban environment can all contribute to reducing it. The creation of Sure Start Children's Centres, Health Action Zones and the New Deal are all examples of policies that can contribute to tackling the impact of poverty on children and families in communities with high levels of deprivation and social exclusion. A clear challenge for any analysis of policy is to consider not only the benefits of individual policies, but also whether different policies complement each other and enhance well-being or, potentially, the complexity leads to confusion and a lack of clarity about the overall aims and objectives.

Does policy represent the perspectives of all stakeholders?

Most policies will impact on a range of stakeholders, including children, parents, practitioners and, often, members of the wider community. Policy can also create differences between stakeholders within the same category. For example, when changes were introduced to childminding, the increased professionalism and impact of regulation caused some childminders to stop working, and led to a significant decline in numbers. This was seen as a problem by some and as an advantage by others. When analysing the impact of policy, it is important to consider whether policies have succeeded or failed in addressing the diverse issues of the different stakeholders who are affected by the policy. Over the past decade, the UNCRC could be seen as one vehicle that has helped policy to move beyond a welfare perspective. For children, this has potentially positive benefits: it sees them as having rights as well as being the recipients of adult protection, and places expectations on governments to ensure the rights of children are respected, addressed in policy and the outcome evaluated. The impact of this is that the interests of children should now be paramount in policy design and implementation, children should be able to exercise rights and their views should be requested and acted upon (Lansdown, 2001). Although this may not happen in all instances, it does provide a basis on which an analysis of policy in respecting and promoting the right of children to be consulted can be assessed.

Activity

Read the following scenario, which describes a typical daily scene for almost every young child in England, and think carefully about the policies that the education provision is based on and how well each of them takes account of the perspective of the child.

Sarah is 6 years old and is in Year 1 with 28 other children. She is with some of her friends from the reception class but her best friend from reception is in the other Year 1 class. She has had some difficulties with reading and now has one-to-one reading support from a teaching assistant three times a week.

She enjoys being at school but misses being able to play with different toys and outside on the bikes and climbing frame. Her favourite lesson is art as she likes to paint the people she has heard about in stories. Sarah likes to write some words on her paintings about the characters in stories and her teacher helps her to do this.

Initially, it may seem that there are very few explicit policies here but this may be because so many policies are taken for granted. Each of the following aspects of policy or practice could potentially impact on Sarah:

- ▶ school starting age
- ▶ the National Curriculum
- ▶ the Primary Framework for literacy and mathematics
- ▶ special educational needs policy
- ▶ legal expectations placed on registered providers against which they are judged by inspectorate bodies in the UK

▸ school results targets

▸ the Primary National Strategy

▸ governing body decisions.

From this list, the only clear reference to the need to consult children is contained in the Special Educational Needs Code of Practice (DfES, 2001b), which emphasizes 'the importance of finding out the ascertainable wishes and feelings of children and involving them when decisions are made that affect them' (section 4: 3). This would only apply if Sarah had been identified as having a special educational need, which may not be the case. The important point from this, however, is that just because there is an expectation, through the UNCRC, that children will be consulted, it does not automatically mean they will be, and this needs to be highlighted in any analysis of policy. Although the National Curriculum and the National Primary Strategy may have strengths, it could be argued that the approach they dictate to learning is not the most appropriate for young children and it is likely that if consulted, children in Key Stage 1 would choose an approach to learning that resembles more closely that of the Early Years Foundation Stage (DfE, 2012b).

Generally speaking, one of the areas in the UK where the impact of various policies is felt most by children is in education, but it is potentially the area where their views have the least impact or are not considered at all. Even where children are consulted, however, this may not equate with their views being respected and acted upon. Tisdall and Davis (2004) raise questions about the effectiveness and ethical considerations of some approaches to consultation based around school councils and whether they lead to democratic communities. This is not meant to suggest that all attempts to consult children are flawed, but it does highlight the need to look systematically at the strategies that are in place to allow organizations to claim that children are consulted. The following questions clearly show how careful analysis can help to appraise the approaches in place to listen to and act upon the views of children:

▸ Do all children have the right to participate, or is participation focused on more articulate or older children?

▸ Do the approaches provide the basis for children to take on decision-making positions?

▸ Is consultation acted on or is it simply tokenistic?

▸ Is feedback provided to the representatives to show what progress has been made?

The Scottish Executive has undertaken a number of consultations with children, in areas such as school food (Shoolbread, 2006) and special educational needs (SEN) policy. The SEN review aimed to involve children at different stages of the process. This was achieved by consulting an initial group of 39 children, further consultation with a group of 46 children and young people, and finally questionnaires completed by a group of over 100 children and young people. The strengths of this process were that it included children with disabilities and those with English as an additional language, and the views of the respondents were used to inform policy-makers at early stages of policy design. During the process, feedback was offered to each group but no regular involvement of children or young people in the policy development group was put in place, although this was asked for. Overall, the involvement of the children and young people led to some changes but there were limitations on what was implemented, which shows that the imbalance of power between children and adults still existed (Tisdall and Davis, 2004). Even though there were limitations in this approach, it does show how children can be involved and provides a basis for analysing whether the perspective of children is in evidence at the policy design, implementation and maintenance stages. In England, the Children's Plan made a greater attempt to include the views of children through the 'Time to Talk' consultation, which is a welcome development given that children are at the heart of planned developments and it is an area in which England has been poor in the past.

Another example of how a major policy can impact on young children is in the introduction of the entitlement to 15 hours' early education a week for 2-year-olds. It is estimated that this will reach 40 per cent of 2-year-olds by 2014–15. This will undoubtedly help parents, particularly working parents, with the cost of childcare, which recent evidence suggests is expensive in Britain (Truss, 2012). However this policy may seem to only have potential benefits for young children.

Activity

Think about the increase in entitlement for free early education for 2-year-olds. List some of the potential benefits and disadvantages of this policy for support staff, teaching staff and children.

Your benefits and disadvantages may have included some of the following:

Table 8.1 Benefits and disadvantages of free early education for 2-year-olds

Potential benefits	Potential disadvantages
Children receive more support to support their educational development at a young age	Children spend more time in formal education and care settings from a younger age
Increased employment opportunities for practitioners	There may not be adequate levels of highly-trained practitioners to provide high-quality care and education for younger children

Table 8.1 continued

Potential benefits	Potential disadvantages
Increased career opportunities for practitioners	Changes are driven by the need to increase the number of parents in work, rather than what is most appropriate for the child
Access to early education and care at a younger age to support parents with childcare	There is less choice for parents with lower income levels in caring for and educating their young children at home full time
Support for working parents through increased funding	Access is initially targeted at areas of high social deprivation, further stigmatizing these communites as being in need of support

The fact that there are potential benefits and disadvantages to increasing government funding for the provision of early education for 2-year-olds does not mean that this policy is bad. It does illustrate, though, that analysis of these points is important as it can highlight the potential advantages and disadvantages from the perspective of the different stakeholders that are affected and help to identify where further developments are necessary. Eyres et al. (2004) support many of these

points as their research found that even young children were aware of the many different adults in nurseries and found this generally helpful as long as there was a level of stability in staffing. If the split between the role of the teacher and support staff is becoming harder to identify, there may be implications for workforce remodelling and the opportunities and challenges this brings in terms of pay and career structure. This seems particularly important as if there are going to be more young children in early education, it will invariably lead to more staff due to the requirement for increased ratios. The needs and support required by 2-year-old children is also different to that of children 3 years and older. It could be argued that a response to many of these potential disadvantages could be addressed by the introduction of Early Years Professionals (EYPs). Since the introduction of EYP status in 2006, more than 9,000 have been trained and a further 2,000 are in training (Nutbrown, 2012). To achieve the qualification, trainees are required to follow a recognized course of training at degree level, and there is an aim to have an EYP in every day care setting by 2015. EYP status is seen as having equivalency to Qualified Teacher Status (QTS) standards (CWDC, 2007). Undoubtedly these roles, which encourage practitioners to enhance their skills, offer potential benefits, but to achieve the best from these policies careful evaluation will be needed to see how they benefit children, those pursuing the training and other practitioners who work in early years and school settings (Fitzgerald and Kay, 2008). However, the debate over this continues as it is still not clear how this role has equivalency in terms of status, pay or progression opportunities several years after being introduced. In addition, the EYP standards are currently being reviewed under the new Teaching Agency since the CWDC was disbanded in April 2012 (Nutbrown, 2012).

Parents have a pivotal role both within the family and when working in partnership with early years care and education settings. In addition, they are stakeholders in many policies impacting on early years education and care. When parents and practitioners work together, there can be significant benefits for them in terms of self-esteem and for children who see a unified approach between the home and setting. This can also help practitioners to have a greater understanding and respect for each family (Fitzgerald, 2012). The approach of the government to families is about providing opportunities for them to lift themselves out of poverty and break down barriers that lead to social exclusion. To achieve these aims, policies have been implemented to increase childcare provision, offer financial support to parents and provide more public funds for the education and care of young children (OECD, 2011). It is also important to analyse whether there are implicit assumptions within policies, based on idealized images or assumptions of the family. In the past, the government has championed marriage as the most stable environment for children to be raised in (Home Office, 1998), but many children flourish in non-traditional families (Patterson, 2006). Family relationships, the quality of parenting and levels of support are examples of important variables and show the potential negative impact of conveying certain types of families as second best (Roberts, 2001). Analysing the likelihood of policies to enhance these variables, rather than focusing on promoting one type of family structure above another, is clearly important.

Using past reports and service developments to appraise policy

The Children's Plan was published in 2007 by the DCSF. Although there has been a change of government, many of the broad objectives from the plan still align with the policy direction of the government. In addition, the five broad outcomes identified in ECM (2004) still form the cornerstone of child and family policy today.

Activity

Read through the overview of the Children's Plan and consider the following questions before reading this section:

- What are the potential positive impacts of the Children's Plan for children, parents and service providers?

- What are the potential negative impacts of the Children's Plan for children, parents and service providers?

- What evidence can be used to assess whether the targets set out in the Children's Plan have been achieved?

▸ What barriers may exist to achieving the targets set out in the Children's Plan and how could these be overcome?

▸ Are there any difficulties in accessing the overall impact of this national policy?

Children's Plan: Building brighter futures

The Plan, published at the end of 2007, outlines the government's strategy to further improve the lives of children and young people over the next 10 years. The Plan was developed through national consultation.

Key points:

The Plan was implemented by 2011 and proposed to:

▸ strengthen support for all families during the early years of their children's lives

▸ achieve 'world-class' schools and an excellent education for every child

▸ involve parents and carers fully in their children's learning

▸ provide more places for children to play safely.

This will be achieved through each of the outcomes of ECM as follows:

Be healthy

▸ A review of CAMHS will be carried out by the DCSF and NHS.

▸ A child health strategy will be published.

▸ An assessment of the impact of the commercial world on children's well-being will be undertaken.

Stay safe

▸ Local authorities will be encouraged to create more 20 mph. speed limit zones (particularly around play areas).

▸ Additional investment in new home safety equipment will be targeted at the most vulnerable families.

▸ A Staying Safe Action Plan will be published.

Enjoy and achieve

▸ There will be a rise in the entitlement to free nursery care for all 3- and 4-year-olds from 12 to 15 hours per week from 2010.

▸ Additional funding will ensure nurseries in the most disadvantaged areas have at least two graduates by 2015.

Continues

Continued

▶ There will be provision of support for continuing professional development for practitioners in educare settings.

▶ Free childcare for 12,000 2-year-olds from disadvantaged families will be made available.

▶ A review of the primary national curriculum with changes will be implemented from September 2011.

▶ There will be additional resources to support the development of early writing, reading and counting.

▶ 'Stage not age' testing will be implemented if the Making Good Progress trials evaluate successfully.

▶ There will be a move towards a Master's-level teaching workforce and support for developing leadership skills.

▶ There will be provision of up-to-date information for parents about their child's progress, attendance and behaviour.

▶ Additional investment will be sought to improve initial teacher training about special educational needs.

▶ A review into special education needs provision in 2009 will follow the review of language and communication that is taking place (Bercow Review).

▶ There will be new guidance for building to ensure that schools are central to their communities through the collocation of child health services, social care, advice, welfare services and police.

▶ There will be a build or upgrade of more than 3,500 playgrounds (an average of 23 per local authority) and a setting up of 30 supervised play areas for children over 8.

▶ There will be a new national play strategy.

Make a positive contribution

▶ Funding will be allocated over the three years to fund two new expert parenting advisers in every local authority.

▶ There will be an expansion of family learning.

▶ There will be support for young carers and delivery of new support for families with disabled children.

Achieve economic well-being

▶ An action plan will be produced to tackle housing overcrowding and to prioritize children's needs in housing decisions.

The principles of the Children's Plan and the emphasis it places on high-quality health, education and social experiences are vitally important for families and have the potential to have a significant positive impact on children's development (DCSF, 2007). Evidence to support this analysis can be drawn from research and evaluations of service provision. For example, findings from the EPPE project support the aims of the Children's Plan in terms of providing early years care and education for children and emphasize the need to ensure it is of high quality through the provision of a highly-skilled workforce (Sylva et al., 2004). The *Early Years Foundation Stage* (DfES, 2007a) and the *Key Elements of Effective Practice* (DfES/Sure Start, 2005) support many of the principles by emphasizing the need for equal and inclusive access for all children, the need to provide well-structured and appropriate play-based experiences, and the importance of working in partnership with parents. For families, particularly where there is only one adult in the household, strategies to make childcare more adaptable and affordable are likely to be beneficial. There are also wider implications for communities in terms of increased employment opportunities within the childcare workforce. A commitment to ensure there is appropriate training and ongoing support to ensure well-qualified and motivated staff is seemingly given. All in all, the policy sets out a number of ambitious plans that would seem to be welcome to all families with children.

However, the National Childcare Strategy (1998), which can be seen as the preceding overall approach to education and care, set out to improve the number of childcare places and accessibility but this did not result in a similar level of provision in all parts of the UK. The targeted approach of providing additional resources for deprived areas has two significant flaws: it adds to the already fragmented and confusing array of provision within early years and it wrongly assumes that the 20–30 per cent of most deprived families live in the corresponding 20–30 per cent most deprived areas. Some areas have a number of maintained settings, which often include trained teachers who can have a positive impact on overall levels of quality (Sylva et al., 2004). Other areas have a number of integrated Children's Centres, where parents are able to access a range of support services for members of the family. The government has recognized the importance of providing joined-up services with the announcement of the expansion of Children's Centres to one in every community (HM Treasury et al., 2004), but even with this, the majority of children will not receive early years care and education in this type of integrated provision (DCSF, 2008b). So have recent policy developments identified key improvements in this area? The commitment of the government to increase the number of funded places for 2-year-olds identifies that this is still an ongoing challenge. The Early Years Foundation Stage continues to support the aims but the Tickell review in 2011 has led to a vastly reduced number of Early Learning Goals in the revised statutory framework for children from 0–5 from September 2012 (DfE, 2012b). The Children and Families Bill making its passage through

Parliament in the 2012–13 session makes it clear that more joined-up working between health, social care and education for children and families remains elusive. In addition to more recent developments of past policy contributing, a potential difficulty with any national policy, however, is that it may propose similar responses for all families. But children and families are not a homogenous group and policies need to be able to take account of this. Ongoing funds also need to be available to deliver the service and to carry out a systematic evaluation of the benefits it brings (Ghate, 2001). The emphasis on children and families has certainly risen on the political agenda since 1997 and is likely to remain high, whichever party forms the government, but *more* provision does not necessarily equate to *better* provision. To be clear, if there are benefits to increased provision, Ghate (2001) argues for the importance of systematic evaluation that includes the views of service users and providers. In addition, as the number of Children's Centres grows, they are likely to develop in different ways, and a policy concentrating on increased provision does not automatically equate with increased quality.

Perhaps the most fundamental question that policies need to address is 'What works for children?' The Treasury response to this during the 2000s was to impose a number of public service agreements on departments to ensure there were clear accountability measures in place. For example, Sure Start, which has the aim of improving health and well-being and lifting families out of poverty, attracted large amounts of funding to help meet the targets set out in the National Childcare Strategy, many of which are reiterated in the Children's Plan. The Plan also assumes that all families will prefer to access early years care and education rather than care for their child at home. Some families may decide that caring for their child at home is their preferred option but there is far less support available for this choice. This may result in some families, perhaps because of lower income levels, feeling they have no choice but to return to work, as they are not able to manage financially.

To assess the targets set out in government policy for children and families, a range of evidence could be used. Government statistics about the number of early years care and education places, levels of poverty and the average cost of childcare could help to make an assessment. Reports from the Early Years Directorate of Ofsted can look at quality in specific settings and more generally across the sector. Information from evaluations and early years organizations could also be useful. For example, the OECD highlighted how early years care and education provision has improved but families still face a range of logistical difficulties in accessing provision because it is often provided in different locations, at times that may not fit work patterns and at unaffordable cost (OECD, 2011; Truss, 2012). Although this relates to past provision, older evidence can be useful as, when contrasted with more recent evidence, it helps to evaluate the success of a policy over time rather than making a simple judgement that there has been either a complete success or complete failure. The content of provision can also be assessed for quality. It could be argued that a positive development for the early years care and education sector was the introduction of *Birth to Three Matters* (for children from birth to 3) (Sure Start Unit, 2002) and the *Curriculum Guidance for the Foundation Stage* (for children aged 3–6) (QCA/DfEE, 2000), which both take account of the developmental needs of young children and promote an appropriate curriculum. In contrast, the introduction of these two separate curriculum documents and the formal approach of the Key Stage 1 curriculum could be seen as adding to, rather than reducing, the fragmentation of the sector. An alternative response to this could have been to introduce one curriculum that addressed the developmental needs and well-being of children in the early years, similar to the approach being developed in Wales. This also offers a potential comparison with which to analyse the English system (Welsh Assembly, 2004). This has been partially addressed through the combining of the two curricula for children aged 0–5 but there is still a divide between the early years curriculum and Key Stage 1 in England. Contrasting past developments with recent developments demonstrates how evidence over a period of time can help to make a detailed analysis of progress to date and identify, with the support of evidence, where further development could be beneficial.

Overall, there have been benefits that are the direct result of the Children's Plan although it can be difficult to accurately assess these. For example, since 2000 there has been a reduction in child poverty, fewer deaths of children due to injury, lower levels of infant and child mortality and an increase in the number of infants being breast-fed. Alongside this, there has been a rise in childhood obesity, increased levels of asthma and diabetes and a reduction in the number of children being immunized against measles (Bradshaw, 2002; Eisenstadt, 2011). Within different communities, there may have been a number of policies operating, such as Sure Start, neighbourhood renewal initiatives, educational projects, New Deal, Health Action Zones, Primary National Strategy and the Healthy Schools Initiative, which can make it difficult to attribute change to one specific policy. This is discussed by Kurtz in relation to conflicting evidence between policies that aim to reduce social exclusion and the different explanations that can be linked to rises in specific disorders, which 'indicates the complexities in interpreting the relationship between overall national trends in health indicators and policy initiatives' (2003: 176). Although health measures do not relate directly to the Children's Plan, they do clearly highlight the need for caution in attributing specific change to one national policy without the evidence to link outcomes with implementation initiatives. Based on this, it could also be argued that an analysis of any national policy, especially in terms of assessing whether targets have been achieved, is best undertaken through local evaluations that are more able to identify specific benefits and disadvantages in the context of the range of policy initiatives that are likely to be in place.

Approaches to analyse policy: evaluative themes

A range of questions can be asked to promote the analysis of policy. Dowling (1999) suggests that commitment to early years care and education can be seen in terms of four broad themes: insufficiency, diversity, lack of resources and commitment. To analyse the impact of policy, questions can be asked that relate to the level of commitment in terms of provision and resources to implement policy plans at a regional and local level. They can relate to how likely policies are to lead to integrated, high-quality provision for each child and family. This approach to analysing policy can be applied at different levels, for example to evaluate a broad government policy (for example, the EYFS, 2012) or the implementation of policy within a setting (for example, the Special Educational Needs Code of Practice in a nursery setting).

The framework suggests a number of questions in different areas that could be applied to evaluate policy. It is unlikely, and perhaps unnecessary, that all of the questions would be applied to one policy. Decisions will need to be made about what is being evaluated and the purpose of the analysis. If it is for an essay, which is aiming to contrast the approach of central governments pre- and post-1997/2010 to early years care and education, it is likely that a number of commitment and resource questions will be raised. If the aim is to evaluate the level of participation of families and children in issues that affect them in their nursery, the focus may be on questions drawn from the diversity section.

The following questions are not meant to be seen as a definitive response to achieving a comprehensive analysis of policy. They could be seen as offering a starting point to promote in-depth analysis, as a stimulus to add a critical dimension to analysing policies, or as a vehicle to promote critical discussion of specific issues. If the aim is to offer a broad overview, it may be useful to include discussion of questions from each section. For a more in-depth analysis of an aspect of policy, questions may be drawn mainly from one area. It is also likely that the initial questions asked would do two things: provide answers and raise more questions.

Commitment

- ▶ Is there clear leadership at national, regional and local levels?

- ▶ Is there a commitment to integrated services and strategies in place to achieve this?

- ▶ Is there evidence of commitment across central departments and professions to developing integrated services for children and families?

▸ Are messages from research being integrated into policy and practice to raise the quality of early years care and education services?

▸ Is there a commitment to increase the level and quality of early years care and education services?

▸ Is there a commitment to promoting the involvement of children and families in service planning and evaluation?

Insufficiency

▸ Does the level of provision match demand in all areas of the UK?

▸ Are there sufficient early years care and education places for all children who require them?

▸ Are there differences between urban and rural locations?

▸ Does the timing of provision match the needs of children and families?

▸ Are there an adequate number of practitioners with appropriate qualifications?

▸ Are there policies/plans in place to overcome any gaps in insufficiency?

Resources

▸ Does the level of resources from central government recognize and allow the development of the early years care and education sector?

▸ How are resources being allocated and shared at a local level?

▸ Are resources being increased over time to allow the development of early years care and education provision?

▸ Are resources sustainable in the long term, particularly outside the maintained sector?

▸ Are resources appropriate to the requirements of service users?

Diversity

▸ Does the range of provision meet the diverse requirements of children and families?

▸ Do all children and families have equal access to provision?

▸ What support and training are available to practitioners to ensure they have the skills to respond to all children and families?

▸ Do policies value and promote the integration of each child and family?

▸ Are providers aware of the diversity of family structures and do they respond to this appropriately?

▸ Are the voices of each child and family heard equally?

International evidence

As detailed in Chapter 6, several countries now have policy initiatives similar to those of the UK, which are aimed at providing services that respond to the requirements of children and families, particularly those with lower income levels. Another similarity of many of these countries with the UK is the emphasis on preventative responses which address all aspects of support that families may need through the provision of joined-up services (OECD, 2011). This evidence can provide another approach to analysing the likely impact of UK policy and providing a forum to debate the potential impacts of approaches that are similar to those in other countries.

In the USA, there has been an increase in both the number of children using day care facilities and the duration of time they spend there. In response to this, the issue of quality has arisen, but in the absence of a national plan, such as Every Child Matters, individual states have responded in different ways. But evidence of the importance of high-quality environments from the USA is very similar to the UK: the higher the quality of the setting, the better the cognitive, linguistic and social outcomes for children. High-quality indicators include high child/staff ratios, higher levels of qualified staff, knowledge of child development and positive interactions between staff and children. In contrast, research shows that most aspects of provision were of medium to poor quality (Grisham Brown and Hallam, 2004). An important message from this is that just because it is known what contributes to good quality, it cannot be assumed that this will be evident in day-to-day practice. The direction can be set out in policy documents but it will then require substantial effort to embed the principles of the policy into practice. Another message to come out of the evaluation was the importance of consulting day care providers to get an accurate reflection of early care and education initiatives (Grisham Brown and Hallam, 2004). Questions can be asked about how this compares with the UK and may suggest that revisions to quality assurance processes and evaluations are needed to take more account of the views of practitioners. Another contributing factor to quality, possibly the most significant, is the skills, knowledge and experience of the workforce. This is clearly recognized by the government as the Children's Plan contains a number of initiatives aimed at raising the skill base and career development opportunities of the workforce. In a number of countries, particularly across Europe, there are a significant number of pedagogues who are generally trained to graduate level, have both rhetorical and practical training combined, and work throughout a range of child and family services (OECD, 2006, 2011). Initially, it may seem that this evidence would not be useful to help evaluate planned workforce developments in parts of the UK. However, it can offer a platform to compare the similarities and differences that this may have with similar roles in the UK (such as Early Years Professionals or Children's Centre Leaders), which could provide evidence to form a position on how successful ongoing or planned policy developments will prove.

In Australia, the development of early childhood services has followed a similar path to that of the UK. There has been a heavy educational focus on policy and varied initiatives have caused an arbitrary division between caring and teaching. This has led to differences in levels of training, qualifications and philosophies underpinning service provision, which in many respects remain evident. Kindergarten provision, which children usually access the year before school, is seen to be good and has an educational focus. In contrast, childcare and day care is seen to be aimed at the socially disadvantaged and about meeting the health and safety needs of children (Jillian, 1996). Evidence of this arbitrary division and the unsystematic development of early years services mirrors the historical development of UK services and provides comparisons to analyse the potential impact for current policies to move to less fragmented and more integrated early years services. The levels of early years care and education offered in Australia also have some similarities with the targeted approach of providing Sure Start local projects in England, which may result in less advantaged communities feeling stigmatized and raises questions about the need for a national childcare policy that leads to national levels of provision. What is clear, though, from international evidence is that a long-term policy commitment, backed by appropriate funding, will be necessary to bring about sustainable improvements in early years care and education in the UK, and this may not always sit easily alongside the quick-fix approach to societal issues (Vimpani, 2002).

International evidence can be useful for analysing approaches to child and family policy in the UK. Glass (2001) argues that caution needs to be applied if there is an unquestioned assumption that what works in other countries can be directly applied in UK contexts. In addition, there are differences within many aspects of policy between the countries of the UK and this was discussed in Chapter 5. There are likely to be aspects of policy, such as service design and raising the quality of early years care and education provision, that will work, but others may not. Any analysis of policy should consider this and ask what aspects of policy are transferable and what may be culture dependent. For example, the approach to funding in the USA is very different to that in the UK and introducing a policy that works well there may not achieve the same outcomes here. When using international evidence to appraise UK policy, as well as asking 'what works?', Glass (2001) suggests there is another fundamental question that needs to be considered: what is worth doing for children? This question is as valid today when appraising policy as it was in 2001.

Summary ☐

- ▶ Analysing policy is a complex process, particularly in the area of early years as policies have become increasingly complex.

- ▶ Nonetheless, it is important to be able to make an appraisal of the broad issues and how they are likely to impact on the various stakeholders (including those whom polices are intended to have an impact on and those who may be affected indirectly).

- ▶ The inclusion of targets in policies may not reflect achievable results, as evidenced by subsequent policies (e.g. contrasting the targets in the Children's plan with recent government intentions for early education provision.

- ▶ To assist readers with this process, the chapter has suggested a number of approaches that can be helpful. They are by no means the only ways to undertake analysis of policy but it is hoped that they provide a starting point and may generate other ideas. The approaches outlined include:

  - measuring the effectiveness of policies according to outcomes (for example, how many additional childcare places have been created and how long these have been sustained for)

  - assessing the ability of a policy to represent the perspective of different stakeholders, particularly children who may not be empowered through policy

  - a comparison with past developments and evaluation reports

  - assessing the approach of policy against research evidence (for example, examining whether the pedagogical approach of early years curricula is developmentally appropriate for young children)

  - evaluating policy against a range of themes, including the level of commitment from government and policy-makers, the level of resources allocated to implementation and sustainability and the ability of the policy to respond to the diversity of stakeholders

  - comparison with international approaches and evidence, but with attention to the level of transferability within the context of the UK and the policy approach in operation

  - the ability to accurately measure gains and to what extent they can be attributed to a policy.

Further reading

One of the best ways to feel more confident with evaluating policy is to read widely to gain an understanding of how authors have approached it. An approach to evaluating early years policy can be informed by reading magazines such as *Community Care* and newspapers such as *The Guardian* and *The Independent*, all of which can also be found online.

Roberts, M. (2001) 'Childcare policy', in P. Foley, J. Roche and S. Tucker (eds), *Children in Society: Contemporary Theory, Policy and Practice*, Basingstoke: Palgrave.

Provides a useful overview of how the international context, through the UNCRC, has had an increasingly significant impact on policy design and implementation in the UK. Any evaluation of UK policy will need to take account of this.

Another important consideration is how well the views of children are taken account of in policy design and implementation. There is a general consensus that children are now more involved but this may not always be the case.

Tisdall, E.K.M. and Davis, J. (2004) 'Making a difference? Bringing children's and young people's views into policy making', *Children and Society*, 18(2): 131–42.

Discusses a range of issues around the involvement of children and considers at what stages their views are taken account of and, most importantly, the impact that this involvement has.

Finally, the most significant challenge for any policy is translating into practice the aspirations it outlines. This is relevant to the majority of policies within child and family services, particularly in the way services are organized and the implications this has for practitioners. In response to this, the following text discusses the impact of a range of early years policies on the workforce and the challenges this poses for service organization, training and development and working practices. See Fitzgerald, D. and Kay, J. (2008) *Working Together in Children's Services*, Oxford: Routledge.

Chapter 9

Conclusion

In this third edition, we have discussed what early years policy is, how it has developed over time, what influences the development of policy has had and how it is implemented, evaluated and analysed. The development of early years policy has been particularly prolific since 1997 when early years issues became central to the then government agenda. Since the election of the Coalition government in 2010, the broad direction of travel has some similarities. However, a significant development has been the number of reviews that have been completed or implemented and the gradual move to more targeted rather than universal provision, such as Sure Start Children's Centres. The results of these reviews are beginning to emerge, for example in the publication of the newly revised *EYFS Statutory Framework* (2012); the establishment of new executive bodies to administer aspects of provision and direct further development; and extend the remit of the role of the Children's Commissioner for England to align the powers more with commissioners in other parts of the UK. This has posed challenges in the study of early years in terms of understanding the range and complexity of policies affecting young children and their families. This emphasis on early years policy will clearly continue into the future as the Coalition parties and Labour have all placed children and families firmly at the centre of their agendas. Recent developments in policy affecting young children are the most radical for over 30 years and over the past two years the pace of change has quickened, involving wide-ranging changes to structure and practice in children's services. The impact of these developments on service provision is likely to be significant for years to come.

A complex range of factors, which combine to create change, influences policy development. These include historical influences, the perceived effectiveness of existing policy and the impact of lobbying by statutory and voluntary sector children's organizations and the impact of a coalition administration. However, the key factor is the perceived importance of early years issues for the government of the day. This in turn is influenced by many interrelated factors, including meeting wider policy commitments, the role of individual ministers and senior civil servants, and the relationship between key figures in government and the early years sector.

Conclusion

Implementing policy at national and local government levels involves legislating for some areas of policy, disseminating information and guidance, and a comprehensive debate about how policy will work at ground level. The shape of policy is confirmed through these processes and the extent to which there is agreement between policy-makers and those delivering policy at service level. Modern policy-making is based on principles that should produce robust, effective developments that are informed by research evidence and lessons from the past. However, recent policies influencing early years have been large and complex and what exactly the eventual outcomes for children, families and practitioners will be remains unclear. Policy direction has also started to be impacted on by the government's intention to reduce the large budget deficit, and initial evidence suggests that policy decisions based primarily on financial need may be contradictory to the evidence of best practice or outcomes.

As the complexity of policy has increased, it has become important when evaluating policy to consider the impact it has on the various stakeholders. For example, policies may have differing impacts on parents and children. A policy to support parents returning to work may improve their employability and income but result in children spending longer in day care. Similarly, policies that have led to significant expansion in the provision of early years services have not, so far, led to increased access to training for all practitioners, recognition of their skills and experience and the implementation of a systematic career framework to promote progression. Nonetheless, as highlighted, there are potentially plans in place to address some of these issues, which emphasize the need for ongoing evaluation.

The remit of this third edition is to help readers understand their own role in policy development as practitioners, employees and members of children's organizations. Policy is the product of human activity and as such can be influenced by those involved. As stated in Chapter 1, practitioners need to understand policy in terms of how it determines their roles and responsibilities, the structures and policies of their workplaces, and the quality of service provision to children and families. Throughout the book, the content and activities have provided a basis to help the reader engage with the complexity of policy-making, implementation and evaluation across the UK. Chapter 5 deals with the current similarities and differences between policy in the UK countries. Chapter 6 presents a basis for evaluating UK policy by drawing on international examples and evidence. However, as policy develops continually, it is very important to develop strategies for keeping up to date with new initiatives. This third edition provides you with a range of tools to understand and evaluate policy, but keeping up to date is your responsibility.

Glossary

This glossary contains explanations of terms that may not be familiar to the reader. Terms which are used in the text but fully explained or discussed so their meaning is clear are not included.

Area Child Protection Committee (ACPC): a multi-agency committee established in every local authority to determine local policy and oversee child protection processes. ACPCs have been replaced by **Local Safeguarding Children Boards**, which are statutory bodies introduced by the Children Act 2004.

Birth to Three Matters: a framework of effective practice for those working with children aged birth to 3 issued by the Department for Education and Skills (DfES). This was replaced by the **Early Years Foundation Stage** (birth to 6 years) in 2008.

Children's Centre: there is a centre based in each of the 20 per cent most disadvantaged wards in England. There were approximately 3,600 in 2010 although the numbers have fallen recently. Children's Centres provide early education integrated with full day care, identification of and provision for children with special educational needs and disabilities, parental outreach, family support, and health services, among other services.

Children's Trust: a multi-agency body established to ensure that joint planning and implementation of plans for children and young people within local authorities are effective. The philosophy of Children's Trusts is underpinned by the Children Act 2004 duty to cooperate and to focus on improving outcomes for all children and young people.

Children's Workforce Development Council (CWDC): a body set up to promote the development and integration of the children's workforce. The body was disbanded in 2012 and its work was split between the Teaching Agency and the Department for Education.

Civil Service: in Great Britain, the Civil Service helps the government of the UK, the Scottish Executive and the National Assembly for Wales formulate their policies, carry out decisions and administer public services for which they are responsible. Civil servants are servants of the Crown, meaning the government of the UK, the Scottish Executive and the National Assembly for Wales.

Curriculum Guidance for the Foundation Stage: statutory guidance for early years practitioners in the Foundation Stage (3–5 years) on developing a curriculum to support teaching and learning towards the Early Learning Goals. This was replaced by the **Early Years Foundation Stage** (birth to 6 years) in 2008 and this was updated again in 2012.

Daycare Trust: a national childcare charity established in 1980, campaigning for high-quality affordable childcare for all.

Desirable Learning Outcomes: learning goals that set out what children should have achieved by the time they enter compulsory education. These were replaced by the **Early Learning Goals**.

Early Excellence Centre: an early years setting that has been highlighted as offering a level of excellence. These became rebranded as Children's Centres.

Early Intervention: early recognition and assessment of additional needs.

Early Learning Goals: the basis of the Foundation Stage curriculum in any early years setting in England.

Early Years Foundation Stage: the statutory curriculum for children from birth to 6 years.

Early Years Professional Status (EYPS): a graduate status that can be achieved by following one of the recognized training or validation pathways to demonstrate a range of skills and attributes. EYPS is seen as having equivalence with Qualified Teacher Status.

Early Years Professional (EYP): the aim of the Early Years Professional is to lead effective high-quality practice in the early years sector. The government's aim is to have at least one EYP in every early years setting by 2015.

Education and Healthcare Plan (EHCP): the outcome of a multi-professional assessment for children with SEN and/or disabilities.

Foundation Stage: the curriculum in England, for children from birth to 6 years (see **Early Years Foundation Stage**).

Local Government Association (LGA): formed in 1997 to represent the 500 local authorities of England and Wales and to promote better local government.

Local Safeguarding Children Board: a multi-disciplinary statutory body responsible for child protection issues in each local authority (see **Area Child Protection Committee**).

National Childminding Association (NCMA): promotes and supports quality childminding expertise, provides information for parents looking for childminders, and provides information and news updates for childminders.

Office for Standards in Education (Ofsted): a non-ministerial government department established under the Education (Schools) Act 1992, Ofsted has expanded over time and now takes responsibility for the inspection of all schools, LAs, teacher training institutions, youth work, colleges, and early years childcare and education provision in England.

Pre-school Learning Alliance (PLA): an educational charity that represents and supports 15,000 community pre-schools in England.

Primary Care Trusts: 302 free-standing statutory bodies that controlled local health care and received their budgets directly from the Department of Health. These organizations were disbanded in 2012.

Private sector: refers to the business or profit-making sector providing services in the early years, such as private day nurseries and childminders.

Public sector: refers to the local or central government sector providing services in the early years, such as schools.

Standard assessment tests (SATS): are completed at the end of Key Stages 1, 2 and 3 to assess progress in the core subjects of the National Curriculum. At Key Stage 1, they now take a less formal style, with schools having a choice of when pupils complete the assessment tasks. They are also referred to as National Curriculum tests.

Sure Start local programme: an area-based initiative with the aim of improving the health and well-being of families and children from before birth to age 4. There were 524 such programmes in neighbourhoods where a high proportion of children lived in poverty. The majority have now been transformed into **Children's Centres**.

Sure Start Unit: part of the Children, Young People and Families Directorate in the Department for Children, Schools and Families (DCSF), working with a wide range of other agencies to develop services for children and families in line with government policy, including services to socially excluded children and families.

Teaching Agency: an executive agency of the DfE. It is responsible for supply and, with others, retention of the workforce; the quality of the workforce; and regulation of teacher conduct.

Universal services: available to all in a stated category (not means-tested), for example primary education is available to all families with children.

Voluntary sector: non-government or profit-making charitable or voluntary organizations such as the NSPCC and Barnardo's.

References

Allen, G. MP (2011) *Early Intervention: The Next Steps.* Available at /www.dwp.gov.uk/docs/early-intervention-next-steps.pdf (accessed 29 May 2012).

Abbott, L. (2002) *Birth to Three Matters: A Framework to Support Children in their Earliest Years*, London: DfES.

Adams, D. and Swadener, B.B. (2010) 'Early childhood education and teacher development in Kenya: lessons learned', *Child and Youth Care Forum* 29(6): 385–402.

Algava, É. and Rualt, M. (2003) *Les assistants maternelles: une profession en développement: Études et Résultats No.232*, Paris: DREES.

Anning, A. (2004) 'The co-construction of an early childhood curriculum', in A. Anning, J. Cullen and M. Fleer (eds), *Early Childhood Education: Society and Culture*, London: Sage.

Arnold, R. (2005) *Early Years Childcare and Education – the Sure Start Agenda: the Beacon Council Scheme Round 5*, Windsor: NFER.

Artiles, A. and Dyson, A. (2005) 'Inclusive education in the globalisation age', in D. Mitchell (ed.), *Contextualising Inclusive Education: Evaluating Old and New International Perspectives*, London: Routledge.

Ashrof, H. (2005) 'The bigger picture on the Children Act, 2004', *Community Care.* Available at www.communitycare.co.uk/articles/article/asp?/liarticleid=47713&lisectionID=22&skeys='BiggerPicture'+Children+Act&liParentID=26 (accessed 17 January 2008).

Association of Directors of Social Services (ADSS) (2005) *Consultation on Draft Statutory Guidance on the Role and Responsibilities of the Director of Children's Services and Lead Member for Children's Services.* Available at: www.adss.org.uk/publications/consresp/2005/children.shtml (accessed 20 March 2005).

Aubrey, C. (2004) 'Implementing the foundation stage in reception classrooms', *British Educational Research Journal*, 30(5): 633–56.

Audit Commission (2002) *Statuatory Assessment and Statements of SEN: In Need of Review?* London: TSO.

Baldock, P. (2011) *Developing Early Childhood Services: Past Present and Future*, Maidenhead: Open University Press.

Barnardos (2003) *'Green Paper* "Every Child Matters"', 8 September. Available at: www.barnardos.org.uk/newsandevents/media/press/release.jsp?id=1153 (accessed 1 March 2005).

Baudelot, O. and Rayna, S. (2000) *Coordinateurs et coordination de la petite enfance dans les communes: Actes du colloque du Créas*, Paris: Institut national de recherche pédagogique.

BBC (2008a) 'Child protection plans "failing"', BBC News channel, 22 January. Available at: http://news.bbc.co.uk/1/hi/programmes/file_on_4/7200217.stm (accessed 30 July 2008).

BBC (2008b) 'Call to scrap children's database', BBC News channel, 21 February. Available at: http://news.bbc.co.uk/1/hi/uk_politics/ 7256972.stm (accessed 7 July 2008).

Bell, A. and La Valle, I. (2005) *Early Stages of the Neighbourhood Nurseries Initiative: Parents' Experiences*, London: DFES/Sure Start Unit.

Berlinski, S., Galiani, S. and Manacorda, M. (2006) 'Giving children a better start: Pre-school attendance and school-age profiles: Uruguay study shows advantages of pre-school education', *Journal of Public Economics*, 92(5–6): 1416–40.

Bilton, H. (1998) *Outdoor Play in the Early Years: Management and Innovation*, London: David Fulton.

Bingham, J. (2012) '"Baby P panic" helped save thousands of children figures show – but care lottery continues', *The Telegraph*, 29 May.

Blair. T. (1996) *New Britain: My Vision of a Young Country*, London: Fourth Estate Ltd.

Blunkett, D. (2006) *The Blunkett Tapes: My Life in the Bear Pit*, London: Bloomsbury.

Bosire, B. (2006) 'Playing Under the Fig Trees in Kenya', *UNESCO Courier: Learning is Child's Play* October 2006.

Bradshaw, J. (ed.) (2002) *The Well-being of Children in the UK*, London: University of York and Save the Children.

Brandon, M., Howe, A., Dagley, V., Salter, C., Warren, C., Black, J. (2006) 'Evaluating the common assessment framework and lead professional guidance and implementation in 2005–6'. DfES Research Report RR740, University of East Anglia.

Brannen, J. and Moss, P. (eds) (2003) *Rethinking Children's Care*, Buckingham: Open University Press.

Brehony, K.J. (2000) 'The kindergarten in England 1851–1918', in R. Wollons (ed.), *Kindergarten and Cultures: The Global Diffusion of an Idea*, London: Yale University Press, 59–86.

References

Brind, R., Norden, O., McGinigal, S., Garnett, E., Oseman, D., La Valle, I. and Jelicic, H. (2011) *Childcare and Early Years Providers,* London: DfE.

Bromley, C., Curtice, J., McCrone, D. and Park, A. (eds) (2006) *Has Devolution Delivered?* Edinburgh: Edinburgh University Press.

Bruce, T. (2001) 'The north and south divided', *Nursery World*, 12 July: 34.

Cafcass (2012) *Three Weeks in November … .Three Years On … Cafcass Care Application Study 2012.* Available at: www.cafcass.gov.uk/pdf/Cafcass%20Care%20Application%20Study%202012%20FINAL.pdf (accessed 29 May 2012).

Carter, C, Janmohammed, Z., Zhang, J. and Bertrand, J. (2007) *Selected issues concerning early childhood care and education in China: Background paper for the Education for All Global Monitoring Report – 'Strong Foundation: Early Childhood Care and Education'*, Paris: UNESCO.

Children's Workforce Development Council (CWDC) (2007) *Prospectus: Early Years Professional Status.*

CiNI (2010) DE (0-6) *Early Years Strategy Briefing Paper.* Available at: http://cini.killercontent.net/media/cb3d218ce0174d05ac5de922dce9aae4CiNI%20Briefing%20Paper%2015.09.10.pdf (accessed 21 May 2012).

Clark, M.M. and Waller, T. (eds) (2007) *Early Childhood Education and Care: Policy and Practice*, London: Sage.

Cleaver, H., Barnes, J., Bliss, D. and Cleaver, D. (2004) *Developing Information Sharing and Assessment Systems*. Nottingham: DfES Publications.

Close, P. and Wainwright, J. (2010) 'Who's in charge? Leadership and culture in extended service contexts', *School Leadership and Management*, 30(5): 435–50.

Comenius, J.A. (1956) *The School of Infancy* (ed. E.M. Miller), Chapel Hill, NC: University of North Carolina Press.

Community Care (2004) 'Hearts and minds reluctantly follow as bill finally completes passage', 1549, 18 November: 18–19.

Community Care (2005) 'A clash of cultures?', 1660, 17 February: 4.

CPAG (2012) *Poverty in the UK: A Summary of Facts and Figures.* Available at: www.cpag.org.uk/povertyfacts/index.htm (accessed 29 May 2012).

Croll, P. and Moses, D. (2000) *Special Needs in the Primary School: One in Five?*, London: Continuum.

Curriculum Development Institute (1996) *Guide to the Pre-Primary Curriculum*, Hong Kong: Education Department.

Dawson, H. (2004) 'The Children Act obstacle course', *Community Care*, 1552, 9 December: 24.

Daycare Trust (2005) 'Childcare and early years services in 2004', paper 1 of *A New Era for Universal Childcare?* Available at: daycaretrust.org.uk (accessed 15 March 2012).

Deloitte and Touche (2008) *Contact Point Data Security Review Executive Summary*, London: DCFS. Available at: www.parliament.uk/deposits/depositedpapers/2008/DEP2008–0502.pdf (accessed on 15 March).

Department for Children, Schools and Families (DCSF) (2007) *The Children's Plan: Building Brighter Futures*, Norwich: The Stationery Office.

Department for Children, Schools and Families (DCSF) (2008a) *Graduate Leader Fund: Further Information on Purpose and Implementation*. Available at: www.everychildmatters.gov.uk/earlyyearsworkforce/ (accessed 2 July 2008).

Department for Children, Schools and Families (DCSF) (2008b) *Building Brighter Futures: Next Steps for the Children's Workforce*. DCSF: Nottingham.

Department for Education (DfE) (2011a) *Childcare and Early Years Provider Survey 2010 (OSR17/2011)*, London: HMSO.

Department for Education (DfE) (2011b) *Special Educational Needs in England: January 2011*. Available at: www.education.gov.uk/rsgateway/DB/SFR/s001007/index.shtml (accessed 29 May 2012).

Department for Education (DfE) (2011c) *Support and Aspiration: A New Approach to Special Educational Needs and Disability – Progress and Next Steps*, London: DfE.

Department for Education (DfE) (2012a) *Families in the Foundation Years*. Available at: http://www.education.gov.uk/home/childrenandyoungpeople/earlylearningandchildcare/ (accessed August 2012).

Department for Education (DfE) (2012b) *Statutory Framework for Early Years Foundation Stage* (EYFS), The Stationery Office: London.

Department for Education and Employment (DfEE) (1997) *Excellence for All Children – Meeting Special Educational Needs*. Available at: http://www.achieveability.org.uk/files/1270740065/dfes-excellence-for-all-children-2001.pdf. (accessed 20 August 2012:

Department for Education and Employment (DfEE) (1998) *Meeting the Childcare Challenge: A Framework and Consultation Document*, London: HMSO.

DfEC (1993) *The Special Educational Needs Codes of Practice*, London: TSO.

Department of Education Northern Ireland (DENI) (2010), *Early Years 0–6 Strategy*, DENI. Available at: www.deni.gov.uk/english__early_years_strategy_.pdf.pdf (accessed 1 May 2012).

Department for Education and Skills (DfES) (2001b) *Special Educational Needs Code of Practice*, London: TSO.

Department for Education and Skills (DfES) (2003) *Every Child Matters* (Green Paper), London: HMSO.

Department for Education and Skills (DfES) (2004) *Removing Barriers to Achievement: The Government's Strategy for SEN*. Available at:

References

https://www.education.gov.uk/publications/standard/publicationDetail/Page1/DfES%200117%202004 (accessed August 2012).

Department for Education and Skills (DfES) (2004a) *Every Child Matters: Next Steps*, London: DfES.

Department for Education and Skills (DfES) (2004b) *Every Child Matters: Change for Children*, London: HMSO.

Department for Education and Skills (DfES) (2006) *Sure Start Children's Centres: Planning and Performance Management Guidance*. Available at: http://publications.everychildmatters.gov.uk/eOrderingDownload/ SSCC-PERFORM2006.pdf (accessed 30 June 2008).

Department for Education and Skills (DfES) (2007a) *Statutory Framework for the Early Years Foundation Stage*, Nottingham: DfES.

Department for Education and Skills (DfES)/Department of Health (DoH) (2003) *Together from the Start: practical guidance for professionals working with disabled children (birth to third birthday) and their families*, [LEA/0067/2003], Nottingham: DfES.

Department for Education and Skills (DfES)/Department for Health (DoH) (2004) *Children's Trusts*. Available at: www.dfes.gov.uk/childrenstrusts/ (accessed 1 December 2004)

Department for Education and Skills/Local Government Association (DfES/LGA) (2001) *Childcare and Early Education: Investing in All Our Futures*, London: DfES.

Department for Education and Skills (DfES)/SureStart (2005) *Primary National Strategy: Key Elements of Effective Practice*, Norwich: HMSO.

Department of Education and Science (DES) (1967) *Children and Their Primary Schools* (Plowden Report), London: HMSO.

Department of Education and Science (DES) (1990) *Starting with Quality: Report of the Committee of Inquiry into the Educational Experiences Offered to Three and Four Year Olds* (Rumbold Report), London: HMSO.

Department of Health (1991) *The Children Act 1989: Guidance and Regulations. Volume 2: Family Support, Day Care and Educational Provision for Young Children*, London: HMSO.

Department of Health (1998) *Quality Protects: Framework for Action*, London: Department of Health.

Department of Health/Department for Education and Skills (DfES) (2004) *National Service Framework for Children, Young People and Maternity Services: Executive Summary*, London: Department of Health/DfES.

Department of Health/Welsh Office (1997) *People Like Us: the Report of the Review of Safeguards for Children Living Away from Home (Utting Report)*, London: HMSO.

Department of Trade and Industry (DTI) (2004) *Work–Life Balance and Flexible Working: The Business Case.* Available at: www.dti.gov.uk/bestpractice /assets/wlb.pdf (accessed 1 March 2005).

Department of Trade and Industry (DTI) (2005) *Work and Families: Choice and Flexibility.* Available at: www.dti.gov.uk/er/ workandfamilies.htm (accessed 1 March 2005).

Devroye, J. (2009) 'The case of D.H. and others v. the Czech Republic', *Northwestern Journal of International Human Rights* 7(1), 81–101.

Diemet, L. (2009) *Childcare Legislation in the Netherlands*, paper delivered at seminar in London organised by the International Centre for the Study of the Mixed Economy of Childcare.

Direction de la recherche, des etudes, de l'évaluation et des statistiques (2002) *Enquète: Modes de garde et d'acceuil des enfants de moins de 7 ans*, Paris: DREES.

Dowling, M. (1999) 'Early years: then, now and next', *Education 3–13*, 27(3): 5–10.

Dunford, J. (2010) *Review of the Office of the Children's Commissioner (England)*, London: The Stationery Office.

Dutch.News (2010) 'Private equity looks to childcare investments', www.DutchNews.nl. (accessed 2 March 2011).

Dwork, D. (1987) *War is Good for babies and Other Young Children: A History of the Infant and Child Welfare Movement in England 1989–1918*, London: Tavistock.

Dyson, A. (2005) 'Philosophy, politics and economics? The story of inclusive education in England', in D. Mitchell (ed.), *Contextualising Inclusive Education – Evaluating Old and New International Perspectives*, London: Routledge.

Easton, C., Gee, G., Durbin, B. and Teeman, D. (2011) *Early Intervention, Using the CAF Process, and its Cost-effectiveness: Findings from LARC 3*, National Foundation for Education Research. Available at: www.nfer.ac.uk/nfer/publi-cations/LGLCO1/LGLCO1.pdf.

Education Scotland (2012) *The purpose of the curriculum.* Available at: http://www.educationscotland.gov.uk/thecurriculum/whatiscurriculumforex-cellence/thepurposeofthecurriculum/index.asp (accessed 21 May 2012).

Eisenstadt, N. (2011) *Providing a Sure Start: How Government Discovered Early Childhood*, Bristol: The Policy Press.

Elliott, F. (2007) 'Safety fears over new register of all children', *The Times*, 27 August.

End Child Poverty (2005) *Key Facts.* Available at: www.ecpc.org.uk/keyfacts.asp (accessed 10 March 2005).

References

End Child Poverty (2011) *Empty Strategy Leaves Families in Growing Hardship, 5 Apr, 2011*. Available at: www.endchildpoverty.org.uk/news/news/empty-strategy-leaves-families-in-growing-hardship/23/189 (accessed 29 May 2012).

European Commission on Employment, Social Affairs and Equal Opportunities (2008) *Implementation of the Barcelona objectives concerning childcare facilities for pre-school-age children*, Brussels: ECESAEO.

Every Child Matters (ECM) (2008) *Contact Point Q and A Online*. Available at: www.everychildmatters.gov.uk/_files/ContactPointQandA.pdf (accessed 6 July 2008).

Eyres, I., Cable, C., Hancock, R. and Turner, J. (2004) '"Whoops, I forgot David": children's perceptions of the adults who work in their classrooms', *Early Years*, 24(2): 149–62.

Fagnani, J. (2009) 'Childcare Policies in France: The Influence of Organisational Change in the Workplace', in S. Kamerman, S. Phipps, and A. Ben-Arieh (eds), *From Child Welfare to Child Well-Being: An international Perspective on Knowledge in the Service of Policy.* 1: 385–402, New York: Springer.

Family Action (2012) *Born Broke*. Available at: www.family-action.org.uk/uploads/documents/parents%20with%20new%20children.pdf (accessed 29 May 2012).

Family and Parenting Institute (2005) *Making Families Matter: Nine Steps to Make Britain Family Friendly*. Available at: www. familyandparenting.org/Manifesto#3 (accessed 1 June 2008).

Family and Parenting Institute (2008) *About the Fund*. Available at: www.familyandparenting.org/ParentingFundAbout (accessed 1 June 2008).

Faux, K. (2010) '"Excessive weight" is placed on early years says Tory MP', *Nursery World*, 4/3/10, 4.

Featherstone, S. (2004) 'Smooth moves', *Nursery World*, 3919: 14–15.

Fitzgerald, D. (2004) *Parent Partnerships in the Early Years*, London: Continuum.

Fitzgerald, D. (2012) 'Working with parents and families', in J. Kay (ed.), *Good Practice in the Early Years,* London: Continuum.

Fitzgerald, D. and Kay, J. (2008) *Working Together in Children's Services*, Oxford: Routledge.

Frean, A. (1997) 'France shows way with childcare', *The Times*, 13 June.

Frost, N. (2005) *Multi-Agency Teams Working for Children*. Available at: www.rip.org.uk/learningevents/ip_reports/Trusts.asp (accessed 26 February 2005).

Gargiulo, R.M. and Piao, Y. (1996) 'Early Childhood Special Education in the People's Republic of China', *Early Childhood Development and Care*, 41(1), 51–7.

Ghate, D. (2001) 'Community-based evaluations in the UK: scientific concerns and practical restraints', *Children and Society*, 15: 23–32.

Gillen, S. (2008) 'Laming: the verdict five years on', *Community Care*, 17 January: 16–17.

Glass, N. (1999) *Origins of the Sure Start Local Programmes.* Available at: www.surestart.gov.uk/_doc/P0001720.doc (accessed 28 June 2008).

Glass, N. (2001) 'What works for children: the political issues', *Children and Society*, 15(1): 14–20.

Glass, N. (2005). 'Surely some mistake?', *The Guardian*, Available at:. www.guardian.co.uk/society/2005/jan/05/guardiansocietysupplement.childrenservices (accessed 24th May 2010).

Grisham Brown, J. and Hallam, R. (2004) 'A comprehensive report of child care providers' perceptions of a statewide early care and education initiative', *Child and Youth Care Forum*, 33(1): 19–31.

Haut Conseil de l'Éducation (2007) *École primaire: bilans des resultants de l'école*, Paris: HCE.

Henry, J. (2012) *Parents in Scotland Will Get Best Free Nursery Package in the UK. The Telegraph*, 10 March 2012, accessed: http://www.telegraph.co.uk/education/primaryeducation/9136095/Parents-in-Scotland-will-get-best-free-nursery-package-in-the-UK.html

Hill, A. (2005) 'Childcare shake-up will send men into the nursery', *Observer*, 6 March.

HM Government (2006) *Select Committee for Education and Skills, 3rd Report June 2006.* Available at: www.publications.parliament.uk/pa/cm200506/cmselect/cmeduski/478/47802.htm (accessed 4th July 2008).

HM Treasury (2011) *Autumn Statement: Presented to Parliament by the Chancellor of the Exchequer*, London: HMSO

HM Treasury, Department for Education and Skills, Department for Work and Pensions (2004) *Choice for Parents, The Best Start for Children: A Ten Year Strategy for Childcare*, London: HMSO.

Home Office (1998) *Supporting Families: A Consultation Document*, London: HMSO.

Hope, C. (2010) 'Middle classes told to stop using Sure Start', *The Telegraph*, 11/8/20.

Hseuh, Y. and Tobin, J. (2003) 'Chinese early childhood educators' perspectives on dealing with a crying child', *Journal of Early Childhood Research*, 1(1): 73–94.

Hu, B. and Szente, J. (2010) 'In introduction of Chinese Early Childhood Inclusion', *International Journal of Early Childhood*, 42(1): 59–66.

Hunter, T. (2005) 'View from the top: teamwork or turf wars?', *Guardian*, 23 February.

References

Ipsos MORI (2011) *Evaluation of Flying Start: Baseline Survey of Families. Mapping needs and measuring early influence among families with babies aged seven to 20 months – Summary Report*, Welsh Government Social Research. Available at: http://wales.gov.uk/about/aboutresearch/social/latestresearch/EvalFlyStart7–20/?lang=en.

Jackson, B. and Jackson, S. (1979) *Childminder: A Study in Action Research*, London: Routledge and Kegan Paul.

Jackson, L. (2005) 'Region rises to the challenge', *The Guardian*, 16 February.

Jiaxiong, Z. and Nianli, Z. (2005) 'A survey of current Shanghai early childhood education through director's self-assessment', *International Journal of Early Years Education*, 13(2): 113–27.

Jillian, R. (1996) 'Early years provision in Australia in the 1990s: present status, current issues and future trends', *International Journal of Early Childhood*, 28(1): 48–58.

Johnson, R. (1999) 'Colonialism and cargo cults in early childhood education; does Reggio Emilia really exist?' *Contemporary Issues in Early Childhood* 1(1): 61–77.

Joseph Rowntree Foundation (2005) *Policies Towards Poverty, Inequality and Exclusion since 1997*. Available at: www.jrf.org.uk/knowledge/findings/socialpolicy/0015.asp (accessed on 25 March 2005).

Kabiru, M., Njenga, A. and Swadener, B.B. (2003) 'Early childhood development in Kenya: empowering young mothers, mobilising a community', *Childhood Education*, 79(6): 358–63.

Kagan, S.L. and Hallmark, L.G. (2001) 'Cultivating leadership in early care and education', *Child Care Information*, 140: 7–10.

Kullas, J. (2000) 'All God's children need to have some space', *Nursery World*, 14 December: 34.

Kurtz, Z. (2003) 'Outcomes for children's health and well-being', *Children and Society*, 17: 173–83.

La Berge, A.F. (1991) 'Medicalisation and Moralisation: The Crèches of 19th Century Paris', *Journal of Social History*, 25(1): 65–87.

Labour Party (1985) *A Charter for the Under-Fives*, London: Labour Party.

Laming, Lord H. (2003) *The Victoria Climbié Inquiry: Report of an Inquiry by Lord Laming,* London: HMSO.

Laming, Lord H. (2009) *The Protection of Children in England: A Progress Report*. London: The Stationery Office.

Lansdown, G. (2001) 'Children's welfare and children's rights', in P. Foley, J. Roche and S. Tucker (eds), *Children in Society: Contemporary Theory, Policy and Practice*, Basingstoke: Palgrave.

Levin, P. (1997) *Making Social Policy: The Mechanisms of Government and*

Politics, and How to Investigate Them, Buckingham: Open University Press.

Levine, R.L. and Fitzgerald, H. (eds) (1992) *Analysis of Dynamic Psychological Systems, Volume 1: Basic Approaches to General Systems Theory and Dynamics Systems, and Cybernetics*, New York: Plenum Press.

Lindon, J. (2005) 'Early stages', *Nursery World*, 3 February.

Lister, R. (2004) *Poverty*, Cambridge: Polity.

Llambi, C., Perera, M, Piñeyro, L. and Rovira, F. (2009) *Effects of an Expansion of Child Care Services on Female Labour Supply and Income Distribution in Uruguay*, Research proposal presented to the PEP Network.

Lloyd, E. (2008) 'Dutch Childcare Reforms: Informal Care Too Costly', *Nursery World* 6 November 2011.

Local Government Association (LGA) (2004) *Children Bill and Every Child Matters: Next Steps*, LGA briefing, 5 March. Available at: www.lga.gov.uk/Documents/Briefing/Our_Work/social%20affairs/children.pdf (accessed 20 March 2005).

Luo, R, Zhang, L., Liu, C., Zhao, Q., Shi, Y., Rozelle, S. and Sharboro, B. (2009) *Behind before they start: The challenge of early childhood education in rural China – Rural Education Action project, Working Paper 209*, Stamford, CA: Stamford University.

Lynch, M. (2006) *Modern China*, London: Hodder Education.

Manani, H.K (2005) *NACECE Capacity Building programme*, Paper delivered to international conference on children and young people in Stockholm.

Manani, H.K. (2007) *Kenya*. Paper presented at international seminar on 'Accelerated learning: New opportunities for children at risk' held in Addis Ababa.

Marcus, L. (2007) 'Scotland: first children's minister', *Nursery World*, 24 May: 4–5.

Martin, M-H. (2010) 'Equality begins in the crèche: The debate over motherhood is missing the point – British mums should be fighting for the French model of childcare', *The Guardian*, 19 February.

Martinez, P. (2008) *Equidad de opportunidades desde el inicio de la vida. Plan de acción al 2015 para el augmento de la cobertura y la mejora de la calidad en la atenció as la primera infancia*, Montedvideo: MIDES-Infamilia.

Masterson, A., Antrobus, S. and Smith, S. (2004) 'The children's national service framework: from policy to practice', *Nursing Management*, 11(6): 12–15.

Mathers, S., Ranns, H., Karemaker, A., Moody, A., Sylva, K., Graham, J. and Siraj-Blatchford, I. (2011) *Evaluation of the Graduate Leader Fund: Final Report*, London: DfE.

Melhuish, E. et al. (2005) *National Evaluation of Sure Start (NESS)*, London:

Institute for the Study of Children, Families and Social Issues, London: Birkbeck, University of London.

Miniserstvo Präce a Sociálnich Vèci (2009) *12 points on Czech Presidency's effort to open discussion on Barcelona objectives,* Prague: MPSV (Ministry of Labour and Social Affairs).

Ministry of Health, Welfare and Sport and Ministry of Education, Culture and Science (2000) *Early Childhood Education and Care Policy in the Netherlands: Background Report to the OECD Project* (official English language version), The Hague: Government of the Netherlands.

Mittler, P. (2005) 'The global context of inclusive education: the role of the United Nations', in D. Mitchell (ed.), *Contextualising Inclusive Education: Evaluating Old and New International Perspectives*, London: Routledge.

Moore, M. (1996) 'As Europe Grows Grayer, France Devises a Baby Boom', *Washington Post* 18 October.

Morton, K. (2009) '"Cool it" on early years, say Tories', *Nursery World*, 9/7/09, 4.

Moss, P. (2001a) 'Britain in Europe: fringe or heart?', in G. Pugh (ed.), *Contemporary Issues in the Early Years* (3rd edn), London: Paul Chapman Publishing.

Moss, P. (2003) 'Getting beyond childcare: reflections on recent policy and future possibilities', in J. Brannen, and P. Moss (eds), *Rethinking Children's Care*, Buckingham: Open University Press.

Moss, P. (2004) 'Why we need a well-qualified early childhood workforce', paper presented on 16 March at Regents College, London.

Muijs, D., Aubrey, C., Harris, A. and Briggs, M. (2004) 'How do they manage? A review of the research on leadership in early childhood', *Journal of Early Childhood Research*, 2(3): 157–69.

Muncey, J. (1988) 'The special school as part of a whole authority approach', in D. Baker and K. Bovair (eds), *Making the Special Schools Ordinary? Vol. 1: Models for the Developing Special School*, London: Falmer Press.

Munro, E. (2011) *The Munro Review of Child Protection Final Report: The Child's Journey*, London, Department of Education.

Muskens, G. and Peters, D. (2009) *Inclusion and Education in European Countries: INTMEAS Project – Final Report on the Netherlands (No.8)*, Brussels: European Union Directorate General for Education & Culture.

Myrdal, J. (1965) *Report from a Chinese Village*, London: Heinemann.

National Audit Office (NAO) (2001) *Modern Policy Making: Ensuring Policies Deliver Value for Money*, London: NAO.

National Audit Office (NAO) (2004) *Early Years: Progress in Developing High Quality Childcare and Early Education Accessible to All*, NAO, HC 268 Session 2003–2004.

National Audit Office (NAO) (2006) *Sure Start Children's Centres*, London: TSO.

National Childminding Association (NCMA) (2005) *The Support Childminder Pathfinder Scheme: Evaluation Report*, London: DFES/Sure Start Unit.

National Children's Homes (NCH) (2003) *United for Children? How Devolution is Impacting upon Children*, London: NCH.

National College for School Leadership (NCSL) (2008) *National Professional Qualification for Integrated Children's Centre Leadership*. Available at: www.ncsl.org.uk/npqicl-index (accessed 15 June 2008).

National Evaluation of Children's Trusts (NECT) (2004) *Children's Trusts: Developing Integrated Services for Children in England*, Norwich: University of East Anglia/National Children's Bureau/DfES/Department of Health.

National Evaluation of Sure Start (NESS) Research Team (2008) *The Impact of Sure Start Local Programmes on Three Year Olds and their Families*, Annesley, Nottingham: DfES Publications. Available at: www.ness.bbk.ac.uk/documents/activities/impact/42.pdf (accessed 26 June 2008).

Norvez, A. (1990) *De la naissance à l'école: Santé, modes de garde et préscolarité dans la France*, Paris: INED – Presses Universitaires de France.

Nursery World (2001) 'NI children's strategy "could lead the world"', *Nursery World*, 12 July: 6.

Nutbrown, C. (2012) *Review of Early Education and Childcare Qualifications: Interim Report*, London: DfE.

Nyland, B., Zheng, X., Nyland, C. and Tran, L. (2009) 'Grandparents as educators and carers in China', *Journal of Early Childhood Research* 7(1): 46–57.

O'Brien, N. (2011) '"Special educational needs" – or just badly behaved children?', *The Telegraph*, 9 March. Available at: http://blogs.telegraph.co.uk/news/neilobrien1/100079216/special-educational-needs-or-just-badly-behaved-children/ (accessed 29 May 2012).

Office of the United Nations High Commissioner for Human Rights (1989) *United Nations Convention on the Rights of the Child*, Geneva: OUNHCHR.

Office for National Statistics (ONS) (2003) *Labour Force Survey*, London: ONS.

Office for Standards in Education (Ofsted) (2006a) *Extended Services in Schools and Children's Centres*. Available at: www.ofsted.gov.uk/assets/Internet_Content/Publications_Team/File_attachments/extended2609.doc (accessed 30 June 2008).

Office for Standards in Education (Ofsted) (2006b) *Inclusion: Does it Matter Where Pupils are Taught? An Ofsted Report on the Provision and Outcomes in Different Settings for Pupils with Learning Difficulties and Disabilities*. Available at: www.ofsted.gov.uk/publications/index.cfm?fuseaction=pubs.displayfile&id=4235&type=pdf (accessed 4 July 2008).

Office for Standards in Education (Ofsted) (2008) *How Well Are They Doing? The*

Impact of Children's Centres and Extended Schools. Available at: www.ofsted.gov.uk/assets/Internet_Content/Shared_Content/Files/2008/jan/childcentres_exschs.doc (accessed 30 June 2008).

Organisation for Economic Co-operation and Development (2001) *Starting Strong; Early Childhood Education and Care,* Paris: OECD.

Organisation for Economic Co-operation and Development (2004) *Early Childhood Education and Care Policy in France*, Paris: OECD Directorate for Education.

Organisation for Economic Co-operation and Development (OECD) (2006) *Starting Strong II: Early Childhood Education and Care*, Paris: OECD.

Organisation for Economic Co-operation and Development (OECD) (2011) *Doing Better for Families*, Paris: OECD.

Osgood, J. (2004) 'Time to get down to business? The response of early years practitioners to entrepreneurial approaches to professionalism', *Journal of Early Childhood Research*, 2(1): 5–24.

Patterson, C.J. (2006) 'Children of lesbian and gay parents', *Current Directions in Psychological Science,* 15(5): 241–4.

Penn, H. (ed.) (2000) *Early Childhood Services: Theory, Policy and Practice*, Oxford: Oxford University Press.

Penn, H. (2005) *Understanding Early Childhood: Issues and Controversies*, Maidenhead: Open University Press

Penn, H. (2005) *Unequal Childhoods*. Oxfordshire: Routledge.

Penn, H. (2009) 'A mother's place is in the home?', *Nursery World* 12/3/09, 10–11.

Perera, M. and Llambi, C. (2010) *Plan de Acción 2010–2015: Dimensinamiento economico de la universilazación de los servicios de atención y educación a la primera infancia: considerando los modelos existents asi como possibles modelos alternatives. Informe final*, Montevideo: ENIA.

Phillips, J.S. and Bhavnagu, N.P. (2002) 'The Masai's education and experiences: Challenges of a nomadic lifestyle', *Childhood Education*, 78: 140–6.

Pilkington, C. (2002) *Devolution in Britain Today*, Manchester: Manchester University Press.

Platt, D. (2004) 'The Children Bill and what it means for children's services', paper presented at the Inter-Agency Group Conference, Business Design Centre, London, 15 July. Available at: www.csci.org.uk/about_csci/speches/iag_conference_15)07_04.doc (accessed 10 June 2005).

Plaisance, É. (1996) *Pauline Kergomard et l'école maternelle*, Paris: Presses Universitaires de France.

Power, E. (2011) 'Cuts threaten plans for special needs children', *The Guardian*, 9 March. Available at http://www.guardian.co.uk/education/mortar-board/2011/mar/09/cuts-threaten-sen-plans (accessed 29 May 2012).

Pugh, G. (ed.) (2001) *Contemporary Issues in the Early Years: Working Collaboratively for Children* (3rd edn), London: Paul Chapman Publishing.

Pugh, G. and Duffy, B. (2010) *Contemporary Issues in the Early Years: Working Collaboratively for Children* (5th edn), London: Paul Chapman Publishing.

Qualifications and Curriculum Authority/Department for Education and Employment) (QCA/DfEE) (2000) *Investing in Our Future: Curriculum Guidance for the Foundation Stage*, London: QCA and DfEE.

Qingshua, J., Yan, L., You, Z. and Qiong, L. (2009) 'A survey of current pre-school education of and for children from low income families in Beijing', *International Journal of Early Years Education*, 13(2): 157–69.

Quinn, G. and Degener, T. (eds) (2002) *The Current Use and Future Potential of United Nations Human Rights Instruments in the Context of Disability*, Geneva: Office of the United Nations High Commissioner on Human Rights.

Rawstrone, A. (2001) 'Scotland provides a good care model', *Nursery World*, 7 June: 4–5.

Rickford, F. (2005) '0–19: Do the politicians care?' *0–19*, Comment, 1 March. Available at: www.zero2nineteen.co.uk/Home/default.asp (accessed 9 June 2005).

Roberts, M. (2001) 'Childcare policy', in P. Foley, J. Roche and S. Tucker (eds), *Children in Society: Contemporary Theory, Policy and Practice*. Basingstoke: Palgrave.

Ruxton, S. (2001) 'Towards a "children's policy" for the European Union?', in P. Foley, J. Roche and S. Tucker (eds), *Children in Society: Contemporary Theory, Policy and Practice*, Basingstoke: Palgrave.

Sanderson, I. (2003) 'Is it "what works" that matters? Evaluation and evidence-based policy making', *Research Papers in Education*, 18(4): 331–45.

Scottish Executive (2001) *For Scotland's Children*, Edinburgh: Scottish Executive.

Scottish Government/COSLA (2008) *Early Years Framework*. Available at: http://www.scotland.gov.uk/Resource/Doc/257007/0076309.pdf (accessed 21 May 2012).

Senge, P. and Lannon-Kim, C. (1991) *The Systems Thinker Newsletter*, 2(5).

Sharp, C. (2003) 'School starting age: European policy and recent research', *Early Education*, Spring: 4–5.

Sheppard, M., MacDonald, P. and Welbourne, P. (2008) 'Service users as gate keepers in Children's Centres', *Child and Family Social Work*, 13: 61–71.

Shoolbread, A. (2006) *Consulting Children on the Proposed Schools (Nutrition and Health Promotion) (Scotland) Bill*, Edinburgh: Scottish Executive.

Siraj-Blatchford, I. and Sylva, K. (2004) 'Researching pedagogy in English preschools', *British Educational Research Journal*, 30(5): 713–30.

Siraj-Blatchford, I., Taggart, B., Sylva, K., Sammons, P. and Melhuish, E. (2008) 'Towards the transformation of practice in early childhood education: the effective provision of preschool education (EPPE) project', *Cambridge Journal of Education*, 38(1): 23–36.

Skinner, C. (2003) *Running Around in Circles: Coordinating Childcare, Education and Work*. York: Joseph Rowntree Foundation.

Sloper, P. (2004) 'Facilitators and barriers for co-ordinated multi-agency services', *Child: Care, Health and Development*, 30: 571–80.

Smith, M., Oliver, C. and Barker, S. (1998) *Effectiveness of Early Years Interventions: What Does the Research Tell Us?* Comprehensive Spending Review: Cross-Departmental Review of Provision for Young Children, Vol. 2, London: HM Treasury.

Sure Start (2008) *Districts that Participated in the Mainstreaming Pilot.* Available at: www.surestart.gov.uk/_doc/P0001719.doc (accessed 30 June 2008).

Sure Start Unit (2002) *Birth to Three Matters: A Framework to Support Children in their Earliest Years*, London: DfES.

Swadener, B.B., Kabiru, M. and Njenja, A. (2000) *Does the village still raise the child? A collaborative study of changing child-rearing and early education in Kenya*. New York: State University of New York Press.

Swap, S.M. (1993) *Developing Home–School Partnerships: From Concepts to Practice*, New York: Teachers College Press.

Sylva, K., Melhuish, E., Sammons, P., Siraj-Blatchford, I. and Taggart, B. (2004) *The Effective Provision of Pre-School Education (EPPE) Project: Findings from Pre-school to end of Key Stage 1*, London: Sure Start.

Sylva, K., Melhuish, E., Sammons, P., Siraj-Blatchford, I., and Taggart, B. (2012) *Effective Pre-school, Primary and Secondary Education 3–14 Project (EPPSE 3–14): Final Report from the Key Stage 3 Phase – Influences on Students' Development From Age 11–14*, London: DfE.

Taylor, D. and Balloch, S. (2005) 'The politics of evaluation: an overview', in D. Taylor and S. Balloch, *The Politics of Evaluation*, Bristol: The Policy Press.

Teather, S. (2011) 'To each child a fair start', *Nursery World,* 28 October 12

The UK Children's Commissioners' Joint Report (2011) *UK Children's Commissioners' Midterm Report to the UK State Party on the UN Convention on the Rights of the Child*, Children's Commissioners England. Available at: www.childcomwales.org.uk/uploads/publications/277.pdf (accessed 1 May 2012).

Tickell, Dame C. (2011) *The Early Years: Foundations for Life, Health and Learning.* Available at: http://media.education.gov.uk/MediaFiles/B/1/5%7BB15EFFOD-A4DF-4294-93A1-1E1B88C13F68%7DTickell%20review.pdf

Tisdall, E.K.M. and Davis, J. (2004) 'Making a difference? Bringing children's and young people's views into policy making', *Children and Society*, 18(2): 131–42.

Tobin, J.J., Wu, D.Y.H. and Davidson, D.H. (1989) *Pre-school in Three Cultures: Japan, China and the United States*, New Haven, CT: Yale University Press.

Tobin, J, Hsueh, Y. and Karasawa, M. (2009) *Pre-school in Three Cultures Re-visited: China, Japan and the United States*, Chicago, IL: University of Chicago Press.

Truss, E. (2012) *Affordable Quality: New Approaches to Childcare,* Centre Forum. Available at: www.centreforum.org/assets/pubs/affordable-quality.pdf (accessed 20 May 2012).

Turksema, R.W. (2000) *Het aanbod van kinderopvang (met eeen samenvatting in het Nederlands* Doctoral thesis submitted to the University of Utrecht (English-language version).

Tweed, J. (2002) 'Labour's early years' job "is not finished"', *Nursery World*, 14 February, 4.

United Nations Economic and Social Council (2009) *Implementation of the International Covenant on Economic, Social and Cultural Rights: Uruguay,* New York: UNESC.

United Nations Educational, Scientific and Cultural Organisation (1990) *World declaration on Education For All and Framework For Action for Meeting Basic Needs,* Paris: UNESCO.

Valentova, M. (2009) *Employment breaks due to childcare in the Czech Republic. Before and after 1989,* Hartford, CT: IDEAS, University of Connecticut.

Van de Linde, T. and Lenaiyasa, S. (2006) 'Influencing and developing good policy in early childhood development amongst pastoralist communities in East Africa: The case of Samburu in Kenya'. Paper delivered at conference in Nairobi on 'Pastoralism and Poverty Reduction in East Africa' organized by the International Livestock Research Institute (based in Nairobi).

Vimpani, G.V. (2002) 'Sure Start: reflections from down under', *Childcare, Health and Development*, 28(4): 281–7.

Walker, R. (ed.) (1999) *Popular Welfare for the 21st Century?*, Bristol: The Policy Press.

Waller, T. (2009) 'International Perspectives', in T. Waller (ed), *An Introduction to Early Childhood*, London: Sage 63–79.

Warnock Committee (1978) *Special Educational Needs: The Warnock Report*, London: DES.

Warnock, M. (2005) *Special Educational Needs: A New Look*, London: Philosophy of Education Society of Great Britain.

Waterhouse, Sir R. (2000) *Lost in Care: Report of the Tribunal of Inquiry into the*

References

Abuse of Children in Care in the Former County Council Areas of Gwynedd and Clwyd since 1974, London: HMSO (Department of Health).

Waterman, C. and Fowler, J. (2004) *Plain Guide to the Children Act 2004*, Slough: National Foundation for Educational Research.

Welsh Assembly (2004) *Celebrating Progress in Early Years and Primary Education*. Available at: www.learning.wales.gov.uk/scripts/fe/news_details.asp?NewsID=1399 (accessed 15 November 2004).

Welsh Assembly (2007) *Good Practice Guidance for Out of Classroom Learning*, Cardiff: Welsh Government.

White, G., Swift, J. and Bennett, A. (2005) *Sure Start Mainstreaming Pilots: What Can We Learn?*, Annersley: DfES Publications.

White, L.A. (2009) 'Explaining Differences in Child Care Policy Development in France and the USA: Norms, Frames, Programmatic Ideas', *International Political Science Review*, 30(4): 385–405.

Winner, E. (1989) 'How can Chinese children draw so well?', *Journal of Aesthetic Education*, 23(1): 41–63.

Winner, E. (1993) 'Exceptional artistic development: The role of visual thinking', *Journal of Aesthetic Education*, 27(4): 31–44.

Wintour, P. (2006) 'Blair admits failing most needy children', *The Guardian*, 16 May, 2006.

Woodrow, C. (2008) 'Discourses of professional identity in early childhood: movements in Australia', *European Early Childhood Education Research Journal*, 16: 2.

World Education Forum (2000) *The Dakar Framework for Action. Education for All: Meeting Our Collective Commitments*, Paris: UNESCO.

Yao, Y. (2002) 'The Making of a National Hero: Tao Xingzhi's Legacies in the People's Republic of China', *Review of Education, Pedagogy and Cultural Studies*, 24(3): 251–81.

Yim, H.Y.B. and Ebbeck, M. (2009) 'Children's preferences for group musical activities in child care centres: A cross-cultural study', *Early Education Journal*, 37(2): 103–11.

Zhu, J. and Zhang, J. (2008) 'Contemporary trends and developments in early childhood education in China', *Early Years*, 28(2): 173–83.

Useful Websites

As explained throughout the book, policy is constantly developing and new initiatives are being trialled or implemented. One way to keep up to date with policy developments is to consult websites from government departments, professional organizations and other relevant bodies. In addition to the websites mentioned in the text, the following websites are likely to be helpful in this task:

Daycare Trust: www.daycaretrust.org.uk/
A national childcare charity with information and responses to policy developments in childcare.

Department for Education: www.education.gov.uk/
Details current government policy and initiatives in education, including early learning and childcare.

Family and Parenting Institute: www.familyandparenting.org/
A charity offering comment and advice to support parents bringing up their children.

Healthy Child Programme:
www.dh.gov.uk/en/Publicationsandstatistics/Publications/PublicationsPolicyAnd
Guidance/DH_107563

Joseph Rowntree Foundation: www.jrf.org.uk/
A social policy research charity that produces reports on a range of social policy issues, including issues relevant to children and families.

National Children's Bureau: www.ncb.org.uk/
Provides comment, analysis and an overview of issues relevant to children.

Ofsted Childcare and Early Education: www.ofsted.gov.uk/early-years-and-childcare
Provides information about current issues for the registration, regulation and monitoring of early years provision.

In addition, some of the websites above also offer the facility to receive regular email updates on new developments. This is an invaluable way of keeping abreast of ongoing policy developments.

Index

Index